Michel Houellebecq and the
Literature of Despair

Also available from Bloomsbury

Novels of the Contemporary Extreme edited by Alain-
Philippe Durand and Naomi Mandel
Ethics and Desire in the Wake of Postmodernism by Graham Matthews
Bret Easton Ellis's Controversial Fiction by Sonia Baelo-Allu
Toni Morrison and Literary Tradition by Justine Jenny Baillie
Salman Rushdie's Cities by Vassilena Parashkevova

Michel Houellebecq and the Literature of Despair

By Carole Sweeney

Bloomsbury Academic
An imprint of Bloomsbury Publishing Plc

B L O O M S B U R Y
LONDON • NEW DELHI • NEW YORK • SYDNEY

Bloomsbury Academic
An imprint of Bloomsbury Publishing Plc

50 Bedford Square
London
WC1B 3DP
UK

1385 Broadway
New York
NY 10018
USA

www.bloomsbury.com

BLOOMSBURY and the Diana logo are trademarks of Bloomsbury Publishing Plc

First published 2013
Paperback edition first published 2015

British Library Cataloguing-in-Publication Data
A catalogue record for this book is available from the British Library.

ISBN: HB: 978-0-8264-2262-0
PB: 978-1-4742-3913-4
ePDF: 978-1-6235-6298-4
ePUB: 978-1-6235-6918-1

Library of Congress Cataloging-in-Publication Data
A catalog record for this book is available from the Library of Congress.

Typeset by Fakenham Prepress Solutions, Fakenham, Norfolk NR21 8NN

Contents

Acknowledgements

This book was made possible with the kind help and cheerful assistance of many friends and colleagues at Goldsmiths, Department of English and Comparative Literature, to whom I am immensely grateful.

Warmest thanks go to my brother and my colleague Marie-Claude Canova Green for their invaluable help with tricky translations; also to Jackie Clarke for providing me with a bracing reading list for May 1968 and to Carrie Hamilton for similar on sex tourism. Thank you to Sophie Corser for her top-notch editing skills and to Maria Lauret, Nicky Marsh and Tim Parnell for being such exacting and generous readers of my work and especially for the latter's constant loving encouragement and forbearance.

This book is dedicated to my family: to my new and wonderful husband, to Tom and Monique, and to the memory of my father, 1920–2012. Lastly, it is for my beloved daughter, Pascale, who has grown into an adult over the course of its writing.

I am grateful to the following journals for their permission to reproduce earlier versions of some material in this book: *Modern and Contemporary France*, 'Natural Women? Anti-Feminism and Michel Houellebecq's *Plateforme*' 20:3 (2012); *Journal of Modern Literature* '"And yet some free time remains…."': Post-Fordism and Writing in Michel Houellebecq's *Whatever*,' 33.4 (2010).

Introduction

... there's little point in denying that he has some profoundly fascistic tendencies [...] Like Céline, he's a right-wing misanthrope who has produced a genuinely perceptive and resonant picture of French society – obscenified and resonating.[1]

In May 2000 a book appeared in British book shops with a cover featuring a half-naked woman staring dolefully into camera. Inscribed in gaudy embossed gold lettering across her naked breasts was a single word: 'atomised'. The cover was in many ways puzzling, as the woman's state of undress seemed to gesture to sex, or at least to some form of eroticism; but she appears uncomfortable, cold, even sullen, with her gaze turned reproachfully towards the reader. This unsettling combination of sex and dejection suggested by the cover of Michel Houellebecq's second novel *Atomised* (*Les Particules élémentaires* 1998) is fitting for a work that has from the outset been difficult to position aesthetically, politically and intellectually. Almost immediately, the novel made a significant commercial and critical impact but one disputed and applauded in almost equal measures as demonstrated by the division of critical opinion in Houellebecq's native France. Both the writer and his novel attracted front page news and Houellebecq began to appear frequently on television, mumbling his way through interviews, head down, cigarette clamped between middle and ring finger. His physical presence did nothing to dispel the controversial reception of the novel, in fact, quite the opposite: 'the only thing the French seem to agree on about Houellebecq', noted a contemporary reviewer in *The New York Times*, 'is that he is the first French novelist since Balzac whose work captures the social realities of contemporary life'.[2] Accusations of misogyny, obscenity, eugenicism, fascism, racism, misanthropy and general intellectual delinquency levelled against the novel did little to hinder its commercial success and the freshly translated novel arrived in the Anglophone literary world complete with a long tailwind of controversy. With the exception of his first novel *Whatever* (1998) (*Extension du domaine de la lutte*, 1994) which garnered slight but favourable critical attention, Houellebecq's career as a novelist has been beset with an unusual amount of controversy, so much so that the French press gave the commotion around the publication of *Atomised* its very own label: *l'affaire Houellebecq*. Each subsequent novel, *Plateforme* (2001) (*Platform* 2002), *Lanzarote* (2000, 2003), *La Possibilité d'une île* (2005) (*The Possibility of an Island* 2006) and the latest, *La Carte et le territoire* (*The Map and the Territory* 2011), has in turn intensified interest, both positive and negative, in his work. Positioned somewhere on a continuum between indictment and admiration, most critical reactions have largely concurred that, for better or for worse, the novels of Michel Houellebecq are the 'most discussed literary-cultural phenomena of the past decade' and register an important shift in France's intellectual and political climate.[3] This shift, one that is as much political as it is intellectual, is the subject of this book.

In France, the 1998 *rentrée littéraire* was dominated, overwhelmed even, by the rumpus around a single novel: *Les Particules élémentaires*. *Le Monde* devoted several front-page headlines detailing Houellebecq's dismissal from the editorial board of the literary review *Perpendiculaire* for serious ideological differences with his colleagues. The 'differences' that troubled *Perpendiculaire*'s editorial board would prove to be the same as those shaping the novel's sharply divided reception in France, as reviewers and critics rapidly separated into two distinctly opposing camps over what *Atomised* might represent. It was either, they claimed, a deeply reactionary, splenetic treatise that implicitly endorsed the ills of contemporary society on the one hand, or a brilliantly sharp Balzacian social satire condemning these same ills on the other. Reaction to the novel was, as Marion Van Renterghem observed in *Le Monde*, extensive and intense: 'Rarely has a novel caused so much ink to flow, incited such passions, outbursts of anger and hate.'[4] More than a decade on from the publication of *Atomised*, the critical quarrels around Houellebecq's work have subsided somewhat but have by no means disappeared, as recently demonstrated by the pejorative comments of Tahar Ben Jalloun, a member of the Prix Goncourt jury that had just awarded Houellebecq this most prestigious of French literary prizes for his latest novel *La Carte et le territoire*. Unequivocal in his distaste for the novel, Jalloun derided it for its uninspired prose style, lack of imagination and a spiritually impoverished view of modern life amounting to little more, he claimed, than 'trivial chatter on the human condition in an affected writing style that claims to be some sort of cleansing.'[5] Far from being a routine spat among literary prize jurors, Jalloun's comments made headline news in France. It is precisely the nature of this 'chatter' about the human condition, trivial or otherwise, that has landed Houellebecq in political and artistic trouble almost continuously since 1998. The same question seems to run through all contemporary critical and popular reception of his work in newspapers, literary reviews and magazines, from one side of the ideological spectrum to the other: is Houellebecq saying what he really means or is it a form of ironic mockery that deploys the attitude and language of its subject to mount its critique? Does he belong to a tradition of satirical writers who turn a caustic eye over their own society or is he articulating a new form of genuinely held masculine *ressentiment*? Either way, Houellebecq's novels represent important, if highly contentious, responses to the changed climate of post-'68 France and, as such, he very quickly obtained the status of *provocateur littéraire*, achieved most famously by Céline and Flaubert before him.[6]

I will argue in this book that critical attention, positive and otherwise, and popular success have accrued to Houellebecq's novels in part because they can be read across the political spectrum, troubling all sides simultaneously. Putting his finger on a basic contradiction inherent in the 'liquid times' of late capitalism, that is the ontological tension between moral and personal freedom and the intense commodification of all human life under such conditions, Houellebecq offers a withering critique of neoliberal late capitalism that never manages to extricate itself entirely from accusations of complicity with its object of scrutiny. His fundamental concern is the encroachment of capitalism in its neoliberal biopolitical form into all areas of affective human life; a thesis made explicit early in his oeuvre in *Whatever* where the narrator asserts that 'economic liberalism is an extension of the domain of the struggle, its extension to all ages and all classes of society'.[7] The human subject is, according to Houellebecq's work considered here, now completely permeated by the discourses and logic of exchange: 'we live not just in a market economy, but more generally in a market society: namely, within a form of civilization in which the entirety of human relations, and equally the entirety of the relations between man and the world, are mediated via a simple numerical calculation entailing attractiveness, novelty, and value for money'.[8] His work presents the subsumption of sexual desire and human intimacy into the mechanisms of quantification and exchange as simply the final stage of capitalism that transforms human attributes into commodities to be exchanged in a deregulated market. On the face of it, then, this seems like a standard leftist critique of the alienation and reification of late capitalism and as such amounts to, as some of Houellebecq's less sympathetic critics have noted, little more than an updating of the Communist Manifesto. But, as we shall see, Houellebecq is certainly no Marxist and *le monde houellebecquien*, as it has come to be known, is a stubbornly un-dialectical space, which moves gradually further and further from any vital connection with the human and the social, indeed from any felt contact with the world. He identifies the intensive reshaping of the self in the language of the commodity and of transaction but finally struggles to envisage any space outside of that process where critical thinking might take place. Every last sphere of human thought and behaviour has been recuperated under the sign of exchange leaving humanity nowhere to go save for its own disappearance into a post-metaphysical desubjectivity.

Crossing ideological positions from right to left, the form as much as the content of Houellebecq's writing cannot easily be placed. Speaking directly to a moment in the late twentieth and early twenty-first centuries in its own 'modern stupid' language, his novels can be read, on the one hand, as a reactionary response to the progressive socio-cultural movements of the twentieth century such as feminism and multi-culturalism while on the other, they seem to offer a compelling critique of the totalizing mechanism of the 'market' with its hitherto unparalleled influence on human life. But it is difficult to separate these things out as Houellebecq seems to refuse to condemn properly, ideologically or ethically, what, on the surface, he appears to be critiquing. His writing is thus ideologically forked, as it seems to participate in, even approve of, the very world that it purports to condemn. Narrated in the idiom of its object of enquiry, the narrative elements in Houellebecq's novels are interposed with a series of (possibly) satirical structuring devices that are inconsistently and unevenly deployed in ways that frequently make any critical purchase on the subject matter, if not impossible, then extremely difficult. Herein, then, lies one of the most disquieting effects of his work as he manipulates, what Martin Crowley calls, a 'wilfully scandalous deployment of cultural material', slipping time and again between surface and depth, high and low, concern and indifference.[9] Typically Houellebecq's prose moves between the serious, the introspective and the philosophical only to deflate this with the low comedy of *le monde houellebecquien*: the body, supermarkets and masturbation. The socio-cultural terrain of this world is shaped by reality TV, airport novels, fast food, pornography, short-term flexible working practices and even shorter-term sexual relationships. Discontented with such a world, Houellebecq's work suggests that if alienation is shown to be the condition of the everyday, it is the task of the novelist to show this in a correspondingly alienated language. If it is to say anything worthwhile, the novel must find its voice in the degraded cultural coinage of trash culture. Thus, the technique Houellebecq employs to show this thoroughly alienated world is to enact a banal, familiar, everyday non-literary language. Houellebecq's writing shows little sustained interest in formalistic concerns and certainly suggests that there is no aesthetic consolation to be had from good form.

Arguably as controversial as his provocative pronouncements on sex and race, Houellebecq's novelistic style has both irked and impressed his critics. A detached grey-ish prose, it proceeds by way of a particularly 'un-novelistic' style that seems, at times, to be utterly indifferent to any aesthetic concerns. Being un-novelistic is not, of course, new to modern French literature, indeed anti-novelistic, anti-narrative writing has been the distinctive quality of the last two significant French literary movements, the *nouveau roman* and *autofiction*. Unallied to any particular literary school or movement, Houellebecq feels himself to be quite distinct from theoretically influenced writers, particularly those influenced by post-structuralism, once remarking that 'in terms of literature, I don't feel an affiliation with the preceding generation'.[10] A patchy anti-psychological realism is the default mode of his writing in which essayistic digressions, aphoristic assertions and para-literary exposition are held together within a perfunctory frame of realist narrative, what Houellebecq describes as 'the idea of a kind of realism'.[11] Although his first novel claims that trying to tell a 'story' these days is simply 'pure bullshit', there is nonetheless a veneer of realism in which there remains a will to tell a story (in many ways, it almost always the same story) but one that wholly rejects any form of psychological depth.[12] This de-psychologization is carried out in ways that are light years from the clean lines and cool detachment of the *nouveau roman* that purged the novel of psychological depth and any lingering residues of romanticism as part of the post-war economic and cultural *entreprise de nettoyage* in France. Unlike postmodernist fiction and its self-conscious concerns around microtextuality and metalanguage, Houellebecq has little, if any, time for the parodic, the inter-textual, the playful, the metafictional or pastiche; offering instead a deadpan, sclerotic prose that rarely troubles itself to pursue any rigorous aesthetic (or in places, intellectual) consistency. Despite the occasional cool authorial inter-jections about its own status as writing, *his* novels are not interested in the self-conscious manoeuvres that inhabit the 'properly' postmodernist novel. Aware that the novel form is perhaps not best suited to contemporary condi-tions Houellebecq accepts the ruination of novelistic discourse, as one of his narrators observes we are '... a long way from *Wuthering Heights*, to say the least'.[13] Consequently, with the possible exception of his first novel *Whatever*, there is only a nominal idea of narrative progression or sequence in each of the novels, typically involving a sexual relationship between an unattractive male protagonist and a significantly more attractive and younger woman that results in suicide, desertion, or psychosis. '[G]rinding pointlessly on ...'[14] with little sense of development or aesthetic consideration, the plots are, at best, meagre affairs, where perfunctorily sketched characters function as ciphers for the overarching hypothesis of his writing that 'the goal of life is missed'. [15]

Unallied then, to any genre or movement in contemporary French or European literature, each of Houellebecq's novels depicts what he calls the progressive 'suicide of the west'. Little wonder then that Julian Barnes's back-cover blurb for *Atomised* claims that Houellebecq's novel 'hunts big game while others settle for shooting rabbits'. Macho metaphors aside, this is a largely accurate assessment of *Atomised*'s flawed but grand intellectual ambition in which the novel recounts this 'suicide' in a text that runs an extensive gamut from philosophy, molecular science and post-industrial French history to forensically, even pornographically, detailed sex scenes, occasional ruminations on penis size and the joy of Monoprix food. To engage meaningfully with Houellebecq's vision one needs to be able to distinguish or differentiate between the 'low' surface trashiness and the 'high' intellectual stakes of his writing as the terrain of *le monde houellebecquien* is one where high and low cultures and discourses collide; where a prolonged cogitation on the agnosticism of modern France glides into a discussion of the merits of a particular supermarket ready-meal; forensically detailed pornographic descriptions nestle against eschatological treatises and scientific descriptions of mitochondrial DNA. Precisely the same flat narrative voice articulates the profound joy of watching 'pussy in motion' in a tawdry Parisian peep show as discusses the imperative to decode the genome in evolutionary terms.[16] *Le monde houellebecquien* is one in which Bourdieu's notion of taste and distinction has all but disappeared, where pulp fiction, *bandes dessinées*, retail catalogues and teen magazines are discussed in the same breath as the theories of Max Planck, Kantian ethics, class politics in Agatha Christie novels, the decline of pig farming in Northern France, Comtian positivism and Balzac's renowned contempt for the middle classes. Conversant with Sartre and Deleuze, Houellebecq's characters are as likely to prefer the work of John Grisham and David Baldacci. Thrashed out in a kind of shambolic, makeshift realism, interspersed with *moraliste* essayistic asides producing a uniformly flat-as-a-pancake style, the narrative form of his novels has been described variously as a depressive, flat and 'nonironical lyricism' commensurate with its subject of existential desolation and dejection, mourning a world in which philosophy has died and with it, Houellebecq suggests, our ability to read, to parent and to love, a world 'without expectation'.[17]

This tumbling together of high and low might, at first, appear as a kind of skilfully wrought intertextuality pointing up the interrelatedness of contemporary life but it is, as I will argue in this book, an inventory of the compacted texture of everyday life that, Houellebecq suggests, has been evacuated of distinction and fatally colonized by the rationalizing nexus of exchange. If distinction is in decline, it is because all has been reduced to a state of similitude in a commercial open market in which everything is subject to the dissolution of symbolic meaning. This thesis is summed up in *Rester vivant et autres textes* (1991), a collection of essays that acts as a useful counterpart to the novels and, in several places, is often indistinguishable from them in both theme and tone. The ideas in this collection resonate strikingly with Baudrillard's thinking in his 1968 work *The System of Objects* where he writes that the goal of the consumer society is the imposition of a bland 'uniformula', a 'profound monotony', that constitutes 'a devolution in the bliss of the consuming masses', achieved through the 'functionalization of the consumer and the psychological monopolization of all need …'.[18] This uniformity of everyday life imposed through consumption invokes a sense of devolved bliss, which is no bliss at all, is an idea that permeates all of Houellebecq's work. Bliss, ecstasy, the sublime – all are subsumed into the material of exchange and 'any true, fine sociological distinctions of the Proustian kind have today been replaced' by the 'sober, crystal-clear formulae' of a quantifying commodification. It seems anomalous then, Houellebecq muses, 'that the parameters of sexual exchange should still remain tied to lyrical, impressionistic, and highly unreliable descriptions'.[19] Houellebecq's characters cannot function in such a world stripped of lyricism, or one governed by the banal dynamics of exchange. *Le monde houellebecquien*, then, is one of radical disenchantment.

Contoured by an overwhelming feeling of acedia, and a sense that any possibility of mythic or symbolic transcendence in life has been irrevocably lost, Houellebecq's novels are inhabited, as we shall see, by protagonists who can neither understand nor enjoy the alienating 'sex and shopping' world of consumption around them. Beginning with the caustic precision of *Whatever* in which the unnamed narrator finds the world in which he lives to be profoundly alienating, even mysteriously so, each of Houellebecq's characters, in many ways all the same character, fail either to understand or enjoy the spoils of the consumer society, experiencing 'lifestyle' choices, leisure opportunities and sexual freedom as acutely agonizing. As I argue here, his novels are populated by the failed subjects of late capitalism; failures because they are unable to take even the most fleeting pleasure in the infantilizing festival of commodity consumption. With few kinship ties and working long hours, Houellebecquian characters (if they can even be properly called that) live alone in a quotidian round of ready meals, sexual disappointment, and mail order catalogues.

Economically affluent, they are often erotic paupers, their lives marked either by desultory onanism interspersed with inconsistent sexual encounters or by failed attempts at sexual love. His protagonists live insignificantly and move indifferently within an environment so systematically reified that the quintessence of freedom is now defined as the ability to order a 'guaranteed delivery of hot food at a given hour'.[20] The reduction of the idea of freedom to a simple choice between one act of consumption and another is unequivocally blamed, as I will consider in detail, on the generation of '68.

In France, Houellebecq's work has been considered scandalously controversial for its unapologetically dogged indictment of the generation of 1968 and for what he sees as the wholesale failure of its radical social and cultural politics. His novels blame the *soixante-huitards*, and feminists in particular, for the decline of organized religion, the destruction of the nuclear family and the rise of a narcissistic individualism that has come to define Western society. Moreover, Houellebecq argues that not only did the radical politics of '68 fail to bring about lasting social and sexual changes, but they actually facilitated the progress of a more tenacious version of consumer capitalism that drew much of its energy from the very same individualism promulgated by the *soixante-huitards*. In this view then, subversive theories of commodity fetishism thrown up by post-'68 Marxist thought and the complex psychoanalytical model of the Freudian–Lacanian desiring subject are now used to sell soft furnishings and package holidays, thus opening up ever-proliferating avenues of consumption, making possible the niche marketing of affective capitalism. Writing at a point when the last of the '68 French thinkers – Deleuze, Lyotard, Derrida, Bourdieu, Blanchot, Baudrillard – have died, Houellebecq's work seems to mark these deaths in, what might be called, 'post-theoretical' novels that exemplify a certain strain of reactionary thinking known as *la pensée anti-'68* (anti-'68 thought). Rejecting the linguistically inflected preoccupations of post-structuralism and the textual self-consciousness of postmodernism, Houellebecq's novels are, in many ways, curiously old-fashioned *romans à theses* that have, at heart, a concern with that rather baggy notion, the human condition. Characterized by a quasi-Comtianism that is brusquely dismissive of the sacrosanct generation of '68, the supremacy of 'high' French critical theory is swept aside in his work as he ridicules the linguistically fixated cultural turn of post-structuralism and its post-Nietzschean obsession with difference, textuality and sexual politics – as we shall see, while Houellebecq's work is full of sex, it is completely indifferent to gender.

In many ways his work testifies to the failure of the post-'68 avant garde project to integrate culture and life in an effort to counter the disenchantment and loss of vitality inherent in modernity as *le monde houellebecquien* is characterized by a despairing disenchantment in which everyday life, what Henri Lefebvre terms the 'fragmented activities' of eating, dwelling and dressing, has lost any possibility of revolutionary autocritique. The potentially 'marvellous' or 'mythic' texture of what Lefebvre calls the 'social text' of the everyday has been annihilated in *le monde houellebecquien* and all we are really left with in his novels, after the dark humour, the sex and the forensic perusal of the blasted spaces of the everyday, is the possibility of retreat, withdrawal and silence.[21] Suggesting that there is no longer a point from which any affirmative political or intellectual resistance is possible, Houellebecq mercilessly lampoons the *soixante-huitards* for their allegiance to Freudo-Marxist 'high' theories, singling out psychoanalysis for particular derision, along with the work of Derrida and Foucault. If theory is dead then irony is equally ineffectual. It too has been recuperated by capital, transformed into eminently profitable transgression. The salving potential of ironic laughter is finally unworkable in Houellebecq's novels: '... humour doesn't do anything at all'.[22] Overall, then, the view of '68 as a moment that smoothed the way for the more potent forces of biopolitical neoliberalism places Houellebecq on both the left and the right as this is a thesis that, in different ways, appeals to both conservative and progressive agendas and, as such, characterizes him as a *rouge-brun* or Left-Conservative writer.[23]

What is it in particular, then, that has made Houellebecq's work resonate so intensely with reading publics and literary critics? The shock of graphic sexual description or eccentric narrative form cannot alone account for its exceptional popular and critical success and notoriety as contemporary French fiction has certainly been no less pornographic or anti-novelistic than Houellebecq's. Both Catherine Breillat and Catherine Millet have articulated ideas around sex and sexuality that are at least as, if not substantially more, 'pornographic' than those in *Atomised* and *Platform*. Millet's *The Sexual Life of Catherine M.* (2002) focuses almost entirely on sexual activity. Labelled 'sick' by *Le Monde*, Virginie Despentes' 1999 novel *Baise-moi* is a staggeringly violent sexual odyssey, unflinchingly recounting scenes of rape and murder, that was subsequently turned into a film. In French art-house cinema, sexual explicitness had become, if not quite ubiquitous, then certainly less rare with three controversially sexually graphic films realized in the space of two years, for example Breillat's *Romance* (1999), Despentes' and Coralie Trinh Thi's film version of *Baise-moi* (2000) and Gaspar Noé's *Irréversible* (2002).[24] Similarly, Houellebecq's focus on alienation, both sexual and social, was by no means a unique phenomenon in French fiction of 1990s. Marie Darrieussecq and Igeor Gran have written powerfully of the profound cultural, sexual and social alienation and the loss of national particularity in *fin de siècle*/pre-millennial France. Elsewhere, contemporaries of Houellebecq, Amélie Nothomb, Jean Echenoz, Christine Angot, Maurice Dantec and Michel Rio have all offered similarly bleak, controversial portraits of modern life. Indeed in 1998, the year when *Les Particules éleméntaires* was published, there was anything but a dearth of controversial novelists and it was certainly true that at the time of its publication 'there was nothing in the novel, either thematically or descriptively, that cannot also be found in other works'.[25] And yet it is Houellebecq's writing that has ignited such intense responses, the likes of which have not been witnessed in France since Louis-Ferdinand Céline's *Journey to the End of the Night* (1932).

Atomised and Houellebecq's other novels considered here offer such a compelling yet contentious response to the culture of late capitalism not simply because they up the pornographic stakes whilst mixing in some misogyny and racism to *épater*, if not the bourgeoisie than the leftist critical establishments in France, but because, as noted above, they do not seem to distance themselves sufficiently from their object of enquiry and, further, refuse to come down on one ideological side or another; a refusal exacerbated by the presence of Houellebecq in the media. Far from the death of the author, it seems to matter very much when the author, the living, chain-smoking, rapping, interview-giving, maternally rejected, 'real' Michel Houellebecq appears on television and categorically refuses to defend himself against the charges of anti-feminism and anti-Islam, preferring rather, to fan the flames of controversy by often elaborating on these in some detail. Houellebecq has been, at least in his earlier career, the opposite of a recluse, courting public attention through the media and regularly talking at length about his work on TV, radio and in the print media; he is, what is called in French, *mediatisé*, a term which awkwardly trans-lates as thoroughly represented by all forms of media. His public image has a separate, yet intimately connected, relationship to his writing as time and again Houellebecq, the author, stands accused of holding the views expressed in his novels, thus returning us to Barthes's famous pronouncement that a literary work is 'always in the end, through the more or less transparent allegory of the fiction, the *author* "confiding in us"'.[26] Houellebecq's image, that of the doleful, politically ambivalent *dépressif*, circulates powerfully in the interpretative economy of his work and, as such, is inextricably caught up in its reception. The French editions of many of his novels show not an anonymous woman in her underwear on the cover, but Houellebecq himself, plastic shopping bag gloomily wedged in the crook of his arm, scowling and smoking, his cigarette precariously balanced between the third and fourth fingers, instantly joining the pantheon of iconographic French intellectual smokers. This, of course, perpetuates the ongoing confusion of author with text and with character – most of his novels feature a character called Michel whose biographical details are strikingly close to those of the 'author' and in *La Carte et le territoire*, one of the characters is named Houellebecq.

My arguments in this book begin with the controversies around the publication of first *Atomised* and then *Platform*.[27] In France, the publication of the former saw Houellebecq simultaneously praised and vilified; hailed both as a Camus for the 'internet generation' and as the new Louis Ferdinand Céline. **Chapter 1**, 'Reception: Notes on Two Scandals', traces the trajectory of the reception of these novels in the popular and literary press. I examine the charges of ideological misbehaviour that were levelled against him by his colleagues and certain sections of the press and also how his work has been read as symptomatic of a fallen France, *une France tombée*, part of a more pervasive rhetoric of *déclinisme* both in France and abroad. Looking at literary reviews and magazines, websites, newspapers and magazines in both English-speaking and French contexts, this chapter examines the main tendencies in the popular reception of his work and focuses in particular on what has become known as '*l'affaire Houellebecq*' in 1999 and on the race-hate trial after the publication of *Platform* in which Houellebecq stood accused of insulting Islam.

Chapter 2 examines the overarching hypothesis running through all of the novels considered here; namely, that market principles of commodification and exchange have come to determine and define the entire life world and that neoliberalism, with its subjectifying biopolitical powers, has extended the reach of reification into the every intimate and affective domain of human life. This, then, is what Houllebecq calls the extension of the domain of the struggle. Drawing on a body of critical work on neoliberalism, particularly Luc Boltanksi and Ève Chiapello's *The New Spirit of Capitalism*, Maurizio Lazaretto, David Harvey, Wendy Brown, and Michael Hardt and Antonio Negri's work in *Empire*, I first trace the development of neoliberalism in the post-Cold War era in a more general economic sense in order to follow its transformation into late capitalist post-Fordism that both precedes and overlaps with what we now call neoliberalism. Using Foucault's concepts of governmentality and biopower that suggest that the extension of state power is effected through ostensibly non-ideological means, this chapter looks at the subjectifying mechanisms of neoliberalism that has in its sights not just the transformation of labour practices and patterns of consumption but the total colonization of everyday life into privatized interest and enterprise producing not citizens but the super-rational figure of *homo œconomicus*.

Isolated white, middle class, middle-aged males, economically comfortable but existentially and sexually besieged, Houellebecq's characters live in a society no longer shaped by religion, kinship or the consolations of culture or philosophy but by economic, scientific and technological imperatives. Indifferently shuffling around in this neoliberal world where moral freedom is defined by choice of consumption and everything is available to be consumed, Houellebecq's characters singularly fail to achieve the requisite attachment to their own surplus value. Indifferent to the advantages of free enterprise, flexible working patterns and private ownership, they are set adrift in the networks of social, cultural and sexual deregulation. **Chapter 3** considers the ways in which all his characters are flawed or bad subjects of neoliberalism who flounder and finally malfunction within a system that permits no alternative, no outside, to the regime of the production and circulation of commodities.

One of the enduring 'scandals' of Houellebecq's work in France is his relentlessly negative depiction of the spirit of '68. Examining the trajectory of anti-'68 thought (*la pensée anti-'68*) in French culture beginning in the 1980s, **Chapter 4**, 'Liquidating the Sixties', argues that the novels examined here form part of a wider political and cultural discourse of a 'turn to the right', *droitisation*, that disregards any progressive achievements that came out of the radical politics of '68. Houellebecq argues that with their emphasis on anti-humanism, narcissistic individualism and above all desire, the *soixante-huitards* merely smoothed the way for capitalism's incursion into the private and affective domains. I look here at the ways in which his work singles out feminism for particular opprobrium, blaming it for encouraging a damaging moral relativism that proved to be ruinous not only for the family unit but also for relations between men and women. Reading *Atomised* and *Platform*, this chapter explores Houellebecq's proposition that '68's emphasis on sexual liberation has led us towards Sade rather than Rousseau and has rendered us incapable of either love or compassion.

Continuing to examine some of the concerns of the previous chapter, **Chapter 5** looks at the ubiquity of sex in Houellebecq's novels and argues that it functions in his work as *the* correlative for ideas about the extension of neoliberal economic principles into affective human life. In a world radically desymbolized by the language of capital, of investment and exchange, sex is simply another transaction in which the lover is less a site of intimate relationality than part of a circuit of self-interest. The realm of the erotic has thus been rendered as banally commodified as shopping or tourism. His characters are becoming insensible to intimacy yet are saturated with the possibilities of unattainable sexual ecstasy. Sex is, believes Houellebecq, sociologically determined and, accordingly he provides a sketch of the changing sexual mores in post-'68 France, suggesting that sex now operates above all, as a second system of social and economic differentiation. Tracing the divergent responses to this system through the stories of Michel and Bruno, I examine the libertine versus the acetic response to the changed valency of sex under neoliberalism. I also consider here the *reductio ad absurdum* of *Platform*'s 'modest proposal' that suggests that sex tourism in the Third World is the logical outcome of the commercialization of sex.

Each of Houellebecq's novels considered thus far (*Whatever, Atomised* and *Platform*) examines what happens when economic logic is extended to the private and affective domain and the subsequent suffering that occurs when human feelings and all aspects of human life are reduced to the status of an object. The final chapter, 'The End of Affect', considers the ways in which this state of affairs is managed, not by any social or political or anthropological means, but through a rationally applied scientific solution. The flicker of hope, albeit a faint one, that a solution might be found for the problem of sex, is wholly absent from *The Possibility of an Island*. Beginning where *Atomised* leaves off, this novel appears to give up altogether on the contingency and potentiality of human life and proposes a purely technical solution to the problem of human suffering. This produces a post-theological and post-human world in which the rational determinism of technology is sovereign and the need for sexual and ontological difference has been overcome.

My arguments do not set out to endorse or contradict any one critical position on Houellebecq's work; they aim rather to trace a thematic arc across the four novels that demonstrates a movement away from the affective lifeworld of thinking, feeling and acting in a human way. This trajectory is, I will argue, one of despair at the human condition as whichever way one views his writing, that is, as sincere or satirical, it finally fails to imagine anything other than participation in or withdrawal from the world it describes.

Notes

1 Theo Tait, 'Gorilla with Mobile Phone', *London Review of Books*, 28, 3, 9 February 2006, http://www.lrb.co.uk/v28/n03/tit01.html [accessed 18 January 2011].

2 Emily Eakin, 'Le Provocateur', *The New York Times Magazine*, 10 September 2000,

http://partners.nytimes.com/library/magazine/home/20000910mag-houellebecq. html [accessed 18 June 2011].

3 Keith Reader, *The Abject Object: Avatars of the Phallus in Contemporary French Theory, Literature and Film* (Amsterdam: Rodopi Press, 2006), 105.

4 Marian Van Renterghem, 'Le Procès Houellebecq', *Le Monde*, 8 November 1998.

5 Emmanuel Hect, 'Ben Jalloun flingue Houellebecq', *L'Express*, 20 August 2010, http://www.lexpress.fr/culture/livre/ben-jelloun-flingue-houellebecq_913745.html [accessed 5 March 2011].

6 See Ruth Cruickshank, *Fin de Millénaire French Fiction* (Oxford: Oxford University Press, 2009), 115–22.

7 *Whatever*, 99.

8 Michel Houellebecq, *Rester vivant et autres textes* (Paris: Éditions de la Différence, 1991), 43.

9 Martin Crowley, 'Houellebecq: The Wreckage of Liberation', *Romance Studies*, 20.1 (2002), 17–28, 18.

10 Marc Weitzmann, 'L'entretien des Inrocks', *Les Inrockuptibles* 16 (April 1996), 56–9, 57.

11 *Whatever*, 12.

12 Ibid., 14.

13 Ibid., 40.

14 Crowley, Martin, 'Low Resistance', *On Bathos*, Sara Crangle and Peter Nicholls, (eds) (London: Continuum, 2010), 148–64, 149.

15 *Whatever*, 14.

16 *Platform*, 17.

17 Svend Brinkmann, 'Literature as Qualitative Inquiry: The Novelist as Researcher', *Qualitative Inquiry*, 15, 8 (2009), 1376–94, 1387.

18 Jean Baudrillard, *The System of Objects* (London: Verso, 1996), 14–15.

19 *Rester vivant*, 33.

20 *Whatever*, 39.

21 Henri Lefebvre, *Critique of Everyday Life*, vol. 3 (London: Verso, 1991), 10.

22 *Atomised*, 349.

23 *Rouge-brun* is a French term that describes the meeting point of right and left politics.

24 See Lisa Downing, 'French Cinema's New Sexual Revolution: Postmodern Porn and Troubled Genre', *French Cultural Studies*, 15. 3 (2004), 265–80.

25 William Cloonan, 'Literary Scandal, *Fin du Siècle*, and the Novel in 1999', *The French Review*, 74. 1 (2000), 14–30, 14.

26 Roland Barthes, 'The Death of the Author', *Image–Music–Text*, ed. and trans. Stephen Heath (New York: Hill and Wang, 1977) 142–8, 143.

27 I will refer throughout to English translations of Houellebecq's work, using some translations of my own where indicated.

1

Reception: Notes on Two Scandals

... in practice I speak on behalf of nothing very much.

Michel Houellebecq

... whenever the French talk about Houellebecq, I always feel certain that they mean something else.

Mark Lilla[1]

Born Michel Thomas in La Réunion on 26 February in either 1956 or 1958 – the year of birth is disputed by his estranged mother – Houellebecq is a child of the immediate post-'68 moment assertion. Undoubtedly bullied by older boys at his boarding school under the policy of *autogestion* that was integral to the post-'68 educational reforms, he suffered first-hand the effects of cultural and structural liberalization and, in many ways, his upbringing was almost perfectly exemplary of what he has described as the selfish narcissism of the generation of '68. His anaesthesiologist mother, Lucie Ceccaldi, and mountain guide father, René Thomas, very quickly separated after his birth and 'soon lost all interest in his existence', sending their young son off to live with his maternal grandparents in Algeria then to boarding school in Meaux, France. In 1961, Michel moved to France to live with his paternal grandparents, first in rural Yonne until he was 12, and then moving to Crécy-en-Brie. These early experiences of his grandmother's cooking, the stability of the French rural way of life and the pastoral freedom of the countryside form an important part of Houellebecq's imagined French past, as does the traumatic experience of parental abandonment. He claims not to have a single picture of himself as a child. Significantly, Houellebecq would take his paternal grandmother's name in a doubly symbolic act that affiliated him with the grandparental generation and simultaneously spurned the post-war generation to which his parents belonged. The tale of family dysfunction does not end there, however. Enraged by the thinly-disguised portrayal of her as the feckless Janine in *Atomised*, his mother wrote a damning indictment of her son in a book called *L'Innocente* (2008) asking her rather startled audience during her book tour, 'Who hasn't called their son a sorry little prick?' Who indeed?

After obtaining a degree in agricultural engineering from the Institut Agronomique Paris–Grignon, Houellebecq spent some time unemployed during which he was hospitalized for depression, eventually finding work as a computer programmer at the Assemblée Nationale. He married at the age of 24, but the marriage lasted only briefly, producing a son in 1981 of whom Houellebecq has rarely, if ever, spoken. It was during these longer periods of unemployment in the 1980s that he began writing, setting up his own literary magazine *Karamazov*. In 1985, encouraged by the writer Michel Bulteau, his first published poems appeared in the *Nouvelle Revue de Paris* and he soon became part of the editorial board of the journal *Digraphe* directed by Jean Ristat. In 1991, with Bulteau's continuing encouragement, he published his first literary critical work, an eccentric piece that is part science fiction, part essay, *H. P. Lovecraft: Contre le monde: contre la vie/H. P. Lovecraft: Against the World, Against Life* (2005), for the series *Infrequentables*. Taking unpaid leave from his programming job at the Ministry of Agriculture, Houellebecq worked on his first collection of poetry *Rester vivant, méthode* (*To Stay Alive: Method*) published in 1991. In 1992, a collection of poems, *La Poursuite du bonheur* (*The Pursuit of Happiness*) won the Prix Tristan Tzara. A further collection, *Le Sens du combat* (*The Art of Struggle*), won the Prix Flore in 1996. More poetry followed in 1999 with the publication of *Renaissance*, a collection that met with modest critical success. It was not, however, until the publication of *Les Particules élementaires* in 1998 that Houellebecq gained widespread critical recognition. Awarded the prestigious Irish IMPAC prize in 2002, this was the novel that ignited the phenomenal *succès de scandale* that moved out of Houellebecq's native France into the Anglophone literary landscape.

Critically applauded but not commercially successful, Houellebecq's first novel, *Extension du domaine de la lutte*, was published to positive, if incon-spicuous, reviews in France where it sold a respectable 16,000 copies. Translated into English by the somewhat mystifying, not to say off-putting, single word *Whatever*,[2] this slim novel was published by Serpent's Tail Press in 1998. Moving between litotic black humour and bathetic acedia, *Whatever* initiated what has become known as *le monde houellebecquien*. Evacuated of its post-war excep-tionalism, France is represented as an 'every-nation', no longer a particular cultural or intellectual space but a blandly homogenized Western topography in which literature, culture, food and drink retain no inherently distinctive national qualities. In this homogenous space Houellebecq's depressive protagonists are sexually impoverished but financially comfortable, living with grim resignation in the mid-level managerial ranks of the burgeoning information economy and beleaguered at every turn by the increasing subsumption of all areas of everyday life into the principles of exchange. Merely adumbrated in *Whatever*, this scenario is one which will be repeated and elaborated upon in more detail in both *Atomised* and *Platform*.

Houellebecq's second novel *Les Particules élémentaires* (1998) was quickly translated into English and published in 2000 as *Atomised* in Britain and, with the more literal translation of *The Elementary Particles*, in the United States. Translated into more than 20 languages, the novel had substantial commercial success in 25 countries worldwide but sold most copies in Britain, the United States, the Netherlands and Germany. Extending the thesis of the relationship between the economic, sexual and affective seen in embryonic form in *Whatever*, *Atomised* traces the lives of parentally abandoned half-brothers Bruno and Michel, whose passage to madness and suicide via two different paths takes in the broad historical sweep of post-1945 France and the altered social and cultural configurations of family, economics and sexuality in the post-'68 era. Examining the extension of consumer capitalism into all areas of contemporary life, most particularly into the sexual and affective domain, *Atomised* roundly lambasts the *soixante-huitards* for their encouragement of narcissistic individualism and suggests that there are only two responses to the world that they have created and encouraged: hedonistic libertinism or ascetic retreat. Both responses end in a similarly tragic fashion for Michel and Bruno as the novel moves into the generic terrain of science fiction, a mode that Houellebecq will more fully explore in his fifth novel, *The Possibility of an Island*. Both this novel and *Atomised* suggest that the transformation of human intimacy into a rationalized productive space within late capitalism can only be 'saved' by the biotechnical solution of cloning. The eschatological utopian/dystopian solution presented at the novel's end is that of a cloned post-humanity free from the contingency and disappointment of desire.

With high sales figures and considerable exposure in the popular media, *Atomised*'s unusually mixed critical reception would intensify with the publication in 2001 of Houellebecq's next novel, *Plateforme*, published in English as *Platform* in 2002. Arguably an even more controversial work than *Atomised*, *Platform* continues to a large extent the ideas presented in its predecessor, suggesting that the solution to the encroachment of the materialist ethos into the sexual domain is to extend this logic even further by setting up a demand and supply relationship between the West and the Third World. On the face of it, this might be taken as a satirical treatment of contemporary Western society and its commercialization of sex. It was not, however, the depiction of sex for sale that turned out to be controversial but several comments made in the novel on the subject of Islam which caught public attention and dramatically intensified the maelstrom of controversy around Houellebecq. Compounding these comments in an interview with *Lire*, Houellebecq declared that Islam was 'the stupidest religion' and 'a dangerous religion right from the start', concluding the interview by saying: 'All one can wish for is that it (capitalism) will rapidly triumph. Materialism is a lesser evil. Its values are despicable, but less destructive, less cruel than those of Islam.'[3] Unsurprisingly perhaps, these remarks provoked outrage among Muslim groups in France and he was duly taken to court in September 2002 where he stood accused of 'incitement to religious and racial hatred'. Choosing to defend himself, Houellebecq not only refused to retract his statement but defiantly reiterated his sentiments: 'All I said is that their religion is stupid'. He was finally acquitted with the judge declaring that what he had written in *Platform* had been directed against the religion of Islam and not its followers.

Another, shorter, work, *Lanzarote*, was published in 2000 and translated into English in 2004. A slender piece of work in all senses, it repeats and mixes elements of both *Whatever* and *Platform* but is lacking in the urgency or conviction of either. A depressive, middle-aged urban professional sets off on his travels on which he finds sexual adventure with two German lesbians on a deserted beach. In between highly implausible sexual bouts with Babs and Pam, the central character comes up with some half-baked truths about national characteristics such as 'Belgians are extremely scatological', 'the Englishman is not motivated by a keen appetite for discovery' and the Italian partiality for 'a cute ass'.[4] As a whole, the book has the air of a stopgap project, frequently repeating ideas from the two earlier works with little by way of progression or development. In many ways, it is as if Raphael Tisserand – the sexually unsuccessful character from *Whatever* – survives the car crash that kills him off in that novel, returns to Paris and takes a *fin de siècle* winter holiday in the Canary Islands.

Houellebecq's third novel *La Possibilité d'une île* (2005) translated as *The Possibility of an Island* was published in English in the same year; the rapidity of the translation a marker of Houellebecq's popularity in the Anglophone world. Effectively resuming where *Atomised* left off, the novel is both a reiteration and an extension of earlier ideas around sex, ageing and the impossibility of 'love' in our time, now more fully embedded in an explicitly science fiction genre. Through the figure of the Daniel1, a provocative postmodernist comedian whose shows are entitled *We Prefer the Palestinian Orgy Sluts* and *Munch on My Gaza Strip (My Huge Jewish Settler)*, Houellebecq broaches the emptiness of post-Nietzschean transgressive culture which is, he believes, the sour inheritance of May '68. Possessing an arguably bleaker and more despairing vision than his previous novels, *The Possibility of an Island* depicts an apocalyptic vision of cloning in which all desire and affect has been expunged from human life and where the post-human entities – neohumans – live in isolated, monadic compounds communicating only by means of a virtual network. Despite its desolate eschatological vision and dismissal of any political or ethical solution to the alienation of the subject, the novel attracted very little critical or ideological indignation, giving the impression that critics and readers alike had become more or less inured to this writer-provocateur's output.[5]

Reception

Reviewing Michel Houellebecq's third novel *Platform* in the *London Review of Books*, Theo Tait provides a useful schema in which he categorizes the reception of his work.[6] Referring principally, but not exclusively, to the writer's reception in his native France, Tait identifies two broad categories of reaction. The first of these is a kind of exhilarated reception in which Houellebecq is heralded not simply as a cantankerous chronicler of the contemporary world but as no less than a 'visionary diagnostician', a view that has arisen largely from his apparently 'prophetic' depiction in *Platform* of an Islamic fundamentalist terrorist attack on a Thai beach published in French two years before the Bali bombings.[7] This impression of authorial prescience was enhanced further by the fact that *Platform* was published in English just weeks before the September 11th attacks on the World Trade Center in New York, and, according to at least one account, Houellebecq's editor was actually completing a press release 'designed to pacify French Muslims' when news broke of the attack on the Twin Towers.[8] Despite their fortuitous relation to his novels, these two historical events served to create the perception of Houellebecq as a kind of soothsaying presence on the literary scene. Also lending weight to this category of reception was the representation of human cloning in his second novel, *Atomised*. Published two years before the last chromosome in the Human Genome project was finally deciphered, the novel discussed in some detail the technicalities involved in genetic human cloning, an account which was, according to at least one reviewer in a scientific journal, an accurate 'foretaste of the profound ways that molecular biology and genetic engineering will dominate the philosophical and ethical discourse of the next century'.[9] And finally, his most recent novel, the Prix Goncourt winning *The Map and the Territory*, has been praised for its prognostic depiction of the financial crisis that followed soon after the 2008 stock market crash, a crisis that was merely imminent at the time of writing. 'So is he', asks one of Houellebecq's reviewers, 'a prophet?'[10]

A second category of reception, overlapping significantly with the first, is one in which Houellebecq is regarded as one of a few living writers able to tap into a politically bleak zeitgeist in which his view of the human condition, politically, culturally and sexually, is regarded as giving voice to some 'unspeakable' prejudices for a large number of embattled Western Europeans, predominantly in France, Britain, Holland and Germany where his success has been greatest. Writing of Houellebecq's role as the 'new Rushdie' after he was taken to court for inciting religious hatred, Salman Rushdie himself observes that '*Platform* is a novel to go to if you want to understand the France beyond the liberal intelligentsia, the France that gave the left such a bloody nose in the last presidential election, and whose discontents and prejudices the extreme right was able to exploit'.[11] Houellebecq, then, has been hailed as an ambassador for a cultural and political populism that seems, at every moment, to teeter perilously on the verge of reactionary backlash. His work certainly seems to articulate the *ressentiment* of white, middle-aged, middle-class men, a 'low masculine anger' executed in a volley, not just of 'political incorrectness' (a nebulous term at best) but also of philosophical and intellectual incorrectness too.[12] In a prose style that is as banally flat as it is captivating, he writes of badly dressed and unattractive loners; of men who masturbate frequently but who can't find sex; men who blame their inability to find erotic and romantic fulfilment on the neoliberal economic system that has introduced a Darwinist element into the hitherto protected domains of sexual and affective life. In the novels examined here, there is a remarkably similar narrative trajectory. Living in a world where economic considerations contour personal and affective relations, the male protagonists find themselves frozen out of the sexual marketplace, briefly find sex, describe this sex in minute detail, make a few bitterly disparaging comments about rival ethnic groups and feminism both of which threaten their acquisition and enjoyment of sex; the women providing the sex then die, always directly or indirectly because of sex, and the protagonists spend the rest of their days in abject solitude musing on the fact that what they wanted all along was actually love not sex. At the risk of belittling the novels, this summary of Houellebecq's 'plots', such as they are, is not much of an exaggeration.

Houellebecq is charged, then, with offering a kind of titillating ideological and intellectual *exposé* in which he mischievously reveals a less palatable side of the 'true French'. This reputation of Houellebecq as *provocateur* has proved particularly enduring in the reception of his novels in the United States where his work is seen as speaking to a *France tombée*; a nation that has lost its political and cultural exceptionalism, but perhaps more significantly, one fallen from its lofty role as intellectual leader. In an insightful essay reviewing the latest crop of books tracing the downwards arc of a 'fallen France', Perry Anderson remarks, 'No other nation, after all, has so conspicuously based its identity on culture, understood in the broadest sense. But here too, as much as – in some ways, perhaps even more than – in matters of industry or state, the scene at large is dismal …'. While literature as a 'pure' genre may have 'lost its position at the apex of French culture' under the Fifth Republic, Anderson argues that the intensity and quality of post-1945 cultural production truly 'set France apart for two generations after the war'. During this time, he continues, the generic definition of what constituted the literary became more flexible: 'Letters in the classical sense lost their commanding position within the culture at large. What took their place was an exotic marriage of social and philosophical thought, at the altar of literature. It was the product of this union that gave intellectual life in the decade of De Gaulle's reign its peculiar brilliance and intensity.'

Portraying contemporary France as a transformed nation state in which the role of culture and the public importance of cultural and literary-intellectual discourses have altered, many say deteriorated, beyond recognition, Anderson argues that Houellebecq is the only French writer since Sartre with significant national and international 'public authority'.[13] If, as Anderson suggests, all of this is true, then it is of equal significance to note that this 'exotic marriage' seems to have reached the end of its union in Houellebecq's work as his novels are constructed in such a defiantly *lisible* manner that the *scriptible* formalism of 'high' post-structuralism with its penchant for ludic metafiction, self-consciousness, multiplicity and linguistic aporia seems but a distant memory. Explicitly, and often humorously, attacking the Nietzschean-Freudo-Marxist intellectual axis of '68 thought, Houellebecq sees literature informed by 'theory' as more than a little ridiculous, and it is this mood of intellectual philistinism permeating much of his work, perhaps as much as the salacious content, that has contributed to his reputation as a mulish literary provocateur. Although he acknowledges the significance of Houellebecq's work in contemporary French literature, Anderson observes, not without some hint of regret, that 'the days of Malraux are long gone'.[14]

Houellebecq offers a cultural pessimism served up not in the formally pleasing prose of Beckett, Musil or even Céline, but in a monotonous, often inconsistently textured, drone that seems fitting to ring in the greyish political tenor of twenty-first century France. Commenting on the relationship between literature and politics in France, he has observed, shrewdly but perhaps somewhat hubristically, that 'when a country is strong, self-confident, it is prepared to accept any amount of pessimism from its writers without turning a hair. The France of the 1950s accepted people like Camus, Sartre, Ionesco, Beckett. The France of the 2000s has trouble putting up with people like me'.[15] The France of which Houellebecq speaks here is, of course, ideologically a world away from that of Camus and Sartre, where Right and Left were clearly defined in an oppositional, often acrimonious, relationship. Such ideological differences have, however, become increasingly less clear and, in very many cases, have collapsed into one another producing a blurring of the boundaries between Left and Right, resulting in the now familiar ideological terrain that defines the centre-right ground of mainstream politics. This has certainly been the case in Britain since the re-branding of the left under Tony Blair's New Labour which embraced rather than denounced neoliberalism. With its strong tradition of *dirigisme*, to a large extent France was buffered against the excesses of neoliberalism experienced in Britain and the United States, but post-Chirac, it has been gradually joining the rest of the West in accepting this Anglo-Saxon, centre-left economic model.

In the light of this idea of a 'fallen France', part of an intellectual discourse known in French as *déclinisme*, American reviewers in particular have regarded Houellebecq's writing as a long overdue debunking of a particularly haughty Gallic moral and intellectual relativism, a view made quite explicit in the title of Jacques Derrida's obituary in *The New York Times*: 'Jacques Derrida, Abstruse Theorist, Dies at 74'. Scarcely able to contain his antipathy towards deconstruction, obituarist Jonathan Kandell describes it as one of 'those fashionable, slippery philosophies that emerged from France after World War II' which:

> … asserted that all writing was full of confusion and contradiction, and that the author's intent could not overcome the inherent contradictions of language itself, robbing texts – whether literature, history or philosophy – of truthfulness, absolute meaning and permanence. The concept was eventually applied to the whole gamut of arts and social sciences, including linguistics, anthropology, political science, even architecture.[16]

Viewed in this way, since the post-war period French thought had been stealthily 'robbing' the truth content from not only literature but also society, replacing it with a menacing radical uncertainty in which the world and its citizens are perceived as little more than discursive entities. Ruth Cruickshank has pointed up this intellectual scepticism, predominantly American in origin, towards French theory and cites as an example, the now notorious, publishing hoax carried out by Alan Sokal's 'postmodern' article in *Social Text*, 'Transgressing the Boundaries: Towards a Transformative Hermeneutics of Quantum Gravity'. Saturated with erudite disparagement and impudent references to anti-Enlightenment discourses, interdisciplinary thought and hegemonic epistemologies, the piece attacked what Sokal, a physics professor at NYU, perceived as the linguistically obfuscating and pointlessly anti-establishment values espoused by a Parisian variety of 'high' intellectualism. Commenting on this affair, John Marks notes that 'Sokal and Bricmont might be considered to have uncovered nothing less than a "pathology" lying at the heart of the supposedly rude health of thought in French life [...] the anti-Republican drive to seduce rather than to persuade by rational argument'.[17] In this context, then, Houellebecq's work has been taken as a reaction against the obscurantism of his intellectual forebears; his novels a much-needed 'common sense' unmasking of the abstruse pretensions and tendencies of critical theory that have influenced much of French literature since the 1950s. A review of *Atomised* in the *Economist* seizes on precisely this mood of anti-intellectualism:

> As he inveighs against trendy intellectualism and liberal complacency, you catch something like the rage and calculation of National Front speeches. As a place of grey nightmare, his France is a fictional invention, to be sure, but one that has had an astounding reception. In Mr Houellebecq's success some see confirmation that his main target, France's intelligentsia, has its head dangerously in the sand. Less starkly, his success may simply represent the passing to a new generation of the literary flame—albeit, in this instance, a blowtorch.[18]

Predictably, in France many reviews of Houellebecq's early work were eager to situate him within this 'new generation' of French writers, which included Marie Darrieussecq, Iegor Gran, Virginie Despentes, Christine Angot and Maurice Dantec and it was not long, as William Cloonan observes, before 'the birth of a new school was announced, the decline of morality decried [...] and humanism was once again pronounced dead'.[19] In an article in *Le Monde* in October 1998 called 'Une nouvelle tendance en littérature', Frédéric Badré decried the French novel as essentially 'irrelevant [...] too narcissistic [...] too introverted' and 'turned towards the past', announcing that Houellebecq, along with Darrieussecq and Gran, represented a new school of French writing that eschewed the avant-garde aesthetics of Les Éditions de Minuit.[20] Rejecting the dense and often impenetrable semantic ambiguity and undecidability that still lingered from the days of post-structuralism and the *nouveau roman*, these new writers ostensibly offered a less cryptic depiction of everyday life that had an immediate and visceral connection with a wide reading public.[21] The mood of everyday life they describe, however, is decidedly grim and in an article in *Le Monde* in 1999, surveying this new tendency in French literature in a less than positive light, Michel Guénaire takes Houellebecq to task for being the head boy of a new school of writing, 'apostles' of a new misery who are the last 'inheritors of the spoils of materialism' and who have set out 'to abolish the dream' and 'kill beauty'.[22] Another article in *Le Monde* attributes Houellebecq's emergence at the end of the nineties as illustrative of a wider intellectual vacuum in French culture that favoured 'the proliferation of anti-poetics and anti-fiction' and a sort of literary 'kitsch' well-suited to its politically blank times.[23] Both *Whatever* and *Atomised* were, in many ways, entirely consonant with this 'new tendency' in French literature; indeed as Cloonan notes, 'far from being unique in capturing this feeling whatever one thinks of *Les Particules éléméntaires*, there is nothing in the novel, either thematically or descriptively, that cannot also be found in other works'.[24] Broadly speaking, these are accurate assessments of the content of Houellebecq's novels as it was certainly the case that his literary peers were addressing comparable issues in their writing, namely, the adverse effects of consumerism and social and sexual alienation, but with nothing like the mordant despair and ideological recalcitrance of Houellebecq's work. What further distinguishes his work from his contemporaries is his unremitting, manifest disdain, if not actual contempt, for those modes of post-war French writing that combine the textuality of a Derridean-influenced post-structuralism with a Sartrean political and ethical commitment. Houellebecq's writing is the very antithesis of Sartre's concept of *littérature engagé* defined most clearly in *What is Literature?* (1947): '... by speaking, I reveal the situation by my very intention of changing it; I reveal it to myself and to others in order to change it [...] with every word I utter, I involve myself a little more in the world, and by the same token I emerge from it a little more, since I go beyond it towards the future'.[25] By his own repeated admission, Houellebecq has no interest in involving himself in the world, politically, textually or otherwise; indeed, each of the novels considered here depicts, in one way or another, an inching away from the world and its vicissitudes. Claiming to be possessed of 'an ideological diffidence verging on atheism', Houellebecq is a quietist in every respect, '… happy to live in a peaceable world in which the moral fibre of a man is rarely truly tested', one in which 'most actions are morally neutral'.[26] Houellebecq's impression of his own 'neutrality' is, however, misleading to say the least. What he regards as neutral and indifferent has elicited condemnatory, even outraged, reactions from many critics, particularly in France, who regard the views expressed in his novels as an insolent anti-intellectualism that is integral to his denunciation of the 'would-be Jacobins' of the generation of 1968.[27]

Houellebecq's work, then, is a rejection of a literary tradition that might broadly be called political in which the literary text, typically the novel, offers some kind of engagement with an otherness, a complex term deftly summed up by Derek Attridge as 'that which is, at any given moment, outside the horizon provided by the culture for thinking, understanding, imagining, feeling, perceiving'.[28] In Houellebecq's novels quite the opposite is the case and, as noted by his most perceptive of critics, his writing returns us to a world decidedly closer to both the positivist determinism of the nineteenth-century literary naturalists and the seventeenth-century moralists for whom life is decipherable according to a set of either prescriptive or proscriptive doctrines. *Le monde houellebecquien* appears to be, then, a categorical reversal of the ethical spirit that has characterized some modern French literature shaped by the Derridean concept of a generosity to the *tout autre* of alterity that involves a radical openness to the not-yet-experienced of thought. If, as, Derrida has suggested, ethics and politics 'start with undecidability', then Houellebecq's work could be judged as non-ethical and non-political as it is predicated upon the already decided, situated in an already anticipated ethical landscape of knowability in which otherness is continually excluded.[29] As Jack Abecassis notes of *Atomised*, it is 'No longer a space of the heroic or the exploratory, the difference between the reader and the fictional character has been reduced to a contemplation of the same by the same …'.[30] The world of the same, then, is Houellebecq's narrative territory. But is this a reaction against and a critique of the blandly homogenizing texture of neoliberalism or a kind of surrender to and acceptance of this similitude? Whatever claims Houellebecq may make about himself as politically neutral and passive, his work certainly cannot claim a similar neutrality. Imperfect though it may be deemed stylistically, his writing is possessed of an uncommon sense of polemical urgency that proffers a genuinely unsettling condemnation of its times. Houellebecq's writing is not a neutral take on contemporary culture, a common-sense view of the way things are, but an expression of a disappointed political idealism that suggests that if neoliberalism is regarded as the *pensée unique* of politics then this can be taken to its logical conclusion in a literature that allows no possibility of an outside to the low, monotonous drone of our times. If there is no outside, no space of opposition, then our only options, Houellebecq suggests, are either hedonistic participation or an ascetic retreat. Unsurprisingly, the unwaveringly self-assured intensity with which this message is articulated has earned him the critical reputation, in some quarters at least, of being a reactionary writer. As we shall see, many reviews and articles have mounted a vigorous, and in some cases extremely censorious, ideological condemnation of his work in which he has been 'considered by turns a pornographer, a Stalinist, a racist, a sexist, a nihilist, a reactionary, a eugenicist and a homophobe'.[31] This is an attitude with which Houellebecq has become extremely familiar since the publication of *Atomised*:

> What I do reproach them for isn't bad reviews. It is that they talk about things having nothing to do with my books—my mother or my tax exile—and that they caricature me so that I've become a symbol of so many unpleasant things—cynicism, nihilism, misogyny. People have stopped reading my books because they've already got their idea about me.[32]

Then, there is the performative, *médiatisé* figure of 'Michel Houellebecq' to consider; the louche, shambolic figure in a crumpled anorak who sits slumped in interviews, chain-smoking and inaudibly mumbling between improbably long conversational pauses, has become a familiar image in French culture. The mediated presence of Houellebecq has become a significant element of his reception as a living writer; indeed, the ubiquity of this presence almost constitutes a separate cultural phenomenon in itself. Numerous appearances on television, newspaper and magazine interviews, photos of himself on the covers of his novels and his cyber-persona on the fast-moving online sites that can make up a cultural discourse within days – the whole array of extra-literary material – have created what the sociological literary critic Jérôme Meizoz has called the paratextual field of authorial posture.[33] Building upon Gérard Genette's concepts in *Seuils* (1987) of the paratext as a para-literary 'message that has taken on material form' and that 'necessarily has a location that can be situated in relation to the location of the text itself: around the text and either within the same volume or at a more respectful (or more prudent) distance'. Meizoz updates and elaborates on these categories for the age of the internet, arguing that the paratextual character of Houellebecq has been a powerful aspect of the production of the persona *maudit* of Michel Houellebecq, *née* Thomas, a figure that circulates in and around the economy of texts inevitably influencing their interpretation and reception.[34] The paratextual cloud surrounding Michel Houellebecq is almost overwhelmingly large. It is not, however, particularly difficult to order as it is shaped by two vociferously contrasting receptions, both within the academy and outside, summed up by the striking polarization of the two websites devoted to Houellebecq: *Les Amis de Michel Houellebecq* and *L'Amicale des Ennemis des amis de Michel Houellebecq*.[35]

From the early 1980s into the 1990s, there was a proliferation of outlets for the both the dissemination of literature and for its popular reception in France, part of what has been called '*l'effet Pivot*' after the presenter of the influential television programme *Apostrophes*, Bernard Pivot. The popularization of literature continued with the proliferation of literary reviews and magazines like *La Quinzaine littéraire*, *Le Monde des livres*, *Le Magazine littéraire* and later *Lire*, *L'Atelier du roman* and *Les Inrockuptibles*. More significant perhaps was the gradual incorporation of writers and intellectuals into non-literary arenas. Indeed, by the end of the twentieth century, as Tamara Chaplain notes in *Turning on the Mind: French Philosophers on Television*, around 35,000 programmes had aired on French TV dealing with philosophy and its cognate domains of literature and culture.[36] Little by little then, French writers found themselves, or in some cases put themselves, in the media eye and this began to have a real effect on the ways in which the role of the writer was understood. Meizoz was one of a group of critics influenced by a new understanding of Pierre Bourdieu's concept of habitus who were interested, among other things, in these shifting contexts of reception. Carefully examining Houellebecq's provocative statements in the press such as his (non) defence of the alleged misogyny and racism in his work in an interview given to *Le Monde*: 'Literature's calling is not to appease but rather to worry and to offend. It is there to provoke. Otherwise, what is the point? Nothing human, or inhuman for that matter, is off limits to literature', Meizoz began to theorise the idea of the 'author's posture' which he sees as 'the convergence between a discursive and a non-discursive form of self-presentation (e.g. in behaviour and dress)'.[37] This 'posture' of the author is a mediated performance that is consumed across a variety of media in which text-images of the author accumulate around these public outings and become a separate product or a commodity in their own right.[38] The authorial creation that has become 'Houellebecq the controversialist' is built upon the ongoing confusion around the status of the authorial voice in his novels, a situation neatly and sarcastically summed up by Salhi Abdel-Illah in *Libération*: '... let's start with the hyperrealist storyline where Jospin is called … Jospin, and Chirac is called … Chirac, the same courtesy being extended to Jacques Maillot. But the same equivalence does not hold for the fictional Michel, the hero/narrator, who in no way is to be confused with the real Michel Houellebecq … '[39]

I move on now to examine some of the specifics of the reception of Houellebecq's work in literary magazines, reviews and newspapers in both the online and print media. The contexts of reception in France occupy a significant position in this examination as a result of the nationally specific scandals and controversies surrounding *Atomised* and *Platform*. My intention here is not to provide an exhaustive account of the reception of Houellebecq's work but to focus on its most pertinent aspects from 1998 to the present, broadly following the categories outlined above. Both academic and popular reception is largely in agreement with Gavin Bowd's verdict that Houellebecq, for good or for ill, is 'one of the most powerful voices in contemporary French literature'.[40] In men's magazines, science reviews, scholarly journals in sociology, psychology, anthropology, biological sciences and religious studies, Michel Houellebecq has been weighed up in almost every cultural and intellectual arena from high to low through middlebrow, and ideologically assessed by commentators from the political left to right. The intensity of the controversies generated around the reception of *Atomised* and *Platform* was of a significantly greater magnitude than that of his last two novels, *The Possibility of an Island* and *The Map and the Territory*, and accordingly merits the vast bulk of attention here. His first novel, *Whatever*, caused little rumpus but quietly set in motion what has become known as *le monde houellebecquien* with its characteristic ambience of dejection, caustic attitude to the world, dubious attitudes, to put it mildly, towards women and an interest in detailing sexual activity that, while still embryonic in this work, will escalate into what many of his detractors describe as full-blown pornography. I begin here with the controversies surrounding the publication of *Atomised*, Houellebecq's second novel, which, as Katherine Gantz has rightly noted, 'remains the defining work of Houellebecqian (sic) controversy' and one that may be considered paradigmatic for its 'distinctive brand of controversy questioning the explicit and implicit motives of both the text and the author'.[41] Of greater global import, however, was the furore surrounding *Platform* which, playing out in the immediate aftermath of the September 11th attacks, resulted in a series of legal proceedings against Houellebecq.

'L'affaire Houellebecq'

Writing of his experience, first as a reader then as the translator of Houellebecq's second novel, *Les Particules élémentaires* into *Atomised*, Frank Wynne immediately saw the potential for the success of the work: 'This is an extraordinary novel, in every possible sense of that word. Part dialectic, part polemic, part digest of the twentieth century, it is funny, intelligent, infuriating, didactic, touching, visceral, explicit and, possibly, dangerous'.[42] He predicted that the English translation of the novel might sell, at best, 5,000 copies after already selling 250,000 copies in France in its first five months of publication, but by the time *Platform* was published sales figures for the English translation (in Britain and the US) reached 560,000. To date, Houellebecq's novels have been translated into more than 25 languages and have sold well over three million copies worldwide; impressive figures at a time when novel sales have everywhere fallen dramatically. As previously noted, there were other French writers in the 1990s who, in one way or another, covered similarly controversial ground to Houellebecq but none came close to rivalling him in terms of raw sales figures or global repute. Certainly none of these other writers began their novelistic careers with such a sustained period of highly visible public controversy as marked the reception of Houellebecq's work in the years between 1998 and 2002 that very quickly and rather predictably earned him that most hackneyed of all soubriquets, *l'enfant terrible*. A measure of public controversy has held fast to the trajectory of the critical reception of Houellebecq's work and has continued right up to his most recent novel *The Map and The Territory* (2010) for which he was accused of plagiarism from Wikipedia, a rather puny charge compared to the intensity and public nature of his previous indictments. I focus here on the controversies that surrounded the publication of Houellebecq's second and third novels, *Atomised* and *Platform*.

The first of these scandals, while not without its legal dimensions, was broadly speaking focused on Houellebecq's alleged ideological and intellectual misbehaviour; specifically, it was his gloves-off assault upon the political and cultural legacies of '68 that initially provoked the most heated responses in the media. As I will discuss in Chapter 4, 'Liquidating The Sixties', by the time *Atomised* was published in 1998, 30 years after *les évenements*, anti-'68 sentiment had become commonplace in France, but the fact that Houellebecq launched his *pensée anti-'68* from within a leftist literary context came as a shock, both to his colleagues and to the grandees of the left-leaning literary establishment in France. The second scandal was more specific and potentially more serious, centring on some explicitly derogatory comments on Islam made in *Platform* which, together with some equally inflammatory remarks in subsequent interviews about the novel, resulted in a widely publicized trial in which he stood accused of incitement to religious and racial hatred by several mosques in Paris and Lyon, the National Federation of French Muslims and the World Islamic League. Defending himself in court against these charges, Houellebecq was pugnaciously impenitent before the panel of three judges: 'I have never expressed the slightest contempt for Muslims, but I still have as much contempt as ever for Islam'.[43] I begin here with the first of these two scandals, the commotion around the publication of *Atomised*, promptly dubbed by *Le Monde* as '*L'affaire Houellebecq*', a label which has endured.

In the spring of 1998, the proofs of *Atomised* were sent out to a handful of publications, one of which, *Les Inrockuptibles*, would play a critical part in the early production of Houellebecq's reputation as a subversive writer. Begun in 1986 as an alternative popular music magazine, *Les Inrockuptibles*, known more familiarly by its diminutive *Les Inrocks*, became a cultural weekly in 1995 aimed at a hip youth market. Informed by an ideological stance somewhere between 'the critical left and the social democratic left', epitomized by contemporary cultural theorists like Pierre Bourdieu, Jacques Bouveresse and Anthony Giddens, the magazine has enjoyed considerable success as a taste-former in popular French culture.[44] The political allegiances of this publication are important to note here as *Les Inrocks* was an especially staunch defender of Houellebecq's literary cause which seemed to them to be defiantly countercultural but which appeared to others, notably his colleagues on *Perpendiculaire*, as deeply reactionary. In the August edition of 1998, the magazine published an interview in which Houellebecq's animated, and in places rather theatrically controversial, conversation with the journalist extolled the qualities of Joseph Stalin who knew, Houellebecq insisted, how best to deal with 'dangerous deviations by killing anarchists and Trotskyites'.[45] This confrontational declaration, one of several he made over the course of the interview, fuelled the burgeoning controversies around Houellebecq's work which had, even by now, provoked a flurry of scandalized headlines in newspapers and magazines expressing both outrage and curiosity at this writer's scathing take on contemporary life. Another, more routine controversy, surfaced around the novel in August 1998 when *L'Espace du Possible*, a New Age holiday camp ridiculed in *Atomised* for its crystal healing sessions and angel workshops, objected to the mocking use of its name and took out a successful injunction preventing distribution of the novel. Houellebecq was compelled to change the name of the holiday camp, which he did, to *Le Lieu de Changement*, mischievously close to the original if not in words, then certainly in spirit. This seemingly minor incident generated a perceptible murmur of indignation among a handful of well-known writers and a number of critics who sprang to his defence including Frédéric Beigbeder and Dominique Noguez, the latter of whom wrote in *Le Monde* defending Houellebecq's right to freedom of speech. The incident, at best a relatively mild case of roguish opportunism, may well have passed by without further ado had not another, almost simultaneous, controversy boiled over into the public domain.

'Me, a lefty?'

Gavin Bowd has described Houellebecq's hard-to-determine ideological stance in his novels as those characteristic of the *rouge-brun,* a helpful shorthand French term that describes 'an ideological realm where extremes of right and left meet in anti-Americanism, anti-socialism and racism'.[46] On the face of it, Houellebecq's preoccupation with the deleterious effects of neoliberalism on the private and affective life seems to originate from Marxist or post-Marxist concerns about the reifying effects of capitalism on the subject. Houellebecq's work, then, appears to join that of a long line of thinkers and writers across the twentieth century who have considered the intrusion of market relations to all areas of human life as a process of colonization of the lifeworld where the rich qualitative processes of living, the daily rituals of social intercourse, in short, the entire cognitive and communicative topography of everyday life, have been subsumed by the quantifying logic of capitalism. In such a world, people have become not only human capital but have also been encouraged to be entrepreneurs of themselves, endlessly plugged into a circuit of production and consumption that procures a new kind of subjectivity, one entirely defined by the economic that has gradually blurred the boundaries between work and non-work, between the private and the public.[47] Thus, as we have seen, he writes in *Whatever*, 'Economic liberalism is the extension of the domain of the struggle, its extension to all ages and all classes of society'.[48] So far, so leftist. Indeed, his left-wing credentials were seen as impeccable by his collaborators at a writer's editorial collective, *Perpendiculaire*, the publishing venture of the earlier Société Perpendiculaire. Set up in 1985 by a group of writers who, perturbed by the collapse of French socialism and the growing political commitment to the 'third way' of global neoliberalism, attempted to carve out a space for a new politics of *littérature engagée*. Meeting every Wednesday in a Paris café, Les Marronniers, members of the *Perpendiculaire* collective would, in time-honoured Parisian intellectual tradition, discuss literature and politics for hours at a time. Among these café-philo intellectuals was Houellebecq who, as one of revue's founding members and part of a wider left-wing literary scene, successfully 'passed' as a *bona fide* leftist intellectual. Up to this point, his work had given no real cause for concern as it seemed to be entirely consonant with the review's ideological agenda, expressing a suspicion of globalization and the pernicious effects of the free market on everyday life. A 1996 collection of poems, *Le Sens du Combat* (*The Art of Struggle*), was testament to this, addressing 'human beings' emotional relationship with the fleeting nature of the global free market' and the 'rot and decline of Europe': 'I stick out in a free-market society/Like a wolf on an open plane …'.[49] In a poem of somewhat dubious aesthetic quality, 'A Last Stand Against the Free Market', the ideological stance could scarcely be clearer:

> We reject liberal ideology for failing to show us the way, or
> A route to reconciliation between the individual and his
> Fellow human beings
> […]
> It is unquestionable and widely accepted that all human
> Endeavour is measured against purely economic criteria
> Entirely numerical criteria
> Captured in digital files.
> That is not acceptable. We must fight for an economy re-
> trained by the people
> and subjected to different standards I would venture to call
> ethical.

The idea of Houellebecq calling for anything on behalf of 'the people' is, in retrospect, fairly incongruous, not to say implausible, given the thematic arc of his subsequent work which is, to say the very least, devoid of any idea of praxis let alone a 'furious desire to strangle/Half a dozen financial experts'.[50] But the central sentiments expressed in here are those that will remain central in his later work and again, on the face of it, look to be perfectly in keeping with ideas on the political left.

More consonant perhaps with his later brand of low discontent is the idea of a 'cold revolution', presented in an earlier collection of prose, *Rester vivant méthode* (1991) (*How to Stay Alive: A Method*), as a manifesto of sorts; a programme for an ascetic method of living that necessitates isolating oneself in a cultural and information vacuum in order to staunch, if only momentarily, the white noise of consumerism:

> Every individual is nevertheless in a position to produce by himself a sort of cold revolution, by placing himself for a moment, outside of the flow of information and advertising. It is very easy do to this [...] all it requires is a step to one side [...] All it takes is to stop for a moment; to turn off the radio, unplug the television; to not buy anything else.[51]

Similarly, in *Interventions* (1998) Houellebecq proclaims that 'we are heading towards disaster [...] as long as we remain within a mechanistic and individualistic world view, we will perish'.[52] This is a view strongly articulated in his first novel, *Whatever*, which contained many of the themes and preoccupations that he would go on to broach in *Atomised* and, again, as such presented no cause for ideological concern to his contemporaries in *Perpendiculaire*. *Whatever* extends the idea of this 'cold revolution', locating it in a more specific context, that of the new *informatique* management class, playing out the central ideas through the loser-ish characters of the narrator and his hapless colleague.

Given the evidence of his first novel and right up until the moment when excerpts of *Atomised* were released ahead of its publication, there seemed to be no reason to suspect that Houellebecq was anything other than a paid-up member of a leftist artist-intellectual tradition. In fact, to all intents and purposes, Houellebecq seemed to be as much opposed to the creeping influence of 'la pensée unique' of neoliberalism as his *Perpendiculaire* colleagues.[53] That is until they read the pre-released extracts from *Atomised* and saw the form that this opposition took. What had appeared as grimly humorous in *Whatever* had transmogrified into an altogether more unsettling and rancorous portrayal of the political bankruptcy and duplicity of the *soixante-huitards*, the student radicals of 1968 who raged against the machine of capitalism and who wanted to dig up 'the beach below the pavement', but 'who turned out to be more radical individualists than their parents and bosses'.[54] As already noted and as will be examined in detail in Chapter 4, at this time criticism of '68 was by no means remarkable, and a steady trickle of writers had been addressing the relationship between neoliberalism and the emancipatory politics of '68 since the early 1970s. Houellebecq, however, went far beyond extant anti-'68 criticism. Unequivocally blaming the entire *soixante-huitard* generation for much contemporary social malaise, he singled out feminism and its production of a generation of 'bad' mothers for exceptionally vicious opprobrium. In short, *Atomised* suggested that the politics of '68 with its centrally cherished tenet of the individual's right to self-realization were wholly responsible for smoothing the way for the triumph of aggressive free market capitalism. This was not a completely new stance for Houellebecq and should not have come as much of a shock to his Marxist colleagues who could have read much the same thing in *Rester vivant; suivi de la poursuite de la bonheur* (1997) in which he concludes that 'May '68 only served to break the few moral rules that still served to brake its voracious operation' and further that 'afterwards, the social machine began to turn even more rapidly, pitilessly ... '.[55] What was unanticipated, however, was the ferocity of the misanthropy, misogyny and racism, a 'depressing and disgusted vision of the world' that marked this critique of '68.[56] Already aghast at comments Houellebecq had made in an interview with *Les Inrocks* on 19 August 1998 (the unofficial start of *la rentrée littéraire* in France) in which he confessed a fondness for Stalin, the collective were appalled by what they perceived, quite reasonably, as the deeply reactionary ideological content of the novel. On this evidence, the board of *Perpendiculaire* summarily expelled Houellebecq from their midst. Given that the editors had already read three extracts from the novel and had actually published two of these in issues four and ten of the journal, the last of which appeared in August, just a couple of months before the novel's publication, this might have been considered an unexpected reaction. However, as stand-alone extracts, these pieces did not capture the intensity of Houellebecq's dyspeptic vision of *fin de siècle* France that gained its full meaning only in its entirety; that is, when read from cover to cover, bringing into focus the force of his searing attack on post-war France in which May '68 appears as the crucial turning point in an 'end of history' narrative. Read in isolation, many of his targets in the novel – social alienation, sexual commodification, cultural homogenization and so on – are those typically attacked by the left, but pieced together in the novel they added up to an ideological panorama sufficiently unsettling to provoke the unanimous condemnation of the editorial collective of *Perpendiculaire* that resulted in Houellebecq's dismissal from the journal's board, an outcome which ignited public controversy. The expulsion provoked a media hue and cry that transported him from the literary pages to front page news and, as Marion Van Renterghem noted in *Le Monde*, 'Houellebecq's book became the Houellebecq affair' and from that point onwards any assessment of the novel was caught up in the rapidly accumulating layers of controversy and scandal.[57] The right wing press criticized Houellebecq's dismissal from *Perpendiculaire's* editorial board and branded their invitation to explain himself to the board 'a Stalinist show trial' with *Le Figaro* devoting four articles examining the ideological 'witch hunt' that Houellebecq was undergoing at the hands of his leftist inquisitors.[58] The controversy, now with its official moniker of *l'affaire Houellebecq*, was given front page coverage no less than five times in *Le Monde* in the autumn of 1998 and the crumpled, chain-smoking figure of Houellebecq became ubiquitous on television, in papers and magazines and at literary events. Dominique Noguez pointed out in 'La Rage de ne pas lire' that the scandal had something of the absurd about it as, instead of commenting on the novel itself, critics had become obsessed with the unrepentant and scruffy figure of its author, forgetting 'that *Atomised* is a novel'.[59]

On Saturday 10 October 1998, five days before the publication of *Atomised* and after they had had been able to read the novel in its entirety for the first time, the co-founders of the *Revue Perpendiculaire*, Nicolas Bourriaud, Christophe Duchatelet, Jean-Yves Jouannais, Laurent Quintreau, Christophe Kihm and Jacques-François Marchandise wrote a piece in *Le Monde* called 'Houellebecq et l'ère du flou' in which they explained their position on their erstwhile colleague: 'Houellebecq is not a Nazi, he is not even a Lepeniste; he consider himself by turns, a social democrat, then a Stalinist. What he is *not*, is interested in mere Politics which is for him a set of opinions overdetermined by class and social background. As an alternative approach to politics, this is surely equally dispiriting'.[60] Visible here is a real anxiety over the idea of a rightwards turn, *droitisation*, in French politics that is disguised by a kind of ideological vagueness or fuzziness, 'flou', which might be translated as 'blur' or 'vagueness' and refers to a phenomenon whereby a set of ideological positions can simultaneously belong to both left and right. To take only one example of this, consider the comments of Dominique Strauss-Kahn, the then Socialist Minister for Industry who, when asked in an interview what would change if the Right won in the French elections in 1993, replied 'nothing', 'their economic policies will not be much different to ours'.[61] Not unlike the politics of the *rouge-brun* mentioned above, *Atomised* seems to address broadly left-wing concerns about the dominance of market values in human life and the attendant loss of affective poignancy, but the effect of the whole appears reactionary, not least the novel's conclusion, set in the near future which, in the face of the bankruptcy of philosophy, ethics and culture, suggests that only science can offer a viable 'solution' to the world's ills. The ways in which 'Houellebecq appropriates the language of the Left for what many see as a right-wing attack' is, as Seth Armus suggests, the real and enduring controversy of *Atomised* and, I would add, the reason that the novel enjoyed such a wide appeal as this confluence of left/right/middle is close to the dominant ideological gait of the times; a grey-ish, murky middle ground.[62] *Perpendiculaire's* article attacked Houellebecq's ostensible endorsement of this ideological 'flou' that they saw as defining the direction of mainstream politics in France where the polarized discourses of the right and left were giving way to these centrist positions of the 'third way'. Marion Van Renterghem's piece on *Atomised* in *Le Monde* sums up Houellebecq's ideological stance when she notes that the novel could be embraced by left and right alike; a view typified by *Le Figaro* towards what they regarded as Houellebecq's victimization by the left but who, in the same breath, decried *Atomised* as an 'interminable porno-misère'. He is a writer, Van Renterghem argues, who is 'unclassifiable', one who 'deranges and divides [...] who comes from the left who in turn pays homage to Stalin ...'.[63]

Houellebecq's response to his accusers was contemptuously succinct. Referring to one of the *Perpendiculaire's* members as an imbecile, he said that he simply hoped for the revue's collapse.[64] In Houellebecq's view, the charges that they had brought against him accusing him of being reactionary and misogynist were essentially 'American' as they reflected an Anglo-Saxon concern with political conformity.[65] Dropped unceremoniously by Flammarion, *Perpendiculaire's* last issue was published by Floch à Mayenne in August 1998. In sharp contrast, Houellebecq's career took a dramatic upward turn in ways that few could have predicted for the author of the modest-selling *Whatever*. Whether or not Houellebecq's highly visible public profile and notoriety might have occurred quite so rapidly without the media attention he initially received in France remains open to question, but it is obvious that the extraordinary media interest generated around the controversies of *l'affaire* certainly contributed to the novel's overall reception and to its reputation as 'an important intellectual juncture, not only in terms of the future of the French novel [...] but also in terms of the future of the intellectual paradigm in which the novel is inscribed'.[66] But whatever effect *l'affaire* might have had on the novel's reception, it is clear that controversy alone cannot account for the remarkable success of the novel, either in France or worldwide.

There was, however, one last surprise left in *l'affaire*. Just as the commotion in the media around *Atomised* was gradually subsiding and the novel was beginning to be given serious literary consideration, came the, if not shocking, then certainly extremely startling news that this much talked-about, best-selling novel had been abruptly dropped with no explanation from the 1998 Prix Goncourt shortlist.[67] Although the novel went on to win the Prix Novembre, even this was not without considerable controversy, the prevalent feeling among the literary establishment and the public was that Houellebecq had been pointedly snubbed by the Goncourt jury. Houellebecq would have to wait until his most recent novel *The Map and the Territory* to receive France's most prestigious literary accolade. Outside of France though, *Atomised* was awarded one of the most lucrative international literary prizes in Europe, the International IMPAC Dublin Literary Award, open to books in translation from any language. Drawn from library nominations from all over the world, the entries for that year, 2002, made an imposing shortlist including Carlos Fuentes, Margaret Atwood and Peter Carey. Commending the novel as a perverse morality tale 'filled with energy, mordant humour and … wondrously passionate excess', the panel of judges deemed it 'darkly brilliant' and 'addictively readable': 'For all the frustrations and failings of the brothers' separate experiences, *Atomised* in the end presents a paradoxically (if at times perversely) moral view of these two anti-heroes, each alienated from surrounding society in his own way.'[68] Significantly, this appraisal of the novel took seriously the work's worldview without once connecting it to *l'affaire*.

The end of the *affaire*

Wendy Michallat has pointed out that the early French reception of *Atomised* was almost compulsively focused on the 'desire to locate Houellebecq, his work and sundry controversial utterances within a political ideology or tradition' and further that this desire 'accounts for much of the polemic surrounding both the man and the writer'.[69] The controversial material and Houellebecq's eccentric, often wilfully provocative, interviews in the wake of *l'affaire* threatened to engulf any consideration of book itself and it was some months before the worst of the commotion died away and more sober considerations began to emerge. Among these was a special issue of *Atelier du Roman* in June 1999, publishing a series of critical essays on *Atomised* that testified to the sea-change in the critical climate around the novel. As Cloonan notes, the controversies around *Atomised* were 'pretty much spent' and these articles 'reflect this change in sensibility' and register a mild sense of incredulity at the intensity of the 'furore created around the novelist and his text'.[70]

In Britain, the reviews of *Atomised* were less impassioned, more measured, and most did not become embroiled in the 'for or against' debates that typified much of the French reception. While not without some reservations about the level of sustained provocation in the novel, most reviewers commended the scale of Houellebecq's ambition, the punchiness of his prose and the disquieting atmosphere of decline and fall created in this tale of two half-brothers. In *The Times Literary Supplement*, Adrian Tahourdin reviewed *Les Particules élémentaires* (as yet untranslated) a year after its publication. Describing it as 'the great literary event' of the 1998 *rentreé*, he continues in effusive style, 'not since Michel Tournier's *The Erl King* (1970) has French fiction produced a novel as unsettling, or as rich in ideas as *Les Particules élémentaires*'. Noting that Houellebecq is not 'the sort of ludic writer British readers expect the French to be', Tahourdin's review praises Houellebecq's attention to detail and his determination to tackle 'big themes'; the decline of Christianity, genetic cloning, consumerism and the 'destructive nature of liberal values' in a 'forceful polemical tract'. Like Julian Barnes's reference to 'big game' on the back cover of the English translation of the novel, the word 'big' also looms large in Tahourdin's review, praising Houellebecq on the grand scale of his intellectual ambition with its novelistic 'echoes of both Balzac and Céline'. Noting that the novel will undoubtedly cause offence to the generation of *soixante-huitards* as it is an unrelenting attack on what he calls '68's 'platitudes, its ideals of individualism and free will', he concludes that Houellebecq had struck 'at the heart of the French liberal Establishment'.[71] The kind of assessment of Houellebecq as a debunker of *idées reçues* also appears in Paul Gent's review in *The Sunday Telegraph*:

> Again and again Houellebecq digs below our platitudes to expose the raw and uncomfortable feelings we are often afraid to admit to ourselves. His bitterness is that of the disappointed idealist. You may remain convinced that Houellebecq is wrong in his relentlessly bleak assessment of society and human nature. But the novel makes you re-examine your beliefs, which is the kind of bracing challenge that literature is for.[72]

Misrecognizing, or perhaps misdiagnosing, Houellebecq as a philosopher, Andrew Marr argues that *Atomised*, while finally marked by a 'pronounced conservative opinion', is a work that nevertheless possesses integrity: 'Houellebecq's disgust and horror are not feigned. He is making serious points about the grimmer outcomes of the sexual revolution, the despair of the first sexual revolutionaries as their bodies age and they find they have failed to invest in companionship, family and the dense web of non-sexual connections that keep us fully alive'.[73] Most critics reviewing *Atomised* in the British literary press read the novel, like Marr, against a wide historical and political canvas and value the importance of its social critique over the idiosyncratic style of his prose; a style that James Sallis, however, cannot let pass unnoticed: '... this novel speaks the language of profundity, but speaks it poorly, tenses incorrect, articles awry, phrases misplaced ... ' The criticism of the prose style notwithstanding, Sallis admits that 'it must also be remarked that the novel is compulsively readable – readable almost in spite of itself – not for its profundity but for all the small verisimilitudinous touches against which structure and author seem pitched in Jacob-like struggle'.[74] The banality of the language and idiom set against the grand scale of his ideas, the juxtaposition of the high and the low, has become Houellebecq's literary marque, something recognized by James Harkin who sees the narrative techniques deployed in *Atomised* as an integral part of the novel's success: 'It is his knack of weaving grand themes into the most inauspicious material that gives Houellebecq his distinctive edge'.[75]

Many of the British critics commend Houellebecq for a certain moral bravery and sincerity of intention. Joshua Winter, for example, argues that he is 'perhaps the most talented and contrary writer in Europe today', one who speaks to the 'moral and cultural emptiness of modern France' with a nihilist verve that is neither artificial nor exaggerated: 'Houellebecq means it, both in his life and work'.[76] Similarly, writing in *The Guardian* Alex Clark astutely reads *Atomised* as an 'anti-novel in the sense that it consistently diminishes any sense of its own possibilities'. Houellebecq's treatment of the 'velvet jackboot of consumerism' and the failure of the 'liberal western intellect to come up with any coherent response to the disasters that enfold it' is occasionally rather adolescent in its foot-stamping but it is, she concedes, a novel full of conviction and one 'which immediately invites comparison with writers such as Céline, Beckett and Camus'.[77]

In another view, in the *London Review of Books*, John Sturrock described *Atomised* as 'boldly out of tune with the times', 'aggressive in thought' and 'often enough tacky in deed', and argues that the novel is propelled by a 'radical intolerance of the ways and means of a society that the novelist sees as terminally degenerate'. Speaking to the varied and often contradictory ideological poses struck in the novel, Sturrock concludes: 'How seriously he occupies any one position at all is open to question, but he has clearly stirred things up to promising effect among the dozing adherents of what I've lately seen referred to in France as 'la pensée unique', which makes it sound as though that once heroically fissile community can no longer raise the intellectual energy to dispute the premises of the liberal consensus'.[78] A similar consideration of the novel's challenge to the literary status quo is offered by Melanie McGrath in *The Evening Standard:* 'Literature with a sure and unapologetic confidence in its own ability – its duty, even – to make a difference'.[79] Chase Madar sees *Atomised* as 'an ambitious novel of ideas' and crucially recognizes the 'irresistible' allure of the novel's 'Left-conservative message', a rare observation among British reviewers, many of whom intuit this ideological miscegenation but fall just short of fully identifying the *rouge-brun* tone of Houellebecq's writing.[80]

Translated in the United States more literally as *The Elementary Particles*, *Atomised* made a distinct impact on the literary scene, although the American reviews were consistently more unenthusiastic than their British counterparts, with many reviewers pointing up the cultural differences between Europe and America. Lorin Stein admits that the novel might tax some American readers who are 'accustomed to radical realism on a big scale' and who may be unimpressed by the discrepancy between the large scale of Houellebecq's narrative canvas and 'the small, sad details that animate it'. Stein admits that while *Atomised*'s non-realism is 'grotesque and fantastical, full of loony physics, half-baked history and sociobiology, bad verse and sputtering misanthropy', this is offset by the fact that is 'also very funny, and sharply observed' and what lingers in the reader's mind is the novel's 'childlike capacity for disappointment'.[81] Assessing the impact of Houellebecq's novels on the international literary scene, Michael Orthofer notes that Houellebecq's sense of anomie hits closer to home in Europe where 'readers can relate more readily to the social commentary in his books' whereas for Americans 'much of his worldview still comes across as exotic and fantastical'. The controversy in France around *Atomised*, Orthofer says, helped to propel the novel across the Atlantic with a more than a whiff of scandal in its tailwind along with a touch of anti-Americanism that is 'all bluster and little sting', full of 'basic misconceptions' about America.[82] Writing in *The New Yorker* Adam Gopnik, who lived in Paris for five years from 1995 to 2000, has a more first-hand understanding of the crucial distinctions between ideological terms in France and the US. *Atomised* is, he says 'a more complicated take on liberal and anti-liberal politics' and this must be read in relation to anti-Americanism in Houellebecq's work: to the French left, 'liberalism' (or, as it is often called, 'wild' or 'savage' liberalism, a quaint and comic thought in American terms) has also come to mean, essentially, American civilization, in all its McDonald's, *Friends* and Exxon aspects'. Suggesting that *Atomised* has the urgency of 'real pathos' it is, Gopnik continues:

> ... less a novel than a kind of eighteenth-century *conte moral*, at once a narrative and a philosophical essay, in which an obsession with oral sex oscillates strangely with fatuous ideological posturing, as in a story by Sade or in the proceedings of an American congressional committee. It is obscene, hateful, pretentious, half educated, funny, ambitious, and oddly moving [...] the book's

bitter tone and its readiness to say the unsayable recall Genet, and even Céline, its literary, dystopian feel brings it much closer to Burroughs (who anticipated the sexless clone years ago), or to J. G. Ballard.

Gopnik concludes: 'What is memorable in Houellebecq's book is not the pseudo-scientific incantations, or the potted "theories," but the depth of feeling, the authentic disgust with *fin-de-siècle* liberal materialism'.[83] Acknowledging the specifically French context of Houellebecq's novel, *The New York Times* journalist Alan Riding asks the incisive question that remains after the histrionic media excesses of *l'affaire* have been stripped away: why is Houellebecq so popular? His answer is by no means comforting, suggesting that 'many French share Mr Houellebecq's dark vision of a post-idealistic, post-ideological France gripped by malaise, unemployment and growing insecurity, where materialism, hypocrisy and corruption have long since replaced dreams of a better life'.[84]

While the reviews of the novel were predominantly negative in the major literary columns of *The New York Times Book Review*, *The Washington Post* and *The Wall Street Journal*, this negativity reached something of an apotheosis in Michiko Kakutani's 'Unsparing Case Studies of Humanity's Vileness' in *The New York Times* where the novel is characterized as '… a bad, self-conscious pastiche of Camus, Foucault and Brett Easton Ellis' and a 'deeply repugnant read' attributable to its 'right-wing politics and wilfully pornographic passages'.[85] Kakutani also objects to the fact that Houellebecq frequently conflates his characters' points of view with his own authorial voice, a matter to which I will return in more detail below. Anthony Quinn's objections are similarly unenthusiastic but differently accented: 'What is surprising about the book is not its pessimism but the fantastically boring way it has been couched […] Its intention is so plainly to rile, to *épater*, that any objections one might raise feel like further ammunition to its entrenched misanthropy'.[86] More positively, in *The Washington Post Book World*, Steven Moore concludes that the novel's 'impressive erudition' and 'gutsy willingness […] to re-think and re-imagine the bases for civilization' mitigate the wilder conclusions of the science fiction.[87] In a more ambivalent assessment, Christopher Caldwell writes: 'It is tempting to link Bruno as a character, and Mr Houellebecq as an author, with the midcentury sybaritic fascism of Drieu la Rochelle and Céline. Mr Houellebecq is too nihilistic, and Bruno too insane, for politics', but nonetheless concedes that 'this is a brilliant novel of ideas – many of them bad ones – in which laser-sharp diagnosis jostles with repellent ideology from paragraph to paragraph. It is also a riveting novel by a deft, observant writer'.[88]

Scandal *redux*: *Platform* and 'the most stupid religion'

Appearing to advocate Third World sex tourism for lonely, sex-starved Westerners, Houellebecq's third novel, *Plateforme*, was published in France in August of 2001. With the dust barely settled on the earlier tumult, a further and arguably much graver controversy erupted, a controversy that had finally less to do with sex tourism than with Islam. Swiftly translated into English, it was published as *Platform* the following summer. Again, there were conspicuous differences between the tone of the reviews of the novel in France and in the English-speaking world. The former continued to resonate with the lingering sectarianism of the *Atomised* controversy, many of the reviews charged Houellebecq with the same ideological delinquency; indeed, they saw this novel as an elaboration of many of the objectionable themes laid out in *Atomised* but on the whole seemed to be reconciled to his status as a writer-provocateur borne out by his admission in *Le Figaro*: 'I admit that invective is one of my pleasures. This only brings me problems in life, but that's it. I attack, I insult. I have a gift for that, for insults, for provocation. So I am tempted to use it. In my novels, it adds a certain spice. It's rather funny, no?'[89] Yes, and yet no.

In both major contexts of reception, in Britain and the USA on the one hand and in France on the other, reviews of *Platform* focused, in the first place, on its particularly controversial content that seems to be advocating, satirically or otherwise, Third World sex tourism as a remedy for a pervasive Western sexual ennui. The more insightful of the reviews drew attention to a kind of ideological ventriloquism that has become a distinctive aspect of Houellebecq's writing whereby he 'throws' controversial or contentious views into the mouths or speech of the marginalized group themselves. Thus, a female character opining on feminism rather implausibly declares: 'Never could abide feminists [...] Stupid bitches always going on about the washing up and the division of labour; they could never shut up about the washing up.'[90] This vitriolic denunciation of feminism by a woman has its equivalent in *Platform* where Houellebecq sets up an Arab character to disparage Islam: 'The problem with Muslims, he told me, was that that the paradise promised by the prophet already existed here on earth [...] For him, there was no doubt, the Muslim way was doomed: capitalism would triumph. Already young Arabs dreamed of nothing but consumer products and sex.'[91] And also in *Platform* 'Every time I heard that a Palestinian terrorist, or a Palestinian child or a pregnant Palestinian woman had been gunned down in the Gaza strip, I felt a quiver of enthusiasm ...'.[92] Taking Houellebecq to task for his 'lazy prejudices' towards Islam in a review of

Platform in the *The New York Times*, Jenny Turner makes a particularly shrewd observation about 'the annoying way that most of the nasty digs at Muslims are put in the mouths of friendly Arabs'. This technique points up, she says, 'the changing world order' of political ideology in which 'racism, like everything else, has shifted its shape [...] and is as likely these days to come in a libertine wrapper as any other'. Acknowledging that while Houellebecq is indisputably 'a terrific writer, funny, prophetic, more feverishly alive to the world around him than are many authors more tasteful ...', he nevertheless resorts to using 'unintegrated slabs of rant' which in its 'reactionary and xenophobic' energies are 'reminiscent of no one so much as Pim Fortuyn ...'.[93] All of Houellebecq's fiction presents the reader and critic with the problem of the separation of the characters' voice and the authorial voice of the novel. This problem is, of course, compounded from our knowledge of Houellebecq's own views on such matters expressed in a multitude of interviews which tend to reinforce rather than distance him from the more controversial aspects of his writing. This is, of course, one of the oldest of critical conundrums in literary analysis and one that has taxed literary critics periodically down the ages. It is not only a question of a slippery postmodernist textual surface, as Ralph Schoolcraft and Richard Golsan suggest in their examination of Houellebecq's work. In a discussion of the relationship between contemporary writing and reactionary politics they argue that: 'The question thus is to discern whether the postmodern facets of these novels are mere surface effects, or if they do in fact invite a mitigating re-reading of his ideological content and poetics'.[94] In other words, if the controversial views function as purely polemical or satirical effects does this mitigate the offensive nature of the views themselves?

The words in the novel were one thing – it is, in fact, questionable if those bringing the charges of 'incitement to racial hatred' against Houellebecq had actually had time to read the novel itself – he went on not only to reiterate, but to elaborate upon these provocative assertions thus 'owning' these views in ways that appeared to suggest not a performance of himself as *provocateur* but the outpouring of some kind of genuinely held belief. In an interview published in *Lire* magazine on 6 September 2001 but which had actually taken place some months prior to the publication of *Platform* in France, Houellebecq spoke to journalist Didier Senecal stating, 'It is more than contempt I have for Islam, it is hatred', the reasons for which merit quoting in full:

> ... It was because of a negative revelation I had in the Sinai, where Moses received the Ten Commandments [...] suddenly I experienced a complete rejection of all monotheisms [...] I told myself that to believe in one God,

you had to be a cretin, really, I can't think of another word for it. And the most stupid religion of all would have to be Islam. When you read the Koran, it is a devastating experience! The Bible, at least, is very beautiful; because Jews have a real literary talent, which can excuse many things [...] I have a residual sympathy for Catholicism, because of its polytheistic aspect [...] and all its works of art, churches, paintings, sculptures, stained glass [...] Islam is a dangerous religion, since its very first appearance. Fortunately, it is doomed. First of all, because God doesn't exist, and even if one is a bloody idiot, one finishes up understanding that in the long term, truth triumphs. On another part, Islam is undermined, under attack by capitalism. All one can wish for is that it (capitalism) will rapidly triumph. Materialism is a lesser evil. Its values are despicable, but less destructive, less cruel than those of Islam.[95]

The interview was, according to Houellebecq, six hours in its entirety during which time, according to Sénécal, Houellebecq became drunkenly incoherent. The comments he made became distilled into a single regrettable phrase: 'the most stupid religion of all would have to be Islam', a sentence which, unsurprisingly, made headlines all over the world after being picked up by a Moroccan newspaper, which published a photograph of Houellebecq on its front page topped with the caption 'This man hates you'. The timing could scarcely have been less propitious, as five days later Al-Qaeda flew two planes into the Twin Towers. Houellebecq's remarks ignited immediate protests from Muslim groups in France. The head of the Paris Mosque, Dalil Boubakeur, accused Houellebecq of inciting 'racial and religious hatred', while Mohammed Béchari of the National Federation of French Muslims made a plea to the French intellectual and literary establishment to join them in condemning the writer's 'baseness'. A representative of the Arab League, Nassif Hitti, denounced Houellebecq's comments as 'despicable' and said that they had 'given rise to legitimate outrage among the Muslim leadership of France'. Finally, three Muslim associations and a human rights organization in Paris brought formal charges against Houellebecq.

While his editor Raphael Sorin met the Grand Imam of Paris to attempt some placatory dialogue, Houellebecq fled into hiding. Quick to repudiate charges of racism saying, he issued a statement saying, 'I deny being a racist, I have never confused Arabs and Muslims and I am indignant that certain journalists misrepresent me with words I've never used'.[96] The case also raised legal questions over whether a publication can be held responsible for the views expressed by interviewees especially since France does not have a law of blasphemy in its secular constitution. The editor of *Lire*, Pierre Assouline, stated that literary magazines should not be held accountable for the 'declarations' writers utter in their interviews: 'If we were to be deemed responsible, then we would not be able to conduct any interviews in the future'.[97] However, for the prosecution Boubakeur argued that 'freedom of expression ends where it can hurt […] I think that my community has been humiliated, my religion insulted, and I want justice to be done'.[98] Boubakeur concluded by saying, 'It's part of Islamic doctrine that Islam is inseparable from the community of believers […] the distinction between Islam and individual Muslims is a false one'.[99]

Houellebecq was tried in courtroom number 17 in the Palais de Justice in Paris on 17 September 2002 with five plaintiffs presenting the case against him for 'incitement to religious and racial hatred' including the mosques of both Paris and Lyon, the National Federation of French Muslims (FNMN) and the Mecca-based World Islamic League and the League for the Rights of Man. The plaintiffs sought both financial damages against Houellebecq of around 190,000 Euros and a public condemnation. Wisely or not, Houellebecq chose to defend himself in court, claiming that his words had been taken drastically out of context and distorted by the media. Further, he declared that he had never 'displayed the least contempt for Muslims' but added, perhaps somewhat ill-advisedly, 'I have as much contempt as ever for Islam'.[100] Declaring his hostility towards all monotheistic faiths, Houellebecq defended his right to criticize any religious beliefs but crucially pointed out that the tenor of such criticism is important claiming, rather disingenuously, that 'the whole tone of the interview was one of contempt, not hate'. Essaying an aesthetic argument, he compared the artistic quality of the Koran versus the Bible: 'In literary terms, the Bible has several authors, some good and some as bad as crap. The Koran has only one author and its overall style is mediocre'.[101] One of the presiding judges explained that Houellebecq's remarks in the interview, while neither 'elegant nor subtle', had crucially been 'directed against the religion of Islam, not its adherents'. Requesting Houellebecq's acquittal, deputy Prosecutor Béatrice Angelelli, reinforced this view: 'It cannot be said' she argued, 'that when one expresses an opinion on Islam, it implies that one is attacking the Muslim community'. The panel of three judges concluded that Houellebecq's remarks were 'without a doubt characterized by neither a particularly noble outlook nor by the subtlety of their phrasing'. They found, however, that his remarks did not 'contain any intent to abuse verbally, show contempt for or insult the followers of the religion in question' and therefore were not punishable under French law and on 22 October Houellebecq was acquitted of all charges brought against him.[102]

There is little doubt that this trial, which made newspaper headlines around the world, and the trail of *enfant terrible* scandal that it left in its wake, fortified Houellebecq's reputation as a controversial writer, a situation consolidated by his inclusion on Daniel Lindenberg's list of the 'new reactionaries' in France in his book *Call to Order: Investigation Concerning the New Reactionaries*.[103] A political philosopher, historian and frequent contributor to *Esprit*, Lindenberg defined this group of 'new reactionaries' by their use of an ideological 'double talk' that he believes conceals 'their truly reactionary nature beneath a liberal gloss'.[104] Benjamin Noys offers a persuasive *précis* of this contemporary ideological situation in French culture:

> Conservative and leftist intellectuals, writers and politicians who espouse generally radical arguments around some sets of ideological questions (economic problem-solving; social welfare; Republicanism; sexual liberation and gay rights) may well not be consistent when they identify other issues of social identity and policy planning. Forms of illiberalism might well suddenly appear in the least likely places because thinkers do not hold cardboard cut-out political philosophies across a spectrum of subjects.[105]

Others named alongside Houellebecq were Alain Finkielkraut, Philippe Muray, Maurice Dantec and Pierre-André Taguieff. Houellebecq responded to Lindenberg by writing a scathingly sarcastic article in *Le Figaro* thanking Lindenberg for giving a coherence and agenda to a hitherto disparate band of writers and thinkers. Whatever Houellebecq thought of his inclusion in this 'list', it was an important moment in French literary history as it consolidated a number of overlapping intellectual and political debates in France around the return to a new kind of conservatism that intersected at several important points with the language and concerns of the left.

The impassioned debates generated by Houellebecq's trial focused on the novel's comments about Islam rather than on the, at least equally, if not more, outrageous proposition that sex tourism should be established in many parts of the Third and developing world. As James Meeks argues in the *London Review of Books*, the long shadow cast by the intense media coverage and 'so much selective quotation from the book highlighting its racial and religious content' obscured the fact that the novel is 'a work of political polemic' but rather than race or religion as central preoccupations it is sex that 'pulls the strings together' of the narrative. 'This is a book', Meeks says, 'which subordinates the clash of civilizations (uncivilizations, in *Platform*'s view) to sexual longing'. Indeed, it is sex and not Islam that is the real subject of *Platform* and *Atomised*;[106] more specifically, the impossibility of attaining love through sex. In both novels sex functions as libidinal corollary for economics and is thus traded and exchanged like any other commodity in an increasingly market-defined neoliberal society where the imploded borders between public and private, work and non-work, commodity and affect define a new variant of capitalism, its neoliberal 'third spirit'.

Notes

1 Mark Lilla, 'Houellebecq's *Elementary Particles*', *New Perspectives Quarterly*, 18, 1 (Winter 2001), 53–60, 54.

2 *Whatever*, trans. Paul Hammond (London: Serpent's Tail, 1998).

3 Sophie Masson, 'The Strange Trial of Michel Houellebecq', *The Social Contract* 14.2 (Winter 2003–4), http://www.thesocialcontract.com/artman2/publish/tsc1402/article_1196_printer.shtml [accessed 9 April 2011].

4 *Lanzarote*, 12–13.

5 Houellebecq's most recent novel, *La Carte et le territoire* (2010), is appreciably less obviously controversial than his previous work, straying into the more recognizable postmodernist territory of narrative self-consciousness and a playful condemnation of the art world. Like *Lanzarote*, I do not consider this novel in detail here as it sits just outside of my main arguments. Although it does address many of the themes I attend to in this book, for example, shifting notions of labour and the decline of national culture – and I will mention some of these in passing – the novel is finally a less representative text to include in my examination of the ideological contours of despair in Houellebecq's writing.

6 Theo Tait, 'Gorilla with Mobile Phone', *London Review of Books*, 28, 3, 9 February 2006, 11–13.

7 Bülent Diken, 'Houellebecq, or, the Carnival of Spite', *Journal of Cultural Research*, 11, 1 (2007), 57–73, 57.

8 Tim Martin, 'The Michel Houellebecq phenomenon', *The Daily Telegraph*, 29 September 2011, http://www.telegraph.co.uk/culture/books/bookreviews/8796739/The-Michel-Houellebecq-Phenomenon.html [accessed 18 April 2012].

9 Roger F. Malina, Review of *Les Particules élémentaires*, *Leonardo*, 32, 2 (1999), 147–8, 147.

10 Jonathan Jones, 'Artistic license to thrill: Houellebecq's *The Map and the Territory*', http://www.guardian.co.uk/artanddesign/jonathanjonesblog/2011/oct/03/michel-houellebecq-map-and-territory [accessed 20 July 2012].

11 Salman Rushdie, 'A platform for closed minds', *The Guardian*, 28 September 2002, 7.

12 Ben Jeffery, *Anti-matter: Michel Houellebecq and Depressive Realism* (Winchester: Zero Books, 2011), 5.

13 In the three decades between 1980 and the middle of the 2000s many of the most prominent French thinkers of the twentieth century died: Roland Barthes (1915–80); Jacques Lacan (1901–81); Raymond Aron (1905–83); Michel Foucault (1926–84); Fernand Braudel (1902–85); Michel de Certeau (1925–86); Simone de Beauvoir (1908–86); Henri Lefebvre (1901–91); Guy Debord (1931–94); Gilles Deleuze (1925–95); François Lyotard (1924–98); Pierre Bourdieu (1930–2002); Maurice Blanchot (1907–2003); Jacques Derrida (1930–2004) and Claude Lévi-Strauss (1908–2009).

14 Perry Anderson, *London Review of Books*, 26, 17, 2 September 2004, 3–9, 3.

15 Bernard Henri-Lévy and Michel Houellebecq, *Public Enemies* (New York: Random House, 2011), 65.

16 Jonathan Kandall, 'Jacques Derrida, Abstruse Theorist, Dies at 74', *The New York Times*, 10 October 2004, http://www.nytimes.com/2004/10/10/obituaries/10derrida.html [accessed 15 January 2010].

17 John Marks, 'L'Affaire Sokal' in *French Cultural Debates* (eds) John Marks and Enda McCaffrey (Melbourne: Monash Romance Studies, 2001), 80–93, 80.

18 'France's literary sensation: Generation war', the *Economist*, 23 October 2001, http://www.economist.com/node/378602 [accessed 15 February 2010]. See also *The Death of French Culture*, (eds) Donald Morrison and Antoine Compagnon (London: Polity, 2010).

19 William Cloonan, 'Literary Scandal, *Fin du Siècle*, and the Novel in 1999', the *French Review*, 74, 1 (2000), 14–30, 14.

20 Founded in 1941 in German occupied Paris and famous for its distinctively discreet blue and white image-less covers, Les Éditions de Minuit is an eminent French publishing house renowned for its publication of *nouveau roman* writers Marguerite Duras, Nathalie Saurraute, Alain Robbe-Grillet, and Michel Butor. The publisher of Beckett's major works, Les Éditions de Minuit continues to be a major force in French literary culture with a stable of Goncourt winning authors on its books.

21 Frédéric Badré, 'Une nouvelle tendance en littérature', *Le Monde*, 3 October 1998, 14.

22 Michel Guenaire, 'Beauté cou coupé', *Le Monde*, 4 February 1999.

23 Marc Petit, 'Nouvelle tendance, vieux démons', *Le Monde*, 10 October 1998.

24 Cloonan, 14.

25 Jean Paul Sartre, *What is Literature? And Other Essays*, trans. Bernard Frechtman (Cambridge: Harvard University Press, 1988) 37.

26 *Public Enemies*, 79, 82.

27 John Banville, 'Futile Attraction: Michel Houellebecq's Lovecraft', *Artforum International*, 1 April, 2005, 2.

28 Derek Attridge, *The Singularity of Literature* (London: Routledge, 2004), 19.

29 Jacques Derrida warns against confusing this concept of indecision with the aporetic stalemate of postmodernism. See 'Hospitality, Justice and Responsibility: A Dialogue with Jacques Derrida' in *Questioning Ethics: Contemporary Debates in Continental Philosophy*, (eds) Richard Kearney, Mark Dooley (London: Routledge, 1999).

30 Jack Abecassis, 'The Eclipse of Desire: L'Affaire Houellebecq', *MLN*, 5, 4 (September 2000) 801–26, 806.

31 Emily Eakin, 'Le Provocateur', *The New York Times Magazine*, 10 September 2000, http://www.nytimes.com/2000/09/10/magazine/le-provocateur. [accessed 18 March 2011].

32 Susannah Hunnewell, 'Michel Houellebecq, The Art of Fiction', *The Paris Review*, 206 (Fall 2010), http://www.theparisreview.org/interviews/6040/the-art-of-fiction-no-206-michel-houellebecq [accessed 18 April 2010].

33 Jérôme Meizoz, *Postures littéraires: Mises en scène modernes de l'auteur* (Genève: Slatkine, 2007); 'Le roman et l'inacceptable: Sociologie d'une polémique: autour de *Plateforme* de Michel Houellebecq' in *L'œil sociologue et la littérature* (Genève: Slatkine Érudition, 2004) 181–209. See also Louise Moor, 'Posture polémique ou polémisation de la posture?: Le cas de Michel Houellebecq' *COnTEXTES*, 10 (2012), http://contextes.revues.org/4921 [accessed 28 August 2012]. I am indebted here to my research student Chloe Chourrout, whose work on authorial posture in Houellebecq and Céline brought Meizoz's work to my attention and helped me think through the relationship between the 'living' paratextual presence of Houellebecq and the reception of his novels.

34 Gérard Genette, *Paratexts: Thresholds of Interpretation* (Cambridge: Cambridge University Press, 1997), 4.

35 Respectively, http://www.houellebecq.info and http://aeamh.free.fr [accessed June 10 2010].

36 Tamara Chaplin, *Turning on the Mind: French Philosophers on Television* (Chicago: University of Chicago Press, 1997), 1.

37 Jérôme Meizoz, *Postures littéraires: Mises en scène modernes de l'auteur* (Genève: Slatkine Érudition, 2007), 15–32.

38 See Corina da Rocha Soares, 'Michel Houellebecq, Amélie Nothomb et Jacques Chessex: Performances sous contexts médiatisés', *Carnets, Cultures littéraires: Nouvelles performances et développement* (Autumn/hiver 2009), 207–20, http//:carnets.web.ua.pt [accessed 18 March 2010].

39 Salhi Abdel-Illah, 'Un racisme chic et tendance', *Libération*, 4 septembre 2001, 6. My own translation.

40 Gavin Bowd, 'Michel Houellebecq and The Pursuit of Happiness', *Nottingham French Studies*, 41, 1 (2002), 28–39, 28.

41 Katherine Gantz, 'Strolling with Houellebecq: The Textual Terrain of Postmodern Flânerie', *Journal of Modern Literature*, 28, 3 (2005), 149–61, 141.

42 Frank Wynne, 'Terribleman', http://www.frankwynne.com [accessed 18 June 2010].

43 Nicholas Le Quesne, 'War of Words', *Time*, 22 September 2002, http://www.time.com/time/magazine/article/0,9171,353525,00.html [accessed 11 April 2011].

44 *Popular Music in France from Chanson to Techno: Culture, Identity, and Society*, (eds) Steve Cannon, Hugh Dauncey (Aldershot: Ashcroft Publishing, 2003), 175.

45 *Les Inrockuptibles*, 19 August 1998.

46 Bowd, 37.

47 On the rationalization of the lifeworld see Marcuse (1964); Adorno and Horkheimer (1997, originally published 1972) and on the technocratic consciousness see Habermas, *Toward a Rational Society: Student Protest, Science and Politics*, trans. Jeremy J. Shapiro (Boston: Beacon Press, 1970).

48 *Whatever*, 99.

49 *The Art of Struggle*, trans. Delphine Grass and Timothy Mathews (London: Herla, 2010), ix, 27, 55.

50 Ibid., 85.

51 *Rester vivant, méthode*, 54–5.

52 *Interventions*, 48.

53 'La pensée unique' is a term coined by Ignacio Ramonet, a journalist for *Le Monde diplomatique*, *Le Monde diplomatique*, janvier 1995, http://www.monde diplomatique.fr/1995/01/RAMONET/1144 [accessed 24 October 2011].

54 Mark Lilla, 'Houellebecq's *Elementary Particles*', *New Perspectives Quarterly*, 18, 1 (Winter 2001), 53–60, http://onlinelibrary.wiley.com/doi/10.1111/089–850.00308/full [accessed 18 October 2011].

55 *Rester vivant*, my translation.

56 Marion Van Renterghem 'Le procès Houellebecq', *Le Monde*, 8 November 1998, 10.

57 Van Renterghem, 10.

58 'Les nouveaux inquisiteurs: Le retour des chasses aux sorcières', *Le Figaro*, 25 September 1998, 30.

59 See Dominique Noguez, *Houellebecq, en fait* (Paris: Fayard, 2003), 73. This also has a usefully detailed, if highly subjective, account of the break between *Perpendiculaire* and Houellebecq.

60 Nicolas Bourriaud, Christophe Duchatelet, et al., 'Houellebecq et l'ère du flou', *Le Monde*, 10 October 1998, 16, my translation.

61 *The Wall Street Journal Europe*, 18 March 1993.

62 Seth Armus, 'The American Menace in the Houellebecq Affair', *French Politics and Society*, 17, 2 (1999), 34–42, 34).

63 Marion Van Renterghem, *Le Monde*, 10 October 1998, http://www.lemonde.fr/livres/article/2010/09/09/le-proces-houellebecq_1409163_3260.html [accessed July 8th 2011].

64 'Michel Houellebecq répond à *Perpendiculaire*', *Le Monde*, 18 September 1998, 10.

65 On the anti-American dimension to *l'affaire* see Seth Armus, 'The American Menace in the Houellebecq Affair', 36.

66 Ruth Cruickshank, '*L'Affaire Houellebecq*: Ideological Crime and *Fin de Millénaire* Literary Scandal', *French Cultural Studies*, 14.1 (2003), 101–16, 104.

67 In addition to Cruickshank's detailed study of *l'affaire Houellebecq* and Marion Van Renterghem's contemporary account, Eric Nalleau devotes a whole chapter to these events in *Au secours, Houellebecq revient!* (Paris: Chiflet & Cie, 2005), 61–123. See also Olivier Wicker in *L'Événement de jeudi* and Jean-Luc Douin in *Le Monde*; Dominique Noguez, 'La Rage de ne pas lire', *Le Monde*, 29 October 1998 and 'Le Style de Michel Houellebecq', *Atelier du Roman*, June 1999, 17–22.

68 http://www.impacdublinaward.ie/2002/Winner.html [accessed 30 September 2012].

69 Wendy Michallat, 'Modern Life is still Rubbish. Houellebecq and the Refiguring of "reactionary" Retro', *Journal of European Studies*, 37 (2007), 313–31, 314.

70 Cloonan, 27. See also *Atelier du Roman*, June 1999, 17–82.

71 Adrian Tahourdin, 'Generation '68', *Times Literary Supplement*, 15 January 1999, 23.

72 Paul Gent, 'Human nature: a particle guide', *The Sunday Telegraph*, 29 April 2000, http://www.telegraph.co.uk/culture/4720583/Human-nature-a-particle-guide.html

73 Andrew Marr, 'We're all Doomed … except for middle-aged French philosophers', *The Observer*, 2 May 2000 http://www.guardian.co.uk/books/2000/may/21/ fiction.michelhouellebecq/print [accessed 24 March 2001]. Other important reviews for *Atomised* in the British press include Jason Cowley, '*Atomised*', *The Times*, 7 July 2001; Andrew Hussey, 'Animal Omega: the dubious moral universe of Michel Houellebecq', *Planet Magazine*, 142, 9 December 2001, http://www. planetmagazine.org.uk/html/archive/houellebecq.html [accessed November 2000]; Nicholas Lezard, 'Pick of the Week: Atom Bomb', *The Guardian*, 24 February 2001, 11; Victoria Segal, '*Atomised* by Michel Houellebecq', *The Times*, 10 March 2001; Paul Tebbs, '*Atomised* by Michel Houellebecq', *The Daily Telegraph*, 24 February 2001, 2.

74 James Sallis, 'Michel Houellebecq, *The Elementary Particles*', *Review of Contemporary Fiction*, 21.1 (2001), 19–197.

75 James Harkin, 'Review of *Atomised*, by Michel Houellebecq', *New Statesman*, 129, 4487 (22 May 2000), 57. In a carefully measured review of *Atomised* in the same magazine a year later, Gerry Feehily observes that the novel is 'fiction as diagnosis' told in a blunt, colloquial language' that may owe more to the discursive mode of the 'archetypal Parisian figure, imbued with *l'esprit de contradiction* 'than to any artistic or intellectual genius'. Gerry Feehily, 'A World on the Brink of Collapse', *New Statesman*, 18 June 2001, http://www.newstatesman.com/node/140573 [accessed 20 September 2012].

76 Joshua Winter, 'France: Into the Void'. *New Statesman*, 131, 4586, 6 May 2002, 25–7, http://www.newstatesman.com/node/142882 [accessed 25 January 2012].

77 Alex Clark, 'Atom bomb', *The Guardian*, 13 May 2000, http://www.guardian.co.uk/books/2000/may/13/fiction.michelhouellebecq [accessed 13 June 2006].

78 John Sturrock, 'Agitated Neurons', *London Review of Books*, 21. 2, 21 January 1999 24–5, 24, http://www.lrb.co.uk/v21/n02/john-sturrock/agitated-neurons [accessed 17 January 2011].

79 Melanie McGrath, *The Evening Standard*, http://www.complete-review.com/reviews/houelbqm/partelem.html [accessed 10 October 2011].

80 Chase Madar, 'Review of *Interventions*, by Michel Houellebecq', *Times Literary Supplement*, 22 October 1999, 36.

81 Lorin Stein, 'What to read in October', *Salon*, 23 October 2000, http:/ /www. salon. com/2000/10/23/octoberfiction [accessed 23 November 2003].

82 Michael Orthofer, 'On Michel Houellebecq', *The Complete Review*, 11, 2 (August 2010), http://www.complete-review.com/quarterly/vol11/issue2/houellebecq. htm [accessed 11 November 2010]. This article appeared in translation in *Le Monde* as 'Michel Houellebecq se replie complètement sur lui-même', September 2010, http://www.lemonde.fr/livres/article/ [accessed 11 February 2012].

83 Adam Gopnik, 'Noel Contendere', *The New Yorker*, 28 December 1998, 64–7, 61).

84 Alan Riding, 'Arts Abroad; Roman à Gripe Stirs Flames Among French' *The New York Times*, 2 March 1999, http://www.nytimes.com/1999/03/02/books/arts-abroad-roman-a-gripe-stirs-flames-among-french.html [accessed 28 September 2005].

85 Michiko Kakutani, 'Unsparing Case Studies of Humanity's Vileness', *The New York Times*, 10 November 2000, http://www.nytimes.com/2000/11/10/books/books-of-the-times-unsparing-case-studies-of-humanity-s-vileness.html [accessed 17 April 2013].

86 Anthony Quinn, 'One Thinks, the Other Doesn't', *The New York Times Book Review*, http://www.nytimes.com/books/00/11/19/reviews/001119.19quinnt.html [accessed 28 September 2011].

87 Steven Moore, 'Getting Physical'. *Washington Post Book World*, 31, 3 (21–7 January 2001), 7.

88 Christopher Caldwell, 'Enraged by Licentiousness … And Indulging in It', *The Wall Street Journal*, 15 November 2001, http://online.wsj.com/article/SB974254862463439512.html [accessed 3 July 2011].

89 Alan Riding, 'Arts Abroad; France's Shock Novelist Strikes Again', *The New York Times*, 11 September 2001, http://www.nytimes.com/2001/09/11/books/arts-abroad-france-s-shock-novelist-strikes-again.html [accessed 17 June 2007].

90 *Atomised*, 173–4. All subsequent references to the novel will be abbreviated to *A* and given in parentheses in the text with the page number.

91 Platform, 350.

92 *Platform*, 349. All subsequent references to the novel will be abbreviated to *P* and given in parentheses in the text with the page number.

93 Jenny Turner, 'Club Bed', *The New York Times*, 20 July 2003, http://www.nytimes.com/2003/07/20/books/club-bed.html [accessed 31 October 2011].

94 Ralph Schoolcraft and Richard Golsan, 'Paradoxes of the postmodern reactionary Michel Rio and Michel Houellebecq', *Journal of European Studies*, 37 (2007), 349–71, 359.

95 Quoted in Sophie Masson 'The Strange Trial of Michel Houellebecq', *The Social Contract*, (Winter 2003–4), 110–13, 111. See also Alan Riding, 'France's Shock Novelist Strikes Again', *The New York Times*, 11 September 2001.

96 'Houellebecq in court over race accusations', *The Guardian*, 17 September 2002, http://www.guardian.co.uk/books/2002/sep/17/michelhouellebecq [accessed 8 November 2011].

97 'French author denies racial hatred', *BBC News*, 17 September 2001, http://news.bbc.co.uk/1/hi/world/europe/2260922.stm [accessed 22 November 2001].

98 Koenraad Elst, 'Afterword, The Rushdie Affair's Legacy', http://koenraadelst.bharatvani.org/articles/misc/rushdie.html [accessed 2 May 2012].

99 Nicholas Le Quesne, 'War of Words', *Time Magazine*, 22 September 2002, http://www.time.com/time/magazine/article/0,9171,353525,00.html [17 April 2013].

100 'French author denies racial hatred'.

101 Ibid.

102 See Alan Riding, 'Author Charged for Islam Remarks is Acquitted', *The New York Times*, and Gerry Feehily, 'The Man Who Fell to Earth', *New Statesman*, 131, 4599 (August, 2002), 36–7. See also Julian Barnes, 'Hate and Hedonism: The insolent art of Michel Houellebecq', *The New Yorker,* www.newyorker.com/archive/2003/07/07/030707 [accessed 20 September 2012]. Reviewing *Platform* in *The Guardian* Michael Worton asserts that he cannot engage meaningfully with Houellebecq's 'gratuitously offensive' comments about monotheism in the novel as 'he provides so little evidence to support his view'. His main objection to the novel, however, is principally an aesthetic one: it is 'weakly conceived, badly structured and in narrative terms simply not convincing', http://www.guardian.co.uk/books/2005/oct/29/fiction.michelhouellebecq [accessed 10 April 2013].

103 *Le Rappel à l'ordre: enquête sur les nouveaux réactionnaires* (Paris: Le Seuil, 2002).

104 John Lloyd, 'Is Man Too Wicked to be Free?', *New Statesman*, 16 December 2002, http://www.newstatesman.com/200212160024 [accessed 18 September 2009].

105 Hugo Frey and Benjamin Noys, 'Reactionary Times', *Journal of European Studies* 37, 3 (2007) 243–53, 247.

106 James Meeks, 'Every Boy's Young Dream', *London Review of Books*, 24, 22, 14 November 2002, 26–7.

2

The Extension of the Domain of the Struggle: The Third Spirit of Capitalism

What the philosophers once knew as life has become the sphere of private existence and now of mere consumption, dragged along as an appendage of the process of material production, without autonomy or substance of its own.

Theodor Adorno, *Minima Moralia*

Extending the domain

'Economic liberalism is the extension of the domain of the struggle, its extension to all ages and all classes of society'.[1] With the possible exception of 'the most stupid religion' anti-Islam comment in *Platform*, this is the most frequently cited line from Houellebecq's work, and for good reason. Encapsulated in this simple expository pronouncement is the overarching hypothesis of Houellebecq's entire oeuvre; namely, that market principles have come to determine and define every aspect of human life. We have arrived, he suggests, at an era that permits, indeed demands, the complete subsumption of human life to market forces and where economic subjectification extends into every sphere of human subjectivity. Houellebecq's characters stumble around and finally disintegrate in this world in which human experience is systematically reified from the cradle to the grave and where human desire, above all sexual desire, is the aspect of human life most recently has been drawn into the domain of the market and as such represents a particularly agonizing burden for the subject. Unable to embrace such a world, his protagonists are besieged and beleaguered, able only to half-exist among the affective ruins of relentless commodification, they live what Adorno would call 'damaged lives'. Set in atomized communities of single males and sometimes females, Houellebecq's characters are profoundly emotionally and sexually isolated and have few meaningful kinship relations, weakened societal affiliations and no religious ties to the society in which they live. The morose trajectories of each of their lives register the processes and effects of neoliberalism which, as David Harvey has argued, '... has pervasive effects on the ways of thought to the point where it has become incorporated into the common-sense way many of us interpret, live in and understand the world'.[2] Examining the production of subjectivity in a society increasingly evacuated of Marx's 'heavenly ecstasies', Houellebecq's writing describes a life world in which the dynamics of reification have assumed a sovereignty hitherto unparalleled; a social reality not only where relations between people have progressively become the relation between things, but where, through the processes of neoliberal governmentality, a society is produced in which '[...] the structure of reification progressively sinks more deeply, more fatefully and more definitively into the consciousness of man [...] It stamps its imprint on the whole of consciousness.'[34] Reification, *Verdinglichung*, the transformation of human beings into thing-like objects and by extension the 'thingly quality of human experience' is central to the new spirit of capitalism that emerged in the last half of the twentieth century, functioning literally in the sense of markets but also, as Timothy Bewes has noted, as a '... metaphor for the effects of capitalism on people, relationships, self-image, ideas, social life, art and culture'.[5] If people are transformed into mere things, it is important to examine how their behaviour operates in ways that are in accordance with the laws of this 'thing-world'.[6] This is precisely, I suggest, what Houellebecq's novels do. They are examinations of how refusing this 'thing-world' can have devastating consequences when there is no imaginable liveable alternative.

Under neoliberal capitalism, the dynamics of reification penetrate more fully into the interiority of the subject so that all human life becomes incorporated into the calculable field of rationalization and totalization. This penetration has reached such a point, argues Slavoj Žižek, that we have arrived at a historical phase of capitalism necessitating a renegotiation of the classic Marxist notion of reification as extant Lukácsian terms are no longer adequate for the task of fully addressing the acceleration of the cognitive and affective reach of capitalism in its neoliberal form. Unlike liberalism's more clearly demarcated division between the public and the private, work and leisure, self and state, the sphere of activity of neoliberal capitalism has no such obviously defined beginnings and ends. Its topography, as Catherine Chaput points up, emerges out of the 'imploded borders' of the formerly liberal world and is made up of 'blurred boundaries that fold into one another' in a psycho-economic landscape in which '... time accelerates, space collapses, and distinctions between such classic demarcations as agent and subject or politics and economics erode'.[7] This is, Žižek argues, neoliberalism functioning as what one might call 'cultural capitalism' in which the very stuff of 'social relationality', far from being invisible is the 'direct object of marketing and exchange' and that '… one no longer sells (and buys) objects which "bring" cultural or emotional experiences, one directly sells (and buys) such experiences'.[8] Writing in *Acts of Resistance* (1998), Pierre Bourdieu defines neoliberal capitalism as nothing less than a 'new kind of conservative revolution' which:

> … appeals to progress, reason and science (economics in this case) […] and so tries to write off progressive thought and action as archaic. It sets up as the norm of all practices, and therefore as ideal rules, the real regularities of the economic world abandoned to its own logic, the so-called laws of the market. It reifies and glorifies the reign of what are called the financial markets, in other words the return to a kind of radical capitalism, with no other law than that of maximum profit, an unfettered capitalism without any disguise, but rationalized, pushed to the limit of its economic efficacy by the introduction of modern forms of domination, such as 'business administration', and techniques of manipulation, such as market research and advertising.[9]

Such 'unfettered capitalism' knows no limits to its subsumption and perpetually thrusts the subject into a milieu in which *everything* is reduced to exchange value. While this is by no means a new concern in either modern literature or political thought, it is almost exclusively the focus of Houellebecq's writing. In a prose style commensurate with the flatness and utilitarianism of the disenchanted world of his characters, he plunges them into isolation, madness and death, as a result of their failure or refusal to invest wholeheartedly in this system of exchange that demands we accept the idea of self as a thing. Beneath the graphic descriptions of sex and the deadpan humour, lies a profoundly melancholic despair; a poignant sense of loss that something has passed away in human relations. As the subject is transformed into an economic object of exchange, his characters find the constant negotiation and exchange of the sexual market unsettling and painful. The male protagonists do attempt, for a short while at least, to go along with the pantomime of these relations, always hoping to find some kind of redemptive, authentic alternative to this process of reification through the medium of young woman's bodies. However, in the final account, all of Houellebecq's protagonists are very bad, botched subjects of neoliberalism as they are fundamentally indifferent to the rewards on offer to the victors in this system and have consistently failed to worship at the altar of what Walter Benjamin has called the 'cultic religion' of capitalism'.[10]

Growing up in the 1950s in a post-war France economically and politically shaped by *dirigisme* (state economic control) Houellebecq entered adolescence in the post-'68 era, a beneficiary of many of the consequences and few of the pleasures of the sexual revolution. As such, his views of 1968 and the 'breakdown' of sexual and personal morality are, to say the least, negative. In Houellebecq's estimation, while 1968 represented a progressive movement away from the oppressive strictures of Catholicism, it also marked the definitive end of social collectivity and enduring kinship relations and, most importantly in his view, delivered up the subject to rapacious market forces. Using sexual emancipation to stand synecdochically for 1968, Houellebecq writes: 'The sexual revolution was to destroy the last unit separating the individual from the market'.[11] With the disappearance of the nuclear family, meaningful religious rituals and older social forms of deference and politesse, the individual becomes an entrepreneurial self who operates almost exclusively on an economic plane in every sphere of life. Much of the interest of Houellebecq's work, then, lies in the intensity of his assertion that the commodifying discourses of neoliberalism were invited in by '68 and have subsequently colonized every last fragment of affective human existence, and in particular sex and sexuality. Liberated in the great rush of post-1968 anti-establishment cultural politics, sexuality and human desire have been drawn more systematically into the logic of the market which in its 'permanent state of war' is forever looking for new things to sell.[12] This is a situation commented upon at some length by Jean-Claude Guillebaud who argues that sexual liberation has gone from being 'yesterday's fresh "subversion"' to a pivotal part of a 'commercial machinery' and now '... far from contravening the rest of the great liberal market and the commands of money, the ambient permissiveness indisputably serves one and the other. And in a thousand ways, erotic hedonism, even unwillingly, has become part of a well-defined market'.

In ways that are comparable to an anti-'68 school of thought epitomized in many regards by Gilles Lipovetsky (to whom I shall refer later), Houellebecq locates the origin of the inversion of ethical values in the sexual revolution of the 1960s.[13] Of course a few years before 1968, Herbert Marcuse's *One Dimensional Man* (1964) had famously theorized the relationship between reification and sexuality: 'It has often been noted that advanced industrial civilization operates with a greater degree of sexual freedom—'operates' in the sense that the latter becomes a market value and a factor of social mores'.[14] Although this hypothesis has been elaborated upon and in many ways superseded, its central supposition is remarkably consonant with Houellebecq's ideas in *Atomised* and *Platform*. In a world stripped of the last vestiges of religious communality, Houellebecq's protagonists all suffer from a surfeit of freedom that, far from liberating them sexually, existentially or socially, paralyses them in the knowledge that they must regard themselves and others through the quantitative lens of consumption. This idea of an unbounded freedom, with its 'free-floating' and 'unbound capital' so crucial to the neoliberal project has scant regard for any social consequences or ethical responsibilities and, as Zygmunt Bauman says, represents the abandonment of an idea of social cohesion and an 'unprecedented [...] disconnection of power from obligations: duties towards employees, but also towards the younger and weaker, towards yet unborn generations and towards the self-reproduction of the living conditions of all; in short, the freedom from the duty to contribute to daily life and the perpetuation of the community...'.[15]

The assertion that capitalism is extending ever further into all areas of human life and particularly into relations between humans is, of course, merely an echo of Marx and Engels in *The Communist Manifesto's* declaration that capital 'has resolved personal worth into exchange value' and '... has left remaining no other nexus between person and person than naked self-interest, than callous "cash payment"'. Noting its capacity to engulf and replace the most sublime reaches of human spirituality, Marx and Engels also note the ability of capitalism to drown out 'the most heavenly ecstasies of religious fervour, of chivalrous enthusiasm, of philistine sentimentalism, in the icy water of egotistical calculation [...] and in place of the numberless indefeasible chartered freedoms, has set up that single, unconscionable freedom – Free Trade'.[16] This account of capitalism as an almost infinitely resourceful energy that calculates human worth in monetary terms develops into a complex and highly influential critique of commodity fetishism that has preoccupied many Marxist and post-Marxist accounts of culture and society and, in particular, theories of reification, over the last century.[17] Defining reification as a process that penetrates 'the very depths of man's physical and psychic nature' and in which the 'rationalization of the world appears to be complete', Lukács's seminal description of reification still remains valuable. Under the forces of reification, Lukács argues, relations between people assume 'the character of a thing' and within a totalized society the individual subjectivity of a person is translated into that of a 'thing', a commodity. This process leads to the full 'atomisation of the individual' which is, in fact, 'only the reflex in consciousness of the fact that the "natural laws" of capitalist production have been extended to cover every manifestation of life in society; that – for the first time in history – the whole of society is subjected, or tends to be subjected, to a unified economic process, and that the fate of every member of society is determined by unified laws.[18]

Under neoliberalism, understood as a new and more assiduous form of reification, every subject must be made *both* an effective consumer and entrepreneurial manager, as the self increasingly becomes both an object to be exchanged and consumed just like any other, and also a project of personal development to be inserted into the wider corporate whole. One particularly astute review of *Atomised* summarizes this dynamic in Houellebecq's work: 'Citizens have now turned into customers, who cannot conceive of a future, let alone of an afterlife, except in terms of increasing wealth and the acquisition of consumer products for status and satisfaction [...] Individualism, the antechamber to barbarism, is the grave of communal life and ultimately of civilization.'[19] The world presented in Houellebecq's writing, then, is an ideologically collapsed one in which there are no longer any clearly delineated demarcations between inside and outside, between public and private, and where the mark of a successful life is one where the subject is most fully realized as a viable and profitable entrepreneurial project; but it is a picture that refuses any kind of Marxist explanation, rather it typifies the Left-Conservative concerns of *rouge-brunism*. An ex-Marxist philosopher who describes himself as an advocate of a similarly 'conservative-liberal-socialism', Lesek Kolakowski adopts an ideological position comparable to that of Houellebecq. In deliberately non-Marxist terms, Kolakowski describes reification as the 'transformation of all human products and individuals into goods comparable in quantitative terms' bringing about 'the disappearance of qualitative links between people; the gap between public and private life; the loss of personal responsibility and the reduction of human beings to being executors of tasks imposed by a renationalized system; the resulting deformation of personality; the impoverishment of human contacts, the loss of solidarity ... '.[20] Many of Houellebecq's ideas and words sound close to that of Marxist critique but his steadfast refusal of Marxism, indeed of any political understanding of this dynamic, is integral to the inconsolably bleak timbre of his writing.

I argue here, and in the following chapter, that Houellebecq's writing charts the transformation of subjectivity enacted by neoliberalism in which it imprints the macro-economic system on the private psycho-social domain, which then gradually permeates and subsumes every social, sexual and familial relation. With no viable effective ideological opposition to what Derrida calls its 'manic, jubilatory, and incantatory form', neoliberal capitalism 'repeats and ritualizes itself' until it becomes naturalized as the human condition and as the *only* possibility of living.[21] This reading begins by examining how neoliberalism is distinct from earlier manifestations of capitalism, tracing its emergence out of three successive spirits of capitalism; approximately distinct eras in which the mechanisms of capitalism moved from that of industrial production to a proliferation of the economies of consumption and the exponential intensification of finance capitalism that rendered the working of the market ever more invisible and yet never more pervasive in its reach. I examine the ways in which neoliberalism is not only a theory of political economy but also, and much more importantly, an ideological project that attempts to construct a model subject who willingly submits to increasingly privatized social relations and 'a social reality that it suggests already exists'.[22]

I also suggest that the four novels considered here all, in one way or another, demonstrate the ways in which this most recent mutation of capitalism conceals its more brutishly ideological workings by giving the appearance of offering freedom and choice and the idea of personal autonomy. Houellebecq's work thus recognizes that neoliberalism has managed to assimilate the discourse of its own critique in order to better adapt to the ethical climate of its time by disguising itself in the languages of self-actualization, personal authenticity and moral freedom that were once the very charges mounted against it by its most passionate enemies in the 1960s and 1970s. This tactic allows it to present potentially unsettling changes, for example to labour and workplace practices such as short-term contracts and outsourcing, as 'hip' commendably non-hierarchical, flexible and 'connexionist' labour practices that allow for greater freedom of the individual, all of which were the goals of post-'68 critique.[23] Crucially then, once ingested in this way, critique and resistance are purged of any ideological content and are utilized to allow for the smoother working of the capitalist machine. Thus, business and entrepreneurialism are now made to appear as if they were a cosy chat between equals in an apparently democratized workplace that favours the faux-domesticated and infantilized concept of 'dress-down Fridays'. Houellebecq is one of the first writers of his generation to address some of the implications of this new spirit of capitalism, which has restructured not only the workplace but also more generally labour patterns across a lifetime. In its most sociological mode his writing offers a commentary on the transformation of the socio-economic world and the affective changes wrought by such changes.

First then, I consider the development of neoliberalism from its origins in the immediate post-World War Two period to its consolidation in the Chicago School and the economic thought of Milton Friedman; through its development in the 1970s in the context of the global oil crisis, then to its emergence proper in the 1980s where it was promulgated most famously by Ronald Reagan in the US and by Margaret Thatcher in Britain.[24] Arguing that a particularly subjectifying type of reification lies at the heart of the neoliberal project, I examine Foucault's ideas of governmentality and why the intensification of reification is central to neoliberalism's biopolitics. Very briefly tracing the development of later capitalism from the end of the nineteenth century to its third and most recent mutation in the 1990s, I move on to more recent definitions of neoliberalism drawing on, among others, the influential work of Luc Boltanski and Ève Chiapello's Weber-inspired tome, *The New Spirit of Capitalism* (2005) which offers an analysis of these changes in a specifically French context.

Neoliberalism: A rascal concept

A complex concept to define with any exactitude, the debates around the term neoliberalism have been characterized, as Neil Brenner and Jamie Peck suggest, by 'a perplexing mix of overreach and underspecification' and marked by statements that are 'promiscuously pervasive, yet inconsistently defined, empirically imprecise and frequently contested'. Unsurprisingly then, critics have often tussled over the exact meaning of the term; it has a complex doubled semantic valency in that it designates both policy and ideology or, more simply stated, it is both theory and practice. It has become, then, something of a 'rascal concept' as it is 'simultaneously, a terminological focal point for debates on the trajectory of post-1980s regulatory transformations and an expression of the deep disagreements and confusions that characterize those debates'.[25] Capitalism has undergone several phases of transformation and, inevitably, there are differences of opinion about the exact nature of these changes but for the most part economic commentators are in agreement that there have been three significant stages of development.[26] Broadly speaking then, neoliberalism might be regarded as the third spirit of capitalism. As a theory of political economy, neoliberalism is, says Harvey, a revival of the eighteenth-century liberal doctrine about freedoms and individual liberties 'connected to a very specific view of the market'.[27] Historically rooted in the principles of classical eighteenth- and nineteenth-century economic liberalism propounded in Adam Smith's *The Wealth of Nations* in 1776 and advocated by John Locke, David Hume and Alexis de Tocqueville, it replaced the Keynesian post-war consensus of state regulated capitalism that had largely dominated Western economies from 1945–85, rising to rapid prominence with very little resistance to become, not just a dominant paradigm, but the only way of thinking about political economy. Its turning point, at which it became most strongly politically endorsed and legitimized, came in the decade of the 1980s with a process of deregulation and rapid financialization of both the UK and US economies. As noted, its most famous proselytizers and practitioners in those countries were Margaret Thatcher and Ronald Reagan and then, later, Tony Blair and Bill Clinton.

According to David Harvey, neoliberalism in its contemporary guise had been 'lurking in the wings of public policy' since the late 1940s when its origins can be traced back to the Austrian political philosopher Friedrich von Hayek's creation of the Mont Pelerin Society in 1947. In *The Road to Serfdom* (1944) Hayek writes of the moral basis of this new type of economic thought that is arranged around the central importance of personal freedom. Together with the economist Milton Friedman and a group of like-minded philosophers, historians and academics, Hayek elaborated a new version of liberalism fashioned from existing versions of classical liberal economic theory which had at its heart the core doctrine that insisted on 'individual freedom from coercion and servitude'. Hayek further posited that there is a natural moral link between economic freedom and individualism:

> Only where we ourselves are responsible for our own interests […] has our decision moral value. Freedom to order our own conduct in the sphere where material circumstances force a choice upon us, and responsibility for the arrangement of our own life according to our own conscience, is the air in which alone moral sense grows and in which moral values are daily recreated in the free decision of the individual. Responsibility, not to a superior, but to one's own conscience, the awareness of a duty not exacted by compulsion, the necessity to decide which of the things one values are to be sacrificed to others, and to bear the consequences of one's own decision, are the very essence of any morals which deserve the name.[28]

Notable here is the vehemence of the moral pitch, which although articulated in more secular tones than the earlier Weberian Protestant capitalist spirit, nevertheless continues the quasi-evangelical belief that the free market is the 'well spring of freedom', both moral and physical, which can only be obtained through completely unfettered competition. This idea of unencumbered capital as crucial to moral freedom will become one of the key aspects of neoliberal discourse which urges the individual to be free by plugging into the circuits of choice and self-differentiation in which one can turn oneself into an entrepreneurial project with endless accumulation potential, which in turn guarantees maximum freedom.[29] It is crucial to appreciate fully this emphasis on the importance of freedom that stands at the centre of neoliberal ideology. Its devotees believe that human freedom is achieved by the shrinking back of all state intervention and, further, that this is not ideological but natural as the declining power of the state liberates the 'natural' laws of the market which in many parts of the world had been held in check since the 1920s by either Fascism or Communism.

In its most basic theoretical sense, neoliberalism can be understood as the most recent version of global market capitalism. Unlike the liberal capitalism of the post-war Keynesian era however, it is capitalism with the welfare gloves well and truly off. 'Neoliberalism', Harvey notes, 'seeks to strip away the protective coverings that embedded liberalism allowed and occasionally nurtured.'[30] Neoliberal policies advocate a radical shrinking back of the state in all matters of national governance save for fiscal ones where it actively encourages policies favouring free trade, financial deregulation and the unfettered flow of transnational capital that seeks the lowest possible costs as it roams across the planet looking for cheap labour. There is an economic emphasis on consumption rather than on production and on a global scale, a shift of financial power away from accountable, democratically elected national governments into organizations such as the WTO, the IMF and the Federal Reserve. Above all, neoliberalism advocates the importance of private property and the private rights of the individual and particularly encourages, therefore, strong private property rights among citizens.

Lasting roughly from the sixteenth to the eighteenth century, the first stage of capitalism was a mercantilist one that would develop into the industrial capitalism of the nineteenth century, located in the workshop and the factory. This first spirit of capitalism was, as Max Weber writes in *The Protestant Ethic and the Spirit of Capitalism* (1904–5), guided by Protestant principles that placed a central importance on thriftiness, patrimony and inheritance and especially on the deferral of pleasure in favour of saving. The *summum bonum* of this capitalist ethic was '... the strict earning of more and more money, combined with the strict avoidance of all spontaneous enjoyment of life' is regarded as 'purely as an end in itself'; a goal with such self-discipline and self-denial is 'closely connected with certain religious ideas.'[31] Hence prudence, avoidance of any hedonism or extravagance around either body or capital, was central to this earlier stage of capitalism where saving for the future was consonant with strong religious beliefs.

This first phase developed gradually into the Fordism of the late nineteenth and early twentieth centuries, a model favouring large centralized bureaucratic corporate structures in which capital produces on its own the means of production. The site of Fordist production was the large-scale factory that produced increasingly standardized goods through a very strict division of the workers' labour. Lasting until the Great Depression of the 1930s, this phase ended when the speculative financial bubble burst provoking an intense crisis of financial confidence and significantly altered attitudes towards the moral mission of capitalism. Thus, a second stage of capitalism emerged which would last roughly from the 1930s though to the 1970s. Largely based on the thinking of British economist John Maynard Keynes, this model involved increased state intervention, a strong commitment to social welfare provision and a commitment to full employment.[32] In North America, the recession and oil crises of 1972–3 were the stimuli for the post-war Western economies' movement away from Fordism with its four principle tenets of production: standardization, mechanization, Taylorist scientific management and assembly line, to post-Fordism. Boltanski and Chiapello summarize how the 'ponderous, rigid industrial systems inherited from the Taylorist era, with its concentration of workers, its smoking, polluting factory chimneys, its unions and welfare states' were condemned to 'inevitable decline' around this time by, not only the oil crisis, but also by the emergence of '... new technologies, changes in consumer habits, diversification of demand, increasing rapidity of the life-cycle of products ...'.[33] The late 1970s also began to see the dual characteristics that would come to characterize much of neoliberal policy: the retrenchment of the state and a deregulation of finance capital, both increasingly underpinned by a strong commitment to the free market monetarist zeal that reached its apogee in the post-Cold War Reagan–Thatcher era.[34] At this point, there was a discernible turn away from a managed Keynesian economic policy based on clear boundaries between nation states to increasingly borderless global trade that developed into a more settled 'third way' neoliberalism of the mid-1990s in which the 'third machine age' and the more cognitive aspects of the information economy gradually replaced the Fordist industrial model.

Central to neoliberalism, then, is a shift from industrial capital to an economy serviced by the less visible, even spectral forces of finance capital, which has resulted in, as Fredric Jameson has noted, 'the gradual disappearance of the physical marketplace' and the escalation of activity, often circumventing national politics, around a wider range of financial services, investment, accumulation, hedge funds, futures and derivatives, as creators of wealth rather than the previously used GDP yardstick of goods and industrial production.[35] Alongside this increasing spectrality of capital is the proliferation of avenues of consumption and a growing differentiation in the range of cultural products and the emergence of the knowledge economies. Describing the transition from production to post-Fordist consumption as one of the most important changes in a neoliberal economy, Stuart Hall suggests this involves 'a greater emphasis on choice and product differentiation, on marketing packaging and design, on the "targeting" of consumers by lifestyle, taste and culture rather than by category of social class; a decline in the proportion of male, skilled, manual working class, the rise of the service and white-collar classes'.[36]

Crucially, neoliberalists do not regard their policies as ideological *per se* but as a return to the 'natural' order of things, an order often fraught with insecurity and anxiety as it is only minimally shored up by the social safety-net of the welfare state; under neoliberal policies public projects such as social housing, unemployment and sickness benefits and socialized medical care are whittled back to a bare minimum. In the post-Fordist workplace, there is a insistence on flexibility, a reduction of worker's benefits, sub-contracting, part-time labour, short-termism and (ostensibly) non-hierarchical management structures and a repeated affirmation of the positive potential of this set-up that transforms what might be regarded as undesirable social atomization and labour insta-bility into the illusion of individual choice. Workers become encouraged to interpellate themselves, not as workers in any collective sense, but as individual entrepreneurs of their own labour; private companies of one. In this way, the precariousness of fixed-term contracts and limited workplace rights is sold to them as an opportunity to work on their business spirit and to sharpen their spirit for competition. What is required from the 'restructured' worker in this increasingly precarious workplace, says Maurizio Lazzarato, is that his or her 'personality and subjectivity have to be made susceptible to organization and command'. Thus, what is at stake here is the demand that the whole of the human being be transformed into capital, hence Margaret Thatcher's claim in her *précis* of Chicago neoliberalism: 'Economics are the method; the object is to change the heart and soul.'[37] What Thatcher articulates here is an apposite description for the construction of the neoliberal subject as the logic of political economy is restructured as biopolitics. Post-Fordist labour becomes not only increasingly immaterial but in its strategy of subjectification neoliberalism makes the worker's 'soul become part of the factory' and capitalism is permitted to shape a life-world from the inside out.[38] This reduction of the worker to a singular competitive entity is understood in neoliberal doctrine as the ultimate in individual freedom and autonomy but in practice it is, says Harvey, a 'dissolution of social solidarities' producing a pervasive sense of uncertainty and instability and contributes to the wider sense of anxiety and the dynamics of 'crisis formation' within capitalism.[39]

The production and transfer of knowledge becomes central to much neoliberal economic activity as labour, mostly for the middle classes, moves towards more intangible activities. Central to the radical reorganization of labour, was the rapid development of information technology in the 1980s and 1990s and in particular, of course, the coming of the World Wide Web in 1992. The electronic revolution, as Ferruchio Gambino notes, radically restratified labour, dividing it into 'a relatively restricted upper level of the super-skilled, and a massive lower level of ordinary post-Fordist doers and executors'.[40] Lyotard's *The Postmodern Condition* (1979) presciently outlined the crucial role that the transformation of knowledge into information would play in the new era of Western capitalism where 'learning' and 'knowledge' can 'fit into the new channels and become operational' only if they can be 'translated into quantities of information'.[41] Thus, as Jason Read argues, neoliberalism is unique as an ideological structure as it is not generated by the state or by a dominant class, but 'from the quotidian experience of buying and selling commodities from the market, which is then extended across other social spaces, the "marketplace of ideas", to become an image of society'.[42] All of this, then, contributes to the transition to a post-industrial paradigm that entails a shift to not only immaterial goods, but also to immaterial labour and it is this idea of immateriality that will be important for a biopolitical understanding of neoliberalism.

Neoliberalism has evolved in other very particular ways outside of the purely economic or labour-based concerns that allow its penetration into the affective domain of the individual to shape the corporeal and sensorial spaces of everyday human life. As Mark Fisher states: 'What we are dealing with now is not the incorporation of materials that previously seemed to possess subversive potentials, but instead, their *precorporation:* the pre-emptive formatting and shaping of desires, aspirations and hopes by capitalist culture.'[43] What, then, are the effects of these changes on the subject? How did neoliberalism as an ideology that seemed to be ever-retreating from the realm of the political become, in Foucault's terms, a form of governmentality? And how did the advocates of neoliberalism convince its citizens that 'human well-being can best be advanced by liberating individual entrepreneurial freedoms and skill within an institutional framework characterized by strong private property rights, free markets, and free trade'?[44] In short, how did neoliberalism go from a theory of political economy to a biopolitical advocation on the care of the self? The most comprehensive post-Foucauldian exposition of this new form of decentred and deterritorialized global capitalism is to be found in Michael Hardt and Antonio Negri's millennial work *Empire* (2000). The definition offered of neoliberalism (although it is notable that Hardt and Negri rarely use that term) is one that suggests its focus is as much on 'the production of social life' as it is on the economic, and further that it has created a life where the 'economic, the political, and the cultural increasingly overlap and invest one another'.[45] It is the overlapping and blurring of these boundaries, in particular between the economic and the affective, that might be regarded as one of the most important characteristics of neoliberalism.

While many commentators have pointed up the aggressive rationalizing economic logic of neoliberalism and its broadening of the idea of what constitutes the market, it is not, as political theorist Wendy Brown notes, 'simply a set of economic policies' as it is 'not only or even primarily focused on the economy'. Neoliberalist policies, Brown continues, certainly believe in 'facilitating free trade, maximizing corporate profits, and challenging welfarism' but the deeper incursion of neoliberalism at the level of subjectivity represents a new form of biopolitical governmentality that 'reaches from the soul of the citizen-subject' and 'involves extending and disseminating market values to all institutions and social action …'[46] As much concerned with the psycho-social internalization of this logic at the level of the subject as with fiscal policies promoting deregulation and the separation of the economy and the state, neoliberalism is distinctive from the *laissez faire* economic liberalism characterized by Adam Smith's self-regulating, invisible hand of the market. In its operation everything – the state, culture, the social world and the psyche – is open to market forces and a new kind of subsumption through entrepreneurialism. Subsumed too, is ideology in any meaningful political sense; in such a comprehensively 'marketized' environment the mantra of 'personal freedom' and 'individual choice' replaces any systematic understanding of the political. The neoliberal exhortation to believe in the importance of individual freedom and choice concomitantly urges the subject to view itself not as part of a wider human collective that might share communal rituals based on kinship and belief but as a site of self-organization; a mini-enterprise that invests its energies into maximizing personal and monetary profit. The severing of the subject from the fabric of the social is central to neoliberalist ideology, mirroring the ways in which capital is encouraged to disembed itself from social and political constraints.[47] As noted, one of Houellebecq's most quoted lines effectively functions as the determining hypothesis of his whole oeuvre, namely that 'unrestrained economic liberalism' (he never calls it neoliberalism as the French interferes in the translation) and the 'extension' of the ethos of the market 'to all ages and all classes of society' that 'seeks to bring all human action into the domain of the market' produces little but alienation and anxiety.[48] The focus of Houellebecq's work, however, is clearly not the economic or fiscal aspects of neoliberalism, but rather the ways in which the biopolitical processes of neoliberalism produce subjects in whom the idea of the self as a privatized entrepreneur, culturally, emotionally, professionally, and sexually, has become naturalized and in the process leaches away feelings of sublimity and pathos. In Houellebecq's novels it is in the realm of affective human intimacy, particularly sexuality, that this process of desublimation is most intensely felt, thus, we see in his work a focus on the synergies between the sexual and material economies.

Under neoliberalism, then, we are compelled to be free; an obligation that generates something of a paradox as the stronger the insistence on the importance of individual choice, distinction and freedom the more homogenous, standardized and thoroughly monocultural the fabric of everyday life becomes; any sense of otherness must either assimilate or disappear. Naturally, this has serious consequences, not only for the relationships between one human being and another but also for both culture and religion as both have traditionally, in different ways, offered a sense of transcendence or sublimity that escapes administered life. As Bewes notes, 'a society in […] which no non-administered reality exists any longer – in which there is no sublimity, no aura is possible – is one in which art becomes untenable except purely as an institutional, instrumental or commercial pursuit'.[49] Again, while this is scarcely a ground-breaking revelation, it is nevertheless something to which Houellebecq's writing continually gestures.

It is crucial to the neoliberal mission in a society in which everything is open to the forces of the market, to emphasize that privatization and individualism are understood by its subjects not as disintegrative or negative moral forces prising apart the deep vertical structures of kinship, collectivity and cooperation, but as an intensification of freedom, the calling card of neoliberalism. Indeed, one might argue that it neoliberalism's ability to present itself as utterly non-ideological, to produce the 'appearance of ideology as its own opposite', that could be called, in its own commercial vernacular, its unique selling point (USP).[50] Neoliberalism is not then, simply a 'new ideology', as Jason Read points up, but rather 'a transformation of ideology in terms of its conditions and effects', a process whereby the ideological content is wholly concealed by its transposition into an ethical discourse.[51] Such a transformation is at the core of the neoliberal hegemony as it eradicates all sense of itself as ideological by its seductively normative veneer that has allowed it to become the most 'successful ideology in history'.[52] As noted at several points so far, central to what might be called the ethical dimension of the neoliberalist project is the quasi-evangelical conviction that human freedom can only be achieved through economic competition and that competition is one of the greatest goods. In this way then, neoliberalism becomes 'an ethic in itself, capable of acting as a guide to all human emotions and substituting for all previously held beliefs'.[53] Thus, the withdrawal of the state from vast areas of public life through increased privatization is presented not as a regressive movement but rather as the opportunity for greater personal freedom and individual self-governance. In a speech from 1976 in which he emphasizes the moral, even philosophical, imperative behind the idea of freedom and private choice, Valéry Giscard d'Estaing declares that the free market can 'deepen [...] the new liberties of everyday life' and that society should 'decentralize boldly in enterprise' and in everyday life:

> If we want the individual to become master of his own destiny and free to take an increasing number of decisions, here is what should *not* be done: increase the powers or the dimensions of an already multi-tentacled administration; nationalize enterprises which do not perform a public service – to do so would be either to deliver them to the technocracy, or to '*étatize*' them and have them be directed by a small number of bureaucrats of the central administration not responsible to anyone; planify the economy, which would be the same as to give a few men the power to decide for several millions; suppress initiative and competition.[54]

In his examination of what comprises the 'spirit' of capitalism, Weber suggests that the moral dimension motivating and sustaining capitalism in its earlier manifestations was provided by the external moral and psychological system of Protestantism. Without such a clear religious doctrine on which to call, neoliberalism has drawn on the increasingly secular aspects of Western society, presenting the benefits of the free and unregulated market – freedom, authenticity, flexibility, autonomy and self-actualization – as moral and philosophical ones and in doing so has substituted the market for religion; indeed, it offers the market *as* religion.

Central to this 'new spirit of capitalism' is a diminishment of any sense of a viable exteriority or opposition to this system summed up of course by Margaret Thatcher's evangelical apophthegm 'There is no Alternative' that has been deployed in French as *la pensée unique*. This overpowering sense of a lack of an outside, of any kind of elsewhere, is the topography of Houellebecq's novels as they articulate the sense of entrapment within an infernal circuit of individualism and materialism, one that denies any possibility of an outside to the logic of the neoliberal cultures, that is, the complete disappearance of *any* opposition to this process. Houellebecq shows that the process itself can endlessly assimilate and use this resistance, now in its weak, non-ideological form, to ensure its continued smooth working. The success of 'standard neoliberal toolkit' has transformed political thinking, says Susan George, successfully inverting theories of political economy in less than fifty years. 'The transformation of thinking has been dramatic', she argues, and its most troubling aspect is the lack of any viable opposition to the idea that '... the market should be allowed to make major social and political decisions, the idea that the state should voluntarily reduce its role in the economy, or that corporations should be given total freedom [...] that citizens be given much less rather than more social protection', all of this has been neutralized as *the* only political, cultural and economic reality of our times.[55] Resistance is futile. Metaphysical resistance is particularly ineffectual as the possibility of a philosophical alternative is equally shattered, as Martin Crowley notes, '... we have locked ourselves into a reductive materialism of performance and profit which relentlessly pulls the rug out from under our metaphysical impulses'. Any aesthetic or cultural solace is even less tenable; at every turn, Houellebecq's work narrates the futility of culture to offer anything other than a stark reminder of the state of things.[56]

Neoliberalism as biopolitics

Michel Foucault's series of lectures from 1978 to 1979 on 'The Birth of Biopolitics' at the Collège de France are highly persuasive accounts of what he termed the governmentality of everyday life. The lectures develop his ideas on the mechanisms of biopolitical subjectification, providing an explanation of how neoliberalism seeks to govern subjectivity or mentalities, thus reaching much further into the processes of subject formation than any previous forms of capitalism have ever managed. Foucault's focus here, then, is how this neoliberal subject is produced through increasingly non-ideological (in the traditional sense of the word) forces. While there are obvious philosophical discontinuities between Marx and Foucault, there is nonetheless a productive relationship to be harnessed between the two, and one which, as Bob Jessop argues, may help us to understand via Marx 'the *how* of economic exploitation and political domination' and 'the *why* of capital accumulation and state power' provided by Foucault's 'analyses of disciplinarity and governmentality'.[57] In his analytics of power offered in these lectures, Foucault moves away from his earlier genealogical approach to an analysis of the modern sovereign state that encompasses the Ancient Greeks to modern neoliberalism. Any analysis of the subject in Western civilization, Foucault argues, has to acknowledge not 'only techniques of domination but also techniques of the self' and, crucially, the interaction between these two. Such an explanation would:

> ... take into account the points where the technologies of domination of individuals over one another have recourse to processes by which the individual acts upon himself [...] The contact point, where the individuals are driven by others is tied to the way they conduct themselves, is what we can call, I think, government. Governing people, in the broad meaning of the word, governing people is not a way to force people to do what the governor wants; it is always a versatile equilibrium, with complementarity and conflict between techniques which assure coercion and processes through which the self is constructed or modified by himself. [58]

In Foucault's conceptualization of governmentality, neoliberalism is understood, as Thomas Lemke explains, not just as the 'extension of economy into the domain of politics, the triumph of capitalism over the state' but as an altered state of the political where the apparent retreat of the state is in reality an expansion of government that acts on the private body – the self – rather than the body politic. Foucault further suggests that neoliberalism, despite its outward appearance to the contrary, is a form of anti-humanism that has profoundly negative social and affective consequences for human society through its demotion of the importance of 'traditional' experiences in favour of individualism and the promotion of 'flexibility, mobility and risk taking' that endangers 'collective bonds' and threatens 'family values and personal affiliations'.[59] Many affective and kinship relations are replaced by relations of utility and rationalization and in this way a population comes to be defined as human capital rather than as a society. Acknowledging the severing of institutional and familial ties and filiations in the later stages of modernity, Foucault describes this as the beginning of the reign of *homo œconomicus* marked by, among other things, the political investment of the body as capital. Houellebecq's work, then, examines the possibility of any intimate bonds in such a scenario. Specifically, he asks what happens when love and sex are no longer protected by the taboos and prohibitions that marked earlier generations but are now determined by the logic of commercial transaction. Sexual liberation was simply 'another stage in the rise of the individual' that allowed sex and desire to be fully opened up to market forces.[60] The destruction of collectivism at the level of the workplace is mirrored, then, in the domestic and personal domain where the collective of the family has been assailed by the incitement to pursue individual pleasures and desires that are incompatible with the ethos of the family unit. Paradoxically, just at the moment that sexuality is liberated from demands for restraint and moral compliance, especially for women, it is folded into an economic dynamic of exchange which has also become increasingly unworkable for those who are failing to profit through a new sexual entrepreneurialism. Sexual desire is no longer spontaneously or freely given (if indeed it ever truly was) and has moved away from any sense of the 'natural' into the realm of the cultural and the economic. Thus, sex and sexuality function as a kind of yardstick with which to measure the effects of neoliberalism on the private body.

Hardt and Negri refine Foucault's concept of biopower as that which seeks to regulate 'social life from its interior, following it, interpreting it, absorbing it, and rearticulating it. Power can achieve an effective command over the entire life of the population only when it becomes an integral, vital function that every individual embraces and reactivates of his or her own accord' and further state that it is, in essence, the culmination of capitalism's long-term project in which '… the increasingly intense relationship of mutual implication of all social forces that capitalism has pursued throughout its development has now been fully realized'.[61] The individual subject is produced by the 'invisible' biopower of neoliberalism in which the idea of any outside or exteriority is almost unthinkable; it is now nigh on impossible to separate capital from any idea of the superstructure beloved of old-school Marxist critique, as Jason Read notes: 'Capital production today has either directly appropriated the production of culture, beliefs, and desires or it has indirectly linked them to the production and circulation of commodities'.[62]

Situating his work in a longer literary tradition, Houellebecq's work is not, as some critics have suggested, a direct heir to the politically engaged French novel that has offered critiques of commodity fetishism and reification in ways seen, for example, in Georges Perec's *Les Choses* (1965) or de Beauvoir's *Les Belles images* (1966).[63] Neither is it a contemporary incarnation of Guy Debord and Raoul Vaneigem's Situationist ethos that fulminated against the 'extension of commodification'.[64] Houellebecq's vision is exponentially bleaker, more despairing, than that of his predecessors, as in his view there exists no point of exteriority to the system as any outside is always already in the process of being assimilated into the all-encompassing logic of consumer materialism. As Maurizio Lazzarato notes of neoliberalism, 'We are here far beyond the various theories of domination (e.g. Frankfurt school, Situationism, Bourdieu's sociology)'.[65] For better or for worse, all the metanarratives really have died this time; religion, family, nation state and ideology have been replaced with promises of individual happiness and freedom delivered by the invincible forces of the market. Without God, Marx or the Father, the human subject is thrown back on itself only to find that the ways of living under such conditions seem to boil down to a stark choice between joining in or withdrawing, hedonism or melancholic asceticism. Houellebecq's response lies caught somewhere between these two seemingly paradoxical stances – his is an ascetic hedonism, one might say, or otherwise put, depressive anhedonia. The results of such an annihilation of any political, ontological or philosophical alternatives are registered in Houellebecq's characters who struggle with living in a world with no sense of any outside or elsewhere, one in which human responses are reduced to the simple binaries of participation or withdrawal, a dynamic reminiscent of Baudelaire's 'spleen and ideal' responses to modernity as Kolakowski notes:

> A hypothetical world from which the sacred had been swept away would admit of only two possibilities: vain fantasy that recognizes itself as such, or immediate satisfaction which exhausts itself. It would leave only the choice proposed by Baudelaire, between lovers of prostitutes and lovers of clouds: those who know only the satisfactions of the moment and are therefore contemptible, and those who lose themselves in otiose imaginings, and are therefore contemptible. Everything is contemptible, and there is no more to be said. The conscience liberated from the sacred knows this, even if it conceals it from itself.[66]

Describing in detail the total subsumption of society by capital, Houellebecq's writing probes the workings of these processes and demonstrates the ways in which the 'incorporation of all subjective potential, the capacity to communicate to feel, to create, to think', is turned into 'productive powers for capital'.[67] Stated differently, and in post-structuralist terms that Houellebecq himself would doubtlessly abhor, his work is an engagement with what Deleuze and Guattari have described as capitalism's ability to affect the micro-spaces of the psyche.[68] Absolutely nothing, according to his novels, is able to avoid the reach of neoliberalism and its promotion of flexibility, differentiation and freedom. Houellebecq's work, then, speaks to a very particular set of historical moments which witnessed not only the 'hegemonic victory of consumer capitalism',[69] but more specifically a fundamental, even irreversible, realignment of the relationships between labour, capital and the social order.

The 1990s witnessed a new era of largely unobstructed neoliberalism that is described in the beginning of *Atomised* as the point at which the 'rise of the global economy' made competition much fiercer among nations (and indeed within them) and perhaps even more significantly put a definitive end to France's political dream of 'integrating the populace into a vast middle-class with ever-rising incomes'. It was also an era, Houellebecq notes, in which 'whole social classes fell through the net and joined the ranks of the unemployed',[70] a historical point at which the French model of state was being threatened, if not exactly superseded, by the Anglo-Saxon free market model, what Pierre Bourdieu described as 'the new global vernacular' of neoliberalism.[71] It would be misleading, of course, to suggest that neoliberalism has been experienced homogenously across the globe and it is important to note that in France it has operated on a different chronological plane and to a different degree to the US and Britain. In many ways, as Alain Touraine has pointed out, it is rather mistaken to 'talk of extreme neoliberalism in a country [...] where the state still controls half its resources, either through the welfare system or by intervening in economic life'.[72] Due in part to public support for the need for state-run industries and utilities across the whole political spectrum France was, to a large extent, sheltered from the more aggressive aspects of the earlier phase of neoliberalism and initially it had nothing like the overall impact that it did on Britain and the US. However, as the 1980s wore on into the 1990s France saw an expansion of privatization which became, as Monica Prasad observes, 'the most noticeable feature of French neoliberalism'.[73]

In their authoritative account of the changing workplace practice and managerial discourse in the periods 1968–75 and 1985–95, Boltanski and Chiapello describe the new workplace in the France of the 1990s as a restructured post-Fordist space emphasizing flexibility, immateriality and affective input from its workers who are asked to emotionally 'invest' in their jobs. Situating their arguments within the wider neoliberal directives of deregulation – privatization and the shrinking back of the state – they demonstrate that the qualities of flexibility, labour immateriality and affective cooperation are crucial to the new neoliberal workplace:

> The flexible network is presented as a distinct form between market and hierarchy, whose happy outcomes include *leanness* of the enterprises, *team-work* and *customer satisfaction*, and the *vision* of *leaders* or *coordinators* (no longer

managers) who *inspire* and *mobilize* their *operatives* (rather than workers). The ideal capitalist unit is portrayed as a self-organized team that has externalized its costs onto sub-contractors and deals more in knowledge and information than in manpower or technical experience.[74]

In their analysis, gone is the Taylorist figure of the mass worker along with the certainty of long-term contracts and jobs for life as expectations of job security are whittled away by the idea that mobility and flexibility represent increased freedom and creativity for workers whose labour is now another commodity to sell on the open market. Boltanski and Chiapello argue that this new, infinitely more precarious, white collar workplace is one in which 'the bureaucratic prison explodes' as the chains of command are fractured into several '*networks* with a multitude of participants'. Post-Fordist workers, all 'self-organized, creative beings', have their labour dispersed over several projects in shifting teams that are led by 'line-managers', rather than the old-fashioned, top-down model of a boss, all possessing the necessary vision and innovative skills to 'mobilize' their workers: 'Now no-one is restricted by belonging to a department or wholly subject to the bosses' authority, for all boundaries may be transgressed through the power of projects [...] With new organizations, discovery and enrichment can be constant.'[75] Thus, one might say that post-Fordism in the workplace is the *parole* to the *langue* of neoliberalism.

The time of the neoliberal or post-Fordist worker is rather paradoxical, as on the one hand it is compelled to be as efficient as possible, organized to squeeze speed and effectiveness out of every last minute of the flexible working day, a day that often extends into 'free' time. On the other, there is a compulsion to treat this free or leisure time as if it were a job and to maximize the pleasure and the intensity of the non-working hours; as Gilles Lipovetsky notes of both work and non-work, 'what counts is self-transcendence, a high-voltage life' in a social domain that is effectively an 'extension of the private sphere'.[76] Conversely, Houellebecq's characters are remarkable for their complete lack of interest in their own surplus value and thus they are, as we shall see in the next chapter, all bad subjects of neoliberalism. His characters are not remotely interested in any form of cultural capital and their failure to achieve what Marcuse calls a 'libidinal cathexis' to any merchandise or services is their one truly distinctive attribute. In a society that depends on 'uninterrupted production and consumption', the bad subject of neoliberalism's failure to cathect to 'the services he has to use (or perform), the fun he has to enjoy, the status symbols he has to carry ...' results in its permanent malfunction.[77] While they are nominally exemplary beneficiaries of this neoliberal system, no matter how hard they try Houellebecq's characters are unable to raise sufficient interest in investing in the concept of the self as entrepreneurial project but soon learn that there is nothing outside of this idea and are faced with a choice between an empty Dionysian hedonistic participation played out through sexual pursuits, the choice of the would-be libertine, or ascetic withdrawal. Demonstrating the undesirability of each of these two options, *le monde houellebecquien* is one suffused with a deep sense of despairing anguish over the lost possibility of plenitude and transcendence. With only minor variations, Houellebecq's writing repeats this thematic in each of his novels, but it is in his first novel, *Whatever*, where this thesis is first articulated.

Notes

1 *Whatever*, 99.

2 David Harvey, *A Brief History of Neoliberalism* (Oxford: Oxford University Press, 2007), 3.

3 Karl Marx and Friedrich Engels, *The Communist Manifesto* (London: Polity, 2008: orig. pub. 1848), 13.

4 Georg Lukács, *History and Class Consciousness: Studies in Marxist Dialectics*, trans. Rodney Livingstone (Boston: MIT Press, 1971), 93, 100.

5 Timothy Bewes, *Reification, or, the Anxiety of Late Capitalism* (London: Verso, 2002), ix, 3.

6 Gajo Petrović, *A Dictionary of Marxist Thought*, (eds) Tom Bottomore, Laurence Harris, V. G. Kiernan and Ralph Miliband (Cambridge, MA: Harvard University Press, 1983), 411–13.

7 Catherine Chaput, 'Rhetorical Circulation in Late Capitalism: Neoliberalism and the Overdetermination of Affective Energy', *Philosophy and Rhetoric*, 43, 1 (2010), 1–25, 2.

8 Slavoj Žižek, *First as Tragedy, Then as Farce* (London: Verso, 2009), 139.

9 Pierre Bourdieu, *Acts of Resistance* (New York: Free Press, 1998), 35.

10 Walter Benjamin, 'Capitalism as Religion' in *Selected Writings: 1938–1940* (Cambridge, MA: Harvard University Press, 1996), 288.

11 *Atomised*, 206.

12 *Platform*, 28.

13 Jean-Claude Guillebaud, *La Tyrannie du plaisir* (Paris: Seuil, 1998), 67.

14 Herbert Marcuse, *One Dimensional Man: Studies in the Ideology of Advanced Industrial Society* (Boston: Beacon Press, 1964), 74.

15 Zygmunt Bauman, *Globalization: The Human Consequences* (New York: Columbia University Press, 1998), 9–10.

16 Karl Marx and Freidrich Engels, *The Communist Manifesto*, 3.

17 The genealogy of important work here includes Georg Lukács, *History and Class Consciousness* (1923); the whole of the Frankfurt school Herbert Marcuse Jürgen Habermas; Henri Lefebvre, *Critique of Everyday Life* (1991) and *Everyday Life in the Modern World* (1994); Guy de Bord's *The Society of the Spectacle* (1967); Fredric Jameson in *Postmodernism, or, the Cultural Logic of Late Capitalism* (1991) and 'Reification and Utopia in Mass Culture'. *Social Text* 1 (1979), 130–48; Jean Baudrillard, *The System of Objects* 1968 (1996), *The Consumer Society* 1970 (1998), *For a Critique of the Political Economy of the Sign* 1972 (1981) and from the standpoint of biopolitical power and governmentality Michel Foucault's *Lectures at the College de France, 1978–79: The Birth of Biopolitics* (2008).

18 Georg Lukács, 'Reification and the Consciousnesses of the Proletariat, in *Cultural Theory: An Anthropology* Imre Szeman and Timothy Kaposy, (eds) (London: Wiley–Blackwell, 2011), 177.

19 David Coward, *Times Literary Supplement* (16 September 2005), 21–2.

20 Lesek Kolakowski, *Main Currents of Marxism, Vol. 1* (Oxford: Oxford University Press, 1978), 334–5.

21 Jacques Derrida, *Specters of Marx* (New York and London: Routledge, 1994), 38.

22 Thomas Lemke, *Foucault, Governmentality, and Critique* (London: Paradigm Books, 2012), 13.

23 For ways in which this has most recently been examined see Thomas Frank, *The Conquest of Cool: Business Culture, Counterculture, and the Rise of Hip Consumerism* (Chicago: University of Chicago Press, 1997) and *One Market Under God: Extreme Capitalism, Market Populism, and the End of Economic Democracy* (New York: Random House, 2000).

24 It is a widely held belief that the first truly neoliberal regime was established in 1973 after Augusto Pinochet's coup against the socialist government of Salvador Allende in Chile.

25 Neil Brenner, Jamie Peck and Nik Theodore, 'Variegated Neoliberalization: Geographies, Modalities, Pathways', *Global Networks*, 10, 2 (2010), 182–222, 283–4.

26 On the history of capitalism in the twentieth century and the rise of neoliberalism see Luc Boltanski and Ève Chiapello, *The New Spirit of Capitalism* (London: Verso, 2005); Giovanni Arrighi, *The Long Twentieth Century: Money, Power and the Origins of our Times* (London: Verso, 1994); Krishan Kumar, *From Post-Industrial to Post-Modern Society: New Theories of the Contemporary World* (London: Blackwell, 1995); Ash Amin, *Post-Fordism: A Reader* (London: Blackwell, 1994); David Harvey, *A Brief History of Neoliberalism* (Oxford: Oxford University Press,

2007); Gilles Lipovetsky, *Hypermodern Times* (2005), and *Le Crépuscule du devoir: L'Ethique indolore des nouveaux temps démocratique* (Paris: Gallimard, 1992). See also Bob Jessop, 'Post-Fordism and the State' in Bent Gaeve, *Comparative Welfare Systems* (London: MacMillan, 1996), 165–85; *Radical Thought in Italy*, (eds) Paolo Virno and Michael Hardt (Minneapolis: University of Minnesota Press, 1996); Zygmunt Bauman, *Globalization: The Human Consequences* (Cambridge: Polity Press, 1998); Susan Strange, *The Retreat of the State: The Diffusion of Power in the World Economy* (Cambridge: Cambridge University Press, 1996). On the relationship between pedagogy and neoliberalism see Henry Giroux, *Against the Terror of Neoliberalism: Politics Beyond the Age of Greed* (Boulder, CO: Paradigm Press, 2008).

27 Sasha Lilley, 'On Neoliberalism: An Interview with David Harvey', *Monthly Review* (June 2006), http://mrzine.monthlyreview.org/2006/lilley190606.html [accessed 2 October 2012].

28 Friedrich von Hayek, *The Road to Serfdom* (London: Routledge, 2005, first pub. 1944), 231–3.

29 *Neoliberalism and Everyday Life*, Susan Braedley and Meg Luxton (eds) (McGill: Queen's University Press, 2010), 10.

30 Harvey, 168.

31 Max Weber, *The Protestant Ethic and the Spirit of Capitalism* (London: Routledge, 2005, first pub. 1930), 53.

32 There are important differences between these three stages in the US/UK and French contexts. On the latter see Richard Kuisel, *Capitalism and the State in Modern France: Renovation and Economic Management in the Twentieth Century* (Cambridge: Cambridge University Press, 1981); Harvey Feigenbaum and Jeffrey Henig, 'The Political Underpinnings of Privatization: A Typology', *World Politics*, 46, 2 (1994), 185–208; Marion Fourcade-Gourinchas and Sarah Babb, 'The Rebirth of the Liberal Creed: Paths to Neoliberalism in Four Countries', *American Journal of Sociology*, 108, 3 (2002), 533–79; Marion Fourcade-Gourinchas and Bob Hancke, 'Revisiting the French Model: Coordination and Restructuring in French Industry', in *Varieties of Capitalism*, Peter A. Hall and David Soskice (eds) (New York: Oxford University Press, 2001), 307–34; Chris Howell, *Regulating Labor: The State and Industrial Labor Relations Reform in Postwar France* (Princeton, NJ: Princeton University Press, 1992); Tony Judt, *Marxism and the French Left: Studies in Labour and Politics in France, 1830–1981* (Oxford: Clarendon, 1986); Michel Marian, 'France 1997–2002: Right-Wing President, Left-Wing Government', *Political Quarterly*, 73, 3 (2002), 258–65; Timothy Smith, *France in Crisis: Welfare, Inequality and Globalization since 1980* (Cambridge: Cambridge University Press, 2004); Bruno Théret, 'Néo-libéralisme, inégalités sociales et politiques fiscales de droite et de gauche dans la France des années 1980', *Revue Française*

de Science Politique, 41, 3 (1991), 342–81; Viven Schmidt, *From State to Market? The Transformation of French Business and Government* (Cambridge: Cambridge University Press, 1996).

33 Boltanski and Chiapello, 195.

34 In Britain, the opening up of the City to outside investors in October 1986 was so momentous that it was named 'The Big Bang'. Many critics and economic historians have argued that financial deregulation has been absolutely crucial to neoliberalism. Deregulation began on 15 August 1971 with the abolition of the Bretton Woods Agreement ending the system of fixed international exchange rates and thus paving the way, as Boltanski and Chiapello argue, for 'The deregulation of financial markets, their decompartmentalization, and the creation of "new financial products"' which has 'multiplied the possibilities of purely speculative profits, whereby capital expands without taking the form of investment in productive activity'.

35 Fredric Jameson, *Postmodernism or, the Cultural Logic of Late Capitalism* (London and New York: Verso, 1991), 275.

36 Stuart Hall, 'Brave New World', *Socialist Review* 91, 1 (1991), 57–84, 57–8.

37 Ronald Butt, 'Mrs Thatcher: The First Two Years', *Sunday Times*, 3 May 1981.

38 Maurizio Lazzarato, 'Immaterial Labour', http://www.generation-online.org/c/fcimmateriallabour3.html and in M. Hardt and P. Virno (eds), *Radical Thought in Italy: A Potential Politics* (Minneapolis: University of Minnesota Press, 1996) 133–47, 30. See also 'From Capital-Labour to Capital-Life', *Ephemera*. 4, 3 (2004), 187–207, 187. For an insightful overview of the Italian laboratory thinkers and autonomous Marxism, see Rosalind Gill and Andy Pratt, 'In the Social Factory: Immaterial Labour, Precariousness, and Cultural Work' *Theory, Culture & Society* 25.7/8 (2008), 1–30.

39 Harvey, 69.

40 Ferruccio Gambino, 'A Critique of the Fordism of the Regulation School', *thecommoner*, 12 (2007), 39–62, 44, http://www.commoner.org.uk/12gambino.pdf [accessed 27 July 2012].

41 Jean-François Lyotard, *The Postmodern Condition: A Report on Knowledge* (Manchester: Manchester University Press, 1984), 4.

42 Jason Read, 'A Genealogy of *homo œconomicus*: Neoliberalism and the Production of Subjectivity', *Foucault Studies*, 6 (2009), 25–36, 26.

43 Mark Fisher, *Capitalist Realism* (London: Zero Books), 9.

44 Harvey, 2.

45 Michael Hardt and Antonio Negri, *Empire* (Cambridge, MA: Harvard University Press, 2000), xiii.

46 Wendy Brown, 'Neoliberalism and the End of Liberal Democracy', *Theory & Event*, 7, 1 (2003), 1–21, 3.

47 Harvey, 3.

48 *Whatever*, 99.

49 Bewes, 122.

50 Žižek, 65.

51 Read, 26.

52 Iain Boal and Michael Watts, 'The Liberal International', *Radical Philosophy*, 140 (2006), 40–4, 41.

53 Paul Treanor, 'Neoliberalism: Origins, Theory, Definition', http:/web.inter.nl.net. users/Paul.Treanor/neoliberalism [accessed 13 July 2011].

54 Valéry Giscard d'Estaing, *Democratie française* (Paris: Arthème Fayard, [1976] 1979), 16–17.

55 Susan George, 'Emerging Opportunities for Structural Change' (1999), www. globalexchange.org/compaigns/econ101/neoliberal.html [accessed 24 July 2012].

56 Martin Crowley, 'Low Resistance', in *On Bathos*, Sara Crangle and Peter Nicholls (eds) (London: Continuum, 2010), 148.

57 Bob Jessop, 'From micro-powers to governmentality', *Political Geography*, 26 (2007) 34–40, 40. Emphasis added.

58 Michel Foucault: *Lectures at the Collège de France, 1978–1979*, trans. Graham Burchell (New York: Palgrave Macmillan, 2008), 203–4.

59 Lemke (2012), 6, 11. See also '"The Birth of Bio-Politics": Michel Foucault's Lecture at the Collège de France on Neo-Liberal Governmentality', *Economy and Society*, 30, 2 (2001), 190–207.

60 *Atomised*, 135–6.

61 *Empire*, 23–24.

62 Jason Read, *The Micro-Politics of Capital: Marx and the Prehistory of the Present* (New York: SUNY Press, 2003), 2.

63 Ruth Cruickshank argues that Houellebecq updates Georges Perec's 'critique of nascent consumption' in his 1965 novel *Les Choses*, 128.

64 Bowd, 31.

65 Lazzarato, 'From Capital-Labour to Capital-Life', 191.

66 Lesek Kolakowski, *Modernity on Endless Trial* (Chicago: University of Chicago Press, 1990), 74.

67 Read, 33.

68 '... civilisation is defined by the decoding and deterritorialisation of flows in capitalist production' Gilles Deleuze and Félix Guattari, *Anti Oedipus: Capitalism and Schizophrenia* (Minneapolis: University of Minnesota Press, 1983), 244.

69 Crowley (2010), 148.

70 *Atomised*, 74.

71 'La nouvelle vulgate planétaire' (my translation). Pierre Bourdieu, *Interventions 1961–2001: Science sociale et action politique* (Marseilles: Agone, 2002) 443–9.

Here, Bourdieu describes Tony Blair and his chosen scribe of neoliberalism, Anthony Giddens, as epitomizing this new global economic order.

72 Alain Touraine, *Beyond Neoliberalism*, trans. David Macy (Cambridge: Polity Press, 2001), 20.

73 Monica Prasad, 'Why is France so French? Culture, Institution, and Neoliberalism, 1974–1981', *The American Journal of Sociology*, 111 (2005), 357–407, 358. Prasad notes that the reforms of Alain Juppé, while opposed by mass strikes against the reform of private sector pensions and healthcare, succeeded in carrying out significant privatization of the financial sector: '80% of the banking sector and 50% of the insurance sector' as well as carrying out major restructuration of the public sector out of which 12.6% of the total workforce were moved into the private sector', 367.

74 Sebastian Budgen, A New 'Spirit of Capitalism', *New Left Review*, 1 (2000), http://www.newleftreview.org/II/1/sebastian-budgen-a-new-spirit-of-capitalism [accessed 15 June 2011].

75 Boltanski and Chiapello, 73, 75, 90.

76 Gilles Lipovetsky, *Hypermodern Times* (London: Polity 2005), 9.

77 Herbert Marcuse, 'Aggressiveness in Advanced Industrial Society' (1967), in *Negations: Essays in Critical Theory* (Boston: Beacon Press, 1968), http://www.wbenjamin.org/marcuse.html [accessed 30 June 2011].

3

(Bad) Subjects of Neoliberalism

I don't like this world. I definitely do not like it. The society in which I live disgusts me; advertising sickens me.

Whatever, 83[1]

'Neoliberalism is not', says Nicholas Kiersey, 'just an authoritative discourse; it is a way of life' and central to this are the twin objectives of free enterprise and private ownership which are the 'essentials of freedom'.[2] As we have seen, under neoliberalism's exhortation to a new 'way of life', modified forms of behaviour and thought are encouraged, both in terms of public and private behaviours, ones that are more thoroughly interpellated by a third spirit of capitalism which sets the subject adrift in a deregulated network of social, cultural and labour relations. Thus, a new form of subjectivity is brought into being. In Thatcher's terms, this is the changed soul, and in Foucault's, the *homo œconomicus* – the 'eminently governable' individual who is willing to regard him or herself as human capital and who is capable of responding 'systematically to systematic modifications artificially introduced into the environment'.[3] The view of the subject as human capital requires individuals to 'invest' in themselves as private individuals rather than social entities and to accept that they are, as workers, no longer dependent on a company, or on a job for life with clearly defined hierarchies and roles, 'but are autonomous entrepreneurs with full responsibility for their own investment decisions and endeavouring to produce surplus value; they are the entrepreneurs of themselves'.[4] Houellebecq's writing, and in particular his first novel, *Whatever*, describes this new biopolitical paradigm of subjectification that produces its subjects within a societal regime of internal control rather than external discipline.

Reading this first novel, then, this chapter examines how the spirit of neoliberal capitalism with its model subject of the *homo œconomicus* has inserted itself into everyday life, into both the physical and the affective domains of human existence. Houellebecq's writing demonstrates a new modality of power

– biopower – which has successfully displaced 'the disciplinary modality of power that is associated with social formations of governmentality'.[5] Articulating the ways in which culture, beliefs and desires are subsumed by neoliberalism's relentless belief in the moral values of 'market society', his writing speaks to an altered context of human relations, one described in *Rester Vivant* as a '… form of civilisation where the entirety of human relations, and equally the entirety of relations between man and the world, are meditated through a simple numerical calculation that involves attractiveness, novelty, and value for money'.[6] Stated otherwise, as Antonio Negri has observed, this is a society in which 'the factory spreads throughout the whole of society […] production is social and activities are productive'.[7] However, as we shall see in this chapter, Houellebecq's protagonists are all, without exception, bad subjects of neoliberalism. Failing to extract any surplus value from their lives by eschewing any interest in the accumulation of any cultural or material capital, they are devoid, one might say free, of any ambition or aspiration. The world around may urge him to compete, consume and to extract the maximum degree of personal freedom from the range of choices of goods and services, but for the protagonist of *Whatever* his 'only real ambition' is to carry on chain-smoking. Unexcited by money and work, bored to tears by the idea of free time, and utterly indifferent to exhortations to distinguish himself professionally or culturally, he is wholly indifferent to the ethos of the 'enterprise society'.

The antithesis of the Foucauldian *homo œconomicus*, the 'man of enterprise and production'[8] who busily makes his entrepreneurial mark on the world, the narrator has a life that seems both 'empty and short', one negatively defined by the almost imperceptible impression that he makes on his world: 'The days slip by indifferently, leaving neither trace nor memory' (*W*, 46). Incapable of being devoured by the seductive lure of consumer products or by consumerism itself, Houellebecq's characters are unmoved by the idea of the production of themselves as an entrepreneurial project. 'Good' neoliberal subjects are those who can be defined by the sum of their choice of goods and services to most fully realize themselves in 'the pursuit of a form of capital'.[9] If a subject is utterly indifferent to most forms of capital, in particular to the gradations and distinctions of cultural capital, as are Houellebecq's characters, then they cannot function easily, or at all, in such a society; they have failed to have their souls altered. I trace here then, the processes and effects of neoliberal subjectification that interpellate individuals as rational units networked into a society in which the boundaries between commodity and non-commodity no longer exist and where those between work and non-work have become blurred. This is a society where all human relations have become subject to the logic of exchange and where we all become buyers and sellers entering into negotiations over the 'numerical calculation' of the 'quality-price relation'.[10]

Whatever: Failure to consume

Defined by their indolent misanthropy and an unremitting *Weltschmerz* that has, as Jerry Varsava rightly points up, a historically specifically inflection, Houellebecq's characters have no aspirational drive whatsoever and are incapable of taking pleasure in anything offered to them. This mood of anhedonia reverberates aesthetically in the peevishly flat prose of Houellebecq's first novel, *Whatever* (*Extension du domaine de la lutte*), which Martin Crowley sees as 'distinguished in particular by its singular receptivity to the mediocrity of its world', it replicates the flattening of a world in which all is commodifed and thus must have a suitable 'limp flatness' that grinds 'pointlessly on ...'.[11] Attracting something of a cult following its publication in both French and in English translation, the novel was arresting for its writing style and eccentric juxtaposition of elements that combined philosophical essayistic asides, pornographic interludes, scraps of moral *fabliaux* and absurd 'management-speak', all couched in a discourse that is banal and un-literary. *Whatever* writes of its world in its own particularly flattened language that does not, or cannot be troubled to distinguish itself from the world it depicts with a 'fluent complicity' of high and low registers that suggest, as Crowley puts it, that the 'game of distinction might itself be bust'.[12] This game holds no interest for our frequently nauseous narrator who relates his account of the workplace in a laconic prose style that is neither fully realist nor sufficiently non-realist to be regarded as connected to its closest corresponding influences of either the brittle aesthetic of the *nouveau roman* or to a 'waning of affect' strain of literary postmodernism; indeed, Houellebecq's novel is generically rather difficult to situate in the French or Anglo-American novelist tradition.

In an attempt to sum up the relationship between the existential disaffection of the novel's protagonist/narrator with the banality of the IT workplace, Tibor Fischer reaches for a somewhat lazy literary comparison on the front cover blurb describing the book as '*L'Étranger* for the info generation'. Translated into English rather puzzlingly by the single word 'whatever', this choice of translation suggests a terse indifference apposite for my concerns here. In the original French, the title may be understood quite literally as the 'extension of the domain of the struggle', therein neatly summarizing the concerns of Houellebecq's slim novel (and indeed of all his subsequent novels), that is to say, the penetration of the economic into the private and affective areas of human life. In this situation then, writing becomes just another activity to be commodified and, as such, cannot be a site of either resistance or transcendence. Such a demystification of literature is, I think, part of Houellebecq's anti-'68 agenda and is something to which I will return in the final chapter, 'The End of Affect'. In contrast to the expository title in the original French, the translated word/phrase in English – 'whatever' – suggests a lack of any appetite for narrative, and its textual surface is pieced together from a makeshift realism to produce what Michel Biron calls a 'a second degree realism' or 'the idea of realism'.[13] A prototype of his later works, part-essay, part-satire, *Whatever*, by most principles of literary convention, barely qualifies as a novel at all; we are indeed, as Houellebecq's narrator observes, '… a long way from *Wuthering Heights*, to say the least' (*W*, 40). However, despite frequent self-conscious interjections about its own status as writing, the narrative is not interested in the self-conscious manoeuvres that might be said to inhabit the 'properly' postmodernist novel; stylistically speaking, Houellebecq has no time for the parodic, the intertextual, the playful, the metafictional or the pastiche. My proposition here is that the novel's lack of narrative appetite emanates from the neoliberal gait of the times, outlined above and in the previous chapter, and traces what Houellebecq calls a moment of 'vital exhaustion', that is as much aesthetic as it is ideological (*W*, 29). This exhaustion inevitably presents certain difficulties for the novelist, as Houellebecq notes: 'the novel form is not conceived for depicting indifference or nothingness; a flatter, more terse and dreary discourse would need to be invented' (*W*, 40). Taken together then, both readings of the novel's title, the translation and the original, sustain my suggestion that the novel addresses the 'bad' subject of neoliberalism – 'no sex drive, no ambition, no real interests either' – a man whose life is one of 'prolonged boredom' and 'vacuity' as he fails to realize his competitive advantage in either the affective or cultural domain (*W*, 30, 46). 'The third millennium augurs well', deadpans the bilious narrator as he vomits silently behind some cushions (*W*, 4).

Just turned 30, the protagonist of *Whatever* is a misanthropic and reclusive computer programmer who has been contracted out to develop a software for the Ministry of Agriculture to assist in the efficient distribution of subsidies to farmers across France. A lucid but dejected witness of the contemporary world, our unnamed, socially isolated narrator is at the centre of this low-spirited novel set in the burgeoning information technology industry of the mid-1990s among a hitherto neglected social group of middle managers (*cadres*) who comprise the 'vast, amorphous masses of the middle classes' eager to please at work and at play.[14] The novel shows the ways in which what Henri Lefebvre calls 'the space of play', the space in which the body rediscovers its use value, has been 'drawn into the heart of exchange' where it has become fully subject to capital and an important site for the 'opportunity for profit ...'.[15] In an economy shaped by the ever-expanding domain of the market, the space of play, of leisure time, becomes part of the whole production of sociability itself within an 'increasingly lucrative regulation' of every aspect of human life; 'personal and affective interactions, emotions, consumer habits and satisfaction' all are measured up in the neoliberal mission that instrumentalizes all 'contexts of interpretation and assessment, forms of identification and membership, interpersonal behaviour and human interaction'.[16] Crucially, these new modes of consumption have shifted from the Protestant, prohibitive ethics that underpinned Fordism to a hedonistic and narcissistic individualism typical of the more secular atmosphere of post-Fordist capitalism. Patterns of consumption are crucially important, if not vital, to the production of neoliberal subjectivity: you are what you consume. This exhortation to consume, however, fails at every turn with Houellebecq's characters.

In an almost perfectly inverse relationship to the rigorous clamour to consume that marks his socio-cultural environment, the narrator of *Whatever* lacks any of the acquisitive desires associated with a man of his age, salary and professional status. Despite a comfortable income and unencumbered leisure time, he is devoid of materialist objectives, shuffling around his unadorned flat in a fog of hopeless boredom in drab, functional clothing, a 'quilted parka and "Weekend in the Hebrides" chunky pullover', apathetic at the prospect of consumption, conspicuous or otherwise (*W*, 53). Wholly impervious to the allure of commodity fetishism, he finds the efforts of others to distinguish themselves though repeated acts of highly differentiated consumption profoundly baffling. Observing the bustle of Rouen city centre on a Saturday afternoon, the apogee of time and space devoted to the ritualistic, eroticized pastime of shopping, the narrator adopts a Camus-like outsider point of view on the action: '... I notice that all these people seem satisfied with themselves and the world [...] All commune in the certainty of passing an agreeable afternoon devoted primarily to consumerism, and thus to contributing to the consolidation of their being [...] I observe, lastly, that I feel different from them, without however being able to define the nature of this difference' (*W*, 69). Lefebvre has described consumption as a process of 'ideological substitutions and displacements' that has 'substituted for the image of active man that of the consumer as the possessor of happiness and of perfect rationality ... ' producing a sense of objectification of the active subject. In this process, he argues, 'Not the consumer nor even that which is consumed is important in this image, but the vision of the consumer and consuming as art of consuming'.[17] A stranger to this art of consumption, the narrator of *Whatever* is painfully alienated from the world; economically comfortable but existentially besieged, he wretchedly inhabits both his professional and social roles. Unconcerned with forging any social connections outside of work, he stays at home to carry out a 'spot of do-it-yourself' and to muse on the hopelessness of life and 'the sensation of all consuming emptiness'; '... the fact is that nothing can halt the ever-increasing recurrence of those moments when [...] the foreboding that your existence is nearing a painful and definitive end all combine to plunge you into a state of real suffering' (*W*, 10, 11). In due course, the suffering undergoes transference from the purely physical public spectacle of vomiting that takes place in the opening pages to psychosomatically induced nausea and eventually to a complete nervous breakdown. Incapable of participating in the carnival of consumption, the narrator is quite literally sickened by it; first, with a physical illness in the form of a pericardial infection, then with a severe psychological breakdown in which he attempts to gouge out his eyes in a botched pseudo-Oedipal manoeuvre. Both physically and psychologically, then, he has profoundly malfunctioned, and is finally unable to assimilate into a world that asks him to be dynamically engaged in everyday life only in the role of a consumer or producer.

Not only failing to acquire pleasure in the new range of affective activity, the narrator is also incapable of producing the necessary desire to reinvest any surplus profit in the affective domain and is thus rendered both neurotic and impotent.[18] 'Lacking in looks as well as personal charm' and 'subject to frequent bouts of depression, he exists almost entirely in social isolation (*W*, 13). 'With no family or friends or sex life and no real interests either', he cannot be enticed in any way to participate in the carnival of the market. 'Nevertheless', the narrator dolefully pronounces, 'some free time remains. What's to be done? How do you use your time? In dedicating yourself to helping other people? But basically other people don't interest you. Listening to records? That used to be a solution, but as the years go by you have to say that music moves you less and less' (*W*, 10). This is, perhaps, a nodding reference to *Nausea* (1938) and Sartre's anti-hero Roquentin who finds a moment of stilled ecstasy, even authenticity, in the tones of a jazz record called *Some of These Days*. Similarly, the narrator of *Whatever* is in search of something 'real', outside the nausea, an unsubsumed authenticity that somehow has remained exterior to the forces of reification. Indifferent to the siren call of culture and consumption, he prefers to remain at home smoking at least four packs of cigarettes a day, an activity he describes rather perversely as, 'the only real element of freedom in my life', doing a 'bit of tidying' and writing animal fables that function as palliatives for his ever-increasing anhedonia. Both writing and reading, it seems, provide a faint hope of succour: 'Writing brings scant relief. It retraces, it delimits. It lends a touch of coherence, the idea of a kind of realism' (*W*, 124). 'An entire life spent reading would have fulfilled my every desire; I already knew that at the age of seven' (*W*, 12). The composition of animal *fabliaux – Dialogues Between a Cow and a Filly, Dialogues Between a Dachshund and a Poodle, Dialogues Between a Chimp and A Stork* – is a defiantly non-utilitarian activity. Essayistic explications of the contrast between the natural and the cultural, these crude fables point up the 'natural' evolutionary violence of sex and natural selection, implying that, under the completely liberated forces of free market sexual competition, humanity is returned, in a counter-evolutionary manoeuvre, to the 'all pervasive agonistic modality of the natural state'.[19] These curious tales are counter-narratives to the ones that dominate in culture as they strip away what Abecassis calls the 'sleek appearance' of the glittering advertising machine that exhorts us to be seductive and to seduce freely whomsoever we desire, to reveal the 'baboon-like hierarchies and symbolic violence' beneath. This slick surface of seductive images that makes up the beguiling vernacular of marketing will always lead back to, what Bourdieu calls, the 'Darwinian world' unleashed by neoliberalism.[20]

Notionally, the narrator is an exemplary beneficiary of affluent mid-1990s France, a fact that his travelling companion Raphael Tisserand points out to him. With their high salaries '… two and a half times the minimum wage; a tidy purchasing power, by any standards' and 'great facility for changing jobs', Tisserand sees them as the fortunate workers in the new knowledge economy: 'It's us guys, the computer experts, we're the kings' (*W*, 6). Our narrator, however, does not have the slightest interest, either financially or culturally, in his 'king-like' surplus, shunning all advice regarding investment opportunities – portfolios or share packages or savings schemes – the mediocrity of which he finds profoundly 'distressing'. For him, free time is the occasion, not for the organized fun of Club 18–30, nor the packaged exotic thrills of Nouvelles Frontières holidays, nor even for a local trip to Paris art galleries, but rather for staying in on drizzly Sundays and getting 'gently depressed' (*W*, 29).

Immune to the allure of product branding, he eats, dresses and drinks in a 'no-name' manner. What he *should* be doing as a good neoliberal consumer is deftly satirized in a scenario entitled *Today's People* from the Galeries Lafayette catalogue:

> After a really full day they snuggle down into a deep sofa with sober lines (Steiner, Roset, Cinna). To a jazz tune they admire the style of their Dhurries carpets, the gaiety of their wall coverings (Patrick Frey). Ready to set off for a frenzied set of tennis towels await them in the bathroom (Yves Saint Laurent, Ted Lapidus). And it's before dinner with intimate friends in kitchens created by Daniel Hechter or Primrose Bordier that they'll remake the world. (*W*, 14)

The tensions of the bourgeois consumer's labouring day are assuaged by a luxury brand sofa. Life is made that bit easier by the availability of matching towels and expensively fitted kitchens with tastefully matching accessories. Disdaining any of the nuances of taste and distinction described in meticulous sociological detail by Bourdieu in *Distinction: A Social Critique of the Judgement of Taste* (1984), Houellebecq's narrator is a kind of anti-distinction machine; wholly indifferent to the marking out of one's bourgeois cultural capital by the acquisition of symbolic goods suggesting 'attributes of excellence' and creating thereby the category of 'good' taste.[21] The cultural capital of an individual is, according to Bourdieu's later work, not only one of the most important aspects of class formation but is central to the operation of the 'neoliberal utopia of a pure and perfect market' in which all citizens are transformed into consumers, urged to define themselves through the proliferating avenues of differentiated consumption.[22]

In contrast to the world of distinction in which he lives, the narrator of *Whatever*, and indeed all of Houellebecq's characters, remain indifferent to all signifiers of excellence, with cultural coordinates that are resolutely functional. Eating 'down-market' canned food from Saupiquet, Monoprix and Unico straight from the tin, they enjoy chips smothered in plentiful mayonnaise at the over-lit tables in Le Flunch, they drink reasonably priced New World wines, and live in domestic spaces unmarked by any aesthetic considerations.[23] Even that most hallowed totem of consumerism, the car, leaves the narrator of *Whatever* unmoved. When he loses his own car, what should be a simple material loss provokes a queasy feeling of Nietzschean over-abundance and moments of extreme existential discomfort in which he is 'gradually overcome by certain weariness in relation to cars and worldly goods' (*W*, 6). Knowing that to admit to losing one's car 'is tantamount to being struck off the social register' and admitting this would constitute social calamity, 'joking about such matters is not the done thing; this is how reputations are made, friendships are made or broken', he tells his work colleagues that the car has been stolen (*W*, 7). The (bogus) announcement of the theft of his car at work the next day is greeted with a reverent compassion and a colleague's hushed counsel to 'hang on in there' (*W*, 23). To admit that he had lost his car would be an admission of weakness in regard to material objects indicative of a lack of grip over the world of things, thus making him appear psychologically suspect. Such seemingly trivial things can, he later confesses to a psychiatrist, trigger the process of social disgrace, leading, in due course, to the 'The death of a professional' (*W*, 134). Immune to the neoliberal imperatives of cultural and social distinction, Houellebecq's characters enact what Crowley calls a 'low resistance' to the mythology of cultural distinction. Almost instinctively repelled by consumerism, they simply observe this world of things, acknowledging that they 'feel different' from others but are unable or unwilling to 'define the nature of this difference' (*W*, 69). Indeed, as Houellebecq's narrator observes, the more one assiduously attempts individuation through cultural distinction the more homogenous, in fact, one becomes:[24]

> Of course, experience has taught me that I'm only called on to meet people who, if not exactly alike, are at least quite similar in their manners, their opinions, their general way of approaching life [...] Despite that I've also had occasion to remark that human beings are often bent on making themselves conspicuous by subtle and disagreeable variations, defects, character traits and the like – doubtless with the goal of obliging their interlocutors to treat them as total individuals. (*W*, 19)

Indistinction

The narrator's refusal to distinguish himself culturally through acts of consumption or workplace behaviour is consonant with the novel's formal refusal to individualize and psychologize any sense of 'character' and situation. From the outset, the narrator ridicules narrative realism as the 'pointless accumulation' of detail with 'clearly differentiated characters hogging the limelight' but admits that even he cannot altogether escape the lure of 'the idea of a kind of realism':

> To reach the otherwise philosophical goal I am setting myself I will need on the contrary to prune. To simplify. To demolish, one by one, a host of details. In this I will be aided, moreover, by the simply play of historical forces. The world

is becoming more uniform before our eyes; telecommunications are improving; apartment interiors are enriched with new gadgets. Human relationships are becoming progressively impossible, which greatly reduces the quantity of anecdote that goes to make up a life. (*W*, 14)

The narrator has no time, either, for the details of individualism in characterization, and accordingly the characters are all more or less interchangeable types: 'My idea is not to try and charm you with subtle psychological observations [...] There are some authors who employ their talent in the delicate description of varying states of soul, character traits, etc. I shall not be counted among these ...' (*W*, 14). While there are often lengthy physical descriptions of characters these are, for the main part, wholly generic, and psychological detail is shunned, suggesting that the attempt to tease out characters' differences realistically in a novel is simply an extension of the fetishizing drive of consumerism.[25] Adorno and Horkheimer assert something very similar in *Dialectic of Enlightenment*: 'The most intimate reactions of human beings have been so thoroughly reified that the idea of anything specific to themselves now persists only as an utterly abstract notion: personality scarcely signifies anything more than shining white teeth and freedom from body odour and emotions.'[26] Functioning, for the most part, as mouthpieces for essayistic digressions on the human condition, characters in Houellebecq's fiction are, at best, meagerly rendered and it is clear that the narrator of *Whatever*, the two Michels, Bruno and Daniel, are the same character. The narratives in which they feature repeat upon themselves with a weary repetition that Svend Brinkmann describes as 'a deep yet non-narrative understanding of contemporary social life' in a prose style that is 'objectivist, sociological, behaviourist, and starkly anti-psychological'.[27]

Whatever searches for a way of articulating this problem of similarity, in many cases an identicalness, in the midst of a cultural pressure for increasing distinction, but it is a search marked by an extreme aversion to a sustained contemplation of the aesthetics of novelistic prose other than an explicitly stated anti-realism, enacting, as John Banville remarks, a distinctly Beckettian manoeuvre, producing a voice that 'seems furious at itself for having begun to speak at all and, having begun, for being compelled to go on to the end'. The novel addresses both the struggle of the protagonist in profound existential alienation (*la lutte*) and the continual annulment of the value of literary discourse to give any meaningful voice to that alienation; hence the foreclosing 'whatever'. It is a work that explicitly and unwaveringly disdains the solace of poetic form prompting Banville to suggest, perhaps somewhat daringly, that

'... Houellebecq is darker even than Beckett, and would never allow himself, or us, those lyric transports that flickeringly illuminate the Beckettian night'.[28] The creation of good form in the novel, the 'accumulation of realistic detail' is, for Houellebecq, nothing but 'pure bullshit [...] Might as well watch lobsters marching up the side of an aquarium ...' (*W*,14). Wilted, disenchanted, testy, Houellebecq's writing nonetheless still clings to the space of the literary text as one that has the potential, however limited, to offer some respite from a debased language that can drive one to the brink of madness. Writing is a corrective, therapeutic process that is capable of rendering everyday life, however banal and futile, intelligible in the space of the literary text: 'The pages that follow constitute a novel; I mean a succession of anecdotes in which I am the hero. This autobiographical choice isn't one, really; in any case I have no other way out. If I don't write about what I have seen I will suffer just the same – and perhaps a bit more so. But only a bit, I insist on this' (*W*, 12). Literature, or some form of writing is necessary, even imperative: 'Literature can cope with anything, it can adapt to any circumstances, it can scrabble around in the dirt, and lick the wounds of misery'.[29] While this may be regarded as contradictory to his views elsewhere on the purpose of culture more generally, what Houellebecq is getting at here is the healing act of writing as a curative for the suffering of the individual.

Any attempt at delineating psychological differences between characters becomes a faintly ludicrous endeavour. Take for example, the sexually incompetent and 'exceedingly ugly' Rafael Tisserand. Still a virgin at 28, Tisserand's character exists with the sole purpose of illustrating a Darwinist take on the primitive sexual economy suggested earlier in the novel as he is presented as the embodiment of the loser's camp in Houellebecq's hypothesis that 'In a totally liberal sexual system certain people have a varied and exciting erotic life; others are reduced to masturbation and solitude' (*W*, 99). The woman that the narrator and Tisserand follow in a night club is referred to as 'the pseudo-Véronique' a copy of the original Véronique, the narrator's former girlfriend whose time spent in psychoanalysis (a Houellebecquian *bête-noire*) merely turned her into an object of egotistical inwardness (*W*, 117). As is frequently the case in Houellebecq's work, narrative events and incidents are merely ruses for essayistic expositions on a particular subject: in this case, the narrator's intense and abiding repugnance for psychoanalysis, which he claims is a 'scandalous destruction of the human being', annihilating the patient's 'capacity to love', replacing it with the mechanical 'process of seduction' that not only avoids the messiness of real human contact but is more readily quantifiable in terms of measuring romantic success (*W*, 102). Thus 'cured', the patient can then be effortlessly re-inserted into the 'proper' circuits of reifiable desire and be returned, fully corrected, to society. In *Minima Moralia*, Adorno argues that psychoanalysis functions as an essentially fraudulent 'privatizing' exercise that interpellates the subject as a more fully atomized, private individual:

> The principle of human domination, in becoming absolute, has turned its point against man as the absolute object, and psychology has collaborated in sharpening that point [...] In appealing to the fact that in an exchange society the subject was not one, but in fact a social object, psychology provided society with the weapons ensuring that this was and remained the case. The dissection of man into his faculties is a projection of the division of labor onto its pretended subjects, inseparable from the interest in deploying and manipulating them to greater advantage ...[30]

As I will discuss elsewhere, the ubiquity of psychoanalysis is attacked in all of Houellebecq's fiction and with it the generation of 1968, routinely depicted as deluded and hypocritical *habitués* of the analyst's couch, are portrayed as being hooked on the 'myths of liberation and individuation' of psychoanalysis and, indeed, see it as part of their right to self-realization.[31] Disparaging psychoanalysis as 'a ruthless school of egotism' that encourages 'pettiness, egoism, arrogant stupidity' and 'a complete lack of moral sense' (*W*, 102), Houellebecq's narrators view psychoanalysis as an essentially egotistical activity and see psychotherapy as part of the wider continuum of consumption, 'selling' the individual an idea of the possibility of a wholesome, healthy psyche in what becomes simply another act of empty choice.

In what Nikolas Rose calls a 'new habitat of subjectification', one characterized by the neoliberal belief that 'individuals can shape an autonomous identity for themselves through choices in taste, music, goods, styles and habit', the market draws in the subject, catering to its idiosyncrasies, peccadilloes and predilections to more thoroughly interpellate it through marketing.[32] There is no escape from this new habitat, but the narrator attempts to resist any direct participation. Shuffling around in his anonymous anorak, the narrator in *Whatever* observes shoppers on the streets of Rouen and their quest for individuation: 'No one group is exactly the same as another [...] Obviously they resemble each other, they resemble each other enormously [...] It's as if they have elected to embody the antagonism which necessarily goes with any kind of individuation by adopting slightly different behaviour patterns ... (*W*, 68)'. Believing in the life-affirming properties of consumption, the shoppers 'commune in the certainty of passing an agreeable afternoon devoted primarily to consumerism, and thus contributing to the consolidation of their being' (*W*, 69). In its fleeting confirmation of agency, not for nothing is shopping often called retail therapy. But it is not in the least therapeutic for our narrator; rather, he is baffled by the seemingly endless desire for differentiation through consumption which merely leaves him feeling distanced and dehumanized, like 'a shrink-wrapped chicken on a supermarket shelf' (*W*, 99).

Paradoxically, as the requirement for differentiation and distinction is thrust ever more urgently on the subject, the sense of a pervasive indistinctness of all things, a general flattening out into a grey, monocultural drone of similitude, becomes more insistent in the novel. The streets of Paris are no exception to this gathering mood in the novel as they too are drawn into a zone of indistinction and similarity. Losing his featureless Peugeot after a party in the midst of identical Parisian streets called Marcel, the narrator is momentarily overwhelmed by a 'violent feeling of identity' brought on by a vertiginous sense of similarity of everything around him (*W*, 6).[33] Unlike the intriguing Parisian streets of the *flanêurs* of Baudelaire, Balzac and the Surrealists, this is a curiously anonymous and charmless Paris; a mundane space, sapped of the marvellous potential of the *derive*.[34] The narrator works 'somewhere in the 13th arrondissement' in a 'totally devastated neighbourhood [...] When you arrive by bus you'd really think World War II had happened. But no, it's only urban planning.' From his office, the windows look out onto a blasted wasteland that 'stretches practically as far as you can see, muddy, bristling with hoardings' (*W*, 16). Urban spaces in *Whatever*, in fact in all of Houellebecq's novels, are hostile, blasted geo-psychic landscapes of social and spatial desolation that emphasize the mounting, and in some cases violent, separation between the winners and the losers under neoliberal capitalism. Houellebecq's Paris is a dreary, bloodless city 'gaudy and repellent' full of 'leprous façades' drained of any mythic or historical particularity in which affluent, educated, single adults live in often rather menacing *quartiers* in their miniscule studio-flats in isolated 'disillusionment and detachment', filling their leisure time with surfing the net (still then in its infancy), evening courses and buying CDs at FNAC (*W*, 40, 82). The northern Gothic city of Rouen where Jeanne d'Arc was burnt at the stake is depicted as similarly undistinguished; a 'dirty, grimy, run down, spoiled ...' town, any historical significance reduced to a pile of 'weirdly curved concrete slabs' (*W*, 67–8).

The more the market moves in on the domains of the personal and the affective, the more painful these spaces become for the novel's narrator; they become, in fact, literally maddening. Instead of 'contributing to the consolidation' of his being, consumption – cultural or otherwise – leaches all vitality from him and he becomes increasingly immaterial and translucent. Incapable of integrating with the world, the narrator's existence becomes increasingly insubstantial and publicly invisible, becoming a life 'without areas of shadow, without substance' (*W*, 146). He is another kind of man without qualities.

Sausages, forks and mobile phones

With the exception of the scientist Michel Djerzinski in *Atomised*, each of the characters in Houellebecq's novels is representative of workers in the age of post-industrialism; their labour, mostly invisible and immaterial, is deployed within a vast and complex network of information that, as Hardt and Negri observe, involves 'creative and intelligent manipulation on the one hand and routine symbolic tasks on the other'.[35] This shift from material industrial production to immaterial labour, mirroring in many ways the transformation in the financial sphere from commodity to fiduciary money, part of what is sometimes called cognitive capitalism, has at its core the constant and invisible exchange of information. This new possibility of exchange is acknowledged with some excitement in *Whatever* by a retiring computer programmer in the Ministry of Agriculture, Louis Lindon, whose favourite subject is the discussion of homological relations between the 'production and circulation of commodities' and information which is, like commodity production, undergoing a shift from 'from the artisanal stage to the industrial stage'(*W*, 43). Lindon's almost boyish enthusiasm for the 'telecommunications revolution' and the progress towards 'the globalization of the network' has its direct inverse in the narrator's compete indifference to the revolutionary potential of networked information (*W*, 39); a fact sarcastically underscored when he notes that the kind of meaningless freedom promised by this technological revolution is summed up by its ability to offer 'the maximum amount of potential choice' to order by computer the 'guaranteed delivery of hot food at a given hour and with relatively little delay' (*W*, 38–9).

Unceremoniously wedged into the sixth chapter of *Platform*, a novel about sex tourism, just as the love affair between Michel and Valérie is getting underway, the reader encounters a mini-essay, no more than a few paragraphs in length, detailing in sociological terms, the shift from industrial production, in this case pig farming in France, to finance capitalism, that is, from material labour to immaterial. No longer able to keep up with the bank repayments on a loan they took out to 'adopt intensive farming methods', Valérie's parents are forced to sell up their pig farm. With the proceeds of the sale they use the money to buy flats in Spain and to invest in unit trusts. Valérie's father comes to realize that the money earned from the rent and the interest 'brought in more money than all his years of work' as they '… lived in a country where, compared to speculative investment, investment in production brought little return'.[36] This short exposition, characteristic of Houellebecq's quasi-sociological novelistic style, is part of a broader discussion in his work that examines the passage from industrial production of the 'real' to the economies of immateriality to an increasing distance from production. Hardt and Negri detail the three types of immaterial labour driving what they call the 'postmodernisation of the global economy':

> The first is involved in an industrial production that has been informationalised and has incorporated communication technologies in a way that transforms the production process itself. Manufacturing is regarded as a service, and the material labour of the production of durable goods mixes with and tends toward immaterial labor. Second is the immaterial labor of analytical and symbolic tasks, which itself breaks down into creative and intelligent manipulation on the one hand and routine symbolic tasks on the other. Finally, a third type of immaterial labor involves the production and manipulation of affect …[37]

For Houellebecq's protagonists, their role in the immaterial labour market of analytic, symbolic and intelligent management of information leaves them feeling useless and redundant; they no longer know how to make anything real or useful. This is remarked upon in both *Atomised* and *Platform*. Chatting with his new lover Christiane over a late night supper of roll-mops and cheese in Les Halles, Bruno muses on his own functional ineffectiveness and on the impossibility of his physical survival outside of the 'industrialised world': 'I'm useless', he begins, 'I couldn't breed pigs, I don't have the faintest idea how to make sausages or forks or mobile phones. I'm surrounded by all this stuff that I eat or use and I couldn't actually make a single thing; I couldn't even begin to understand how they're made. If industrial production ceased tomorrow, I couldn't do anything to start things off again'.[38] Not only is Bruno unable to make any practical object, something with use rather than exchange value, he realizes that his labour, which consists of writing 'dubious articles on outdated cultural issues', is part of this new immaterial economy, and is, to a large extent, utterly pointless. Moreover, Bruno says, most of the people he knows 'are exactly the same'. A similar comment is to be found in *Platform* when Michel (*redux*) is confronted with the practical difficulties of everyday life in Cuba where the inability to fully participate in industrial production (due to sanctions, oil shortages and so on) compels its citizens to become true *bricoleurs*, making do and mending as they go. Michel muses upon his material worthlessness 'completely inept in matters of industrial production. I was perfectly adapted to the information age, that is to say good for nothing'. Imagining himself and his friend trying to outwit an economic blockade, he realizes that they would be defeated by their own lack of practical skills: 'We lived in a world made of objects whose manufacture, possible use and functions are completely alien to us.'[39] These then, are the men who populate *le monde houellebecquien*, men who might be said in some ways to be the result of not only a move to immaterial labour practices but also of a certain feminization of labour that developed in the late twentieth century.

The rapid development of the information economy in the 1990s – we must recall here the Copernican changes instanced by the appearance of the first internet search engine between 1990 and 1995 – signalled the end of the material production of physical commodities for a whole stratum of workers, not only in France, but also across the world, as a new machine age began. Although immaterial labour actually only accounts for a relatively small proportion of employment in developed economies, it has nevertheless become, as Hardt and Negri say, a hegemonic form of labour that now plays 'a foundational role in production processes'.[40] Originating in the thought of Italian Marxists Antonio Negri, Paolo Virno and Maurizio Lazzarato, immaterial labour is a term describing the central importance of information, communication and symbolic or analytical activities in the production and circulation of commodities, summarized in *Empire* as the 'informatization of production'.[41] In *Whatever*, then, labour has become completely immaterial. As a well-paid 'analyst programmer' in the newly emergent informational economy, the narrator works with intangible data relating to French agriculture that are moved around between networks setting up '… the possibility of establishing various interconnections between individuals, projects, organizations and services' (*W*, 38). A very familiar model to us now, at the time of writing this was a new modality of labour; computers would, as the narrator warns the bored secretaries attending his talk on integrated software, completely 'change their lives' (*W*, 55). Hardt and Negri similarly articulate this radical transformation in working practices when they assert that 'In the passage to the informational economy, the assembly line has been replaced by *the network* as the organizational model of production [...]'[42] This reduction of visible, audible, tangible communication to invisible and intangible information extends into the domain of personal relations. '... Most people vaguely admit', says the narrator in *Whatever*, 'that every relationship, in particular every human relationship, is *reduced* to an exchange of information' (*W*, 41). It is certainly true that any human interactions experienced by the narrator are at best etiolated, shrunk down to the most perfunctory exchanges with co-workers and managers in his office and impersonally dry speeches at colleagues' leaving dos. His outlook on the world is boiled down to a set of negativities couched in the language of existential nausea: '... computers make me puke. My entire work as a computer expert consists of adding to the data, the cross-referencing, the criteria of rational decision-making. It has no meaning, it is [...] a useless encumbering of the neurons. The world has need of many things, bar more information' (*W*, 82). Communication, then, becomes reduced to information and, in turn, there is a depreciation of an essentially felt quality to human inter-action, both factors that cause the narrator finally to stop speaking altogether shortly after an encounter with a particularly exasperating example of language reduced to the banalities of management discourse.

Just before undergoing a complete mental breakdown, the narrator visits a colleague in his department and is confronted head on with the ludicrous, obfuscating language of management-speak in a passage worth quoting in its entirety:

> In the afternoon I was due to see the head of the 'Computer studies' department. I don't really know why. As far as I was concerned I had nothing to say to him [...] Before installing myself in this office I'd been handed a voluminous report called Directive on the Ministry of Agriculture Data Processing Plan [...] It was devoted, if the introduction was to be believed, to *an attempt at the predefinition of various architectural scenarii, understood within a targeted objective.* The objectives, which themselves warranted a more detailed analysis in terms of desirability [...] I quickly leafed through the opus, underlining the more amusing phrases in pencil: *The strategic level consists in the realization of a system of global information promulgated by the integration of diversified heterogeneous sub-systems.* Or indeed: *It appears urgent to validate a canonic relational model with an organizational dynamic leading in the medium term to a data-based-oriented project.* (*W*, 27)

Meaning is utterly debased as language breaks down into nonsensical syntactic structures and verb phrases that continue to function within a whole as if an invisible consensus operates within which no one will point out the complete loss of meaning. For the 'bad' subject, that is, one who refuses the logic of the system, it is literally maddening, causing the narrator to malfunction within the system; he can no longer make meaning or produce output and can thus only follow Lyotard's dictum 'Be operational [...] or disappear'.[43] Increasingly alienated from the smooth-working of this meaningless language machine, in which language is made to serve the 'aims and objectives' culture of neoliberalism, a culture where 'targets' assume an unrivalled importance in immaterial labour, the narrator breaks down and contemplates a literal severance from the world. Later, he tells the psychiatrist of his desire to cut off his genitals and to gouge out his eyes and blind himself, to render himself an unsexed, emasculated, unseeing creature that would 'inspire repugnance in other men' (*W*, 145). This desire to maim his body, particularly his genitals, is of particular significance here, as it is the body and its attendant sexuality that will become the focus of the most intensive marketing in these new 'habitats of subjectification' and will be more explicitly the focus of Houellebecq's next novels, *Atomised* and *Platform*. The body is an important part of one's physical or corporeal capital, and as such must be managed and invested in ways that maximize its potential for social profit. 'One manages one's body', Baudrillard notes; 'one handles it as one might handle an inheritance'.[44] The narrator is blithely spending his inheritance, routinely abusing his body with bottle after bottle of alcohol, copious amounts of cigarettes and erratically self-medicating with prescription drugs. For him, both sedation and intoxication are outside of any useful or operational purpose and, as such, offer a kind of way out of living a purely functional existence.

Following the death of Tisserand after a disastrous drunken evening on the beach where the narrator unsuccessfully urges him to murder, the narrator undergoes a devastating mental breakdown. Diagnosing him as suffering from 'ideational decline', his psychiatrist informs him, in a rather uninsightful conclusion, that he is lacking any social connection and is in definite search for identity (*W*, 134). Paradoxically, madness appears as a rational course of action for the narrator and he is able to talk lucidly to the psychiatrist about his desire for self-erasure. In his madness, then, he has become what Zygmunt Bauman calls the 'dirt of postmodern society', a failed subject of neoliberalism who cannot be incited by the seductions of the 'infinite possibility and constant renewal promoted by the consumer market', nor by 'rejoicing in the chance of putting on and taking off of identities' and least of all by the endless 'chase after more intense sensations and even more exhilarating experience'.[45] He is the antithesis of the rationally consuming subject desired by neoliberal governmentality as he fails to produce within himself any governable sense of ambition, interest or aspiration.

The narrator's recovery from the brink of total physical breakdown is accompanied by a kind of resurgence, however tentative, of the urge to re-invest the body with a materiality, a solid quiddity of being to oppose the 'frightening possibility' of seeing life stripped of its metaphysical dimensions; a life entirely 'without substance' – '... I don't understand, basically, how people go on living' – is attenuated by a frenetic bike ride into the Forest of Mazan where nature, fulfilling a kind of primitivist rejuvenating function, gives him '... the impression of being present at a new departure' (*W*, 147, 154). Activity, nature, being outdoors, the feel of his muscles working, sunlight on his embattled body stretched out in a forest meadow, all bring the narrator an epiphany of sorts at the novel's close. Understanding that there is no 'sublime fusion' to be found; that any sense of authentic self outside of an economically dominated reality can never be found, he is reconciled to separation and that despite nature's 'profoundly reassuring' presence there is no sublimity to be had in commune with the natural world (*W*, 154–5). The best he can expect is to become as weightless as digital information, 'an item in a file', compressed and explicable 'between the pages', his reduction or transformation to a text as entry in a textbook of psychiatry brings him solace; he has become information himself (*W*, 150). He is, however, without shame at this thought. Having obtained some clarity of vision out of the process of breakdown, he sees the extent to which some spirit of life, a Spinozan striving (*conatus*), persists:

> A great mental shock restores me to the deepest part of myself. And I take stock, and I ironize, but at the same time I have great respect for myself. What a great capacity I have of grandiose mental images, and of seeing them through! How clear, once more, is the image I have of the world! The richness of what is dying inside me is absolutely prodigious; I needn't feel ashamed of myself; I shall have tried. (*W*, 154)

While the narrator of *Whatever* escapes with his life if not his sanity, the protagonists of Houellebecq's next and most famous novel, *Atomised*, are not quite so fortunate. A more detailed elaboration of the thesis of the extension of the 'free' market into the affective, specifically the sexual, life of the individual, *Atomised* follows the lives of two half-brothers who are even more firmly entrenched in the neoliberal regime and, as such, are driven to find alternatives that are even more drastic. The novel takes in a broad historical panorama of France in the twentieth century and beyond, and one of its central concerns is what happens to the body, sex and love under a biopolitical regime that seeks to subsume all sensual and sexual human experience. This failure, or reluctance, to be the neoliberal *homo œconomicus* takes two distinctive paths. On the one hand, there is an attempt to enjoy the spoils of libidinal hedonism, as attempted by Bruno in *Atomised*, Daniel 1 in *The Possibility of an Island* and, to a certain extent, by the Michel of *Platform*, all of whom attempt to plunge headlong into the libertine world of erotic indulgence and the promise of *jouissance*. Disconnected from any real social relations and unable to derive any pleasure from their material affluence, these characters search for realization and fulfilment in erotic experience, a search inevitably doomed to failure because, as they come to realize, sexual desire has become one of the most thoroughly commodifed domains of affective human life. There is no longer a 'natural' eroticism or sensuality but simply an extension of the market principles of exchange into sexual relations. On the other hand, and in contrast to this quest for meaning through sexual activity, there is the anti-hedonist, ascetic response involving a Spartan-like withdrawal into monadic isolation away from any sensual pleasures of life, most readily identified with Michel in *Atomised* and with the narrator in *Whatever*.

Notes

1 Hereafter, references to *Whatever* will be given in parentheses within the body of the text using the abbreviation *W*.

2 Nicholas J. Kiersey, 'Everyday Neoliberalism and the Subjectivity of Crisis: Post-Political Control in an Era of Financial Turmoil'. *Journal of Critical Globalisation Studies*, 4 (2011), 23–44, 35–6. Hayek cited in Karl Polyani's *The Great Transformation* (Boston: Beacon Press, 1954), 258.

3 Foucault, 'The Birth of Biopolitics', 258.

4 Thomas Lemke, 'The Birth of Bio-Politics: Michel Foucault's Lecture at the Collège de France on Neo Liberal Governmentality', http://www.thomaslemkeweb.de/engl.%20texte/The%20Birth%20of%20Biopolitics%203.pdf [accessed 5 April 2013], 9.

5 Beverley Best, '"Fredric Jameson Notwithstanding": The Dialectic of Affect', *Rethinking Marxism*, 23, 1 (2011), 60–82, 61.

6 Michel Houellebecq, *Rester vivant et autres textes* (Paris: Librio, 2001), 43. Translation my own. Abbreviated henceforth as *RV*.

7 Antonio Negri, 'Interpretation of the Class Situation Today: Methodological

Aspects' in *Open Marxism, Vol. 2: Theory and Practice* (eds) W. Bonefeld, R. Gunn and K. Psychopedis (London: Pluto, 1992), 85.

8 Foucault, 'The Birth of Biopolitics', 147.

9 Kiersey, 35–6.

10 Houellebecq, *Interventions* (Paris: Flammarion, 1998), 27.

11 Martin Crowley, 'Low Resistance', 149.

12 Crowley, 150.

13 Michel Biron, 'L'Effacement du personnage contemporain: l'exemple de Michel Houellebecq', *Études françaises*, 41, 1 (2005), 27–41, 33.

14 *Atomised*, 74. The description is here loosely attributed to President Giscard d'Éstaing.

15 Henri Lefebvre, *The Production of Space*, trans. Donald Nicholson-Smith (Blackwell: Oxford, 1991), 128.

16 Juan Martin Prada, 'Economies of affectivity', http://www.vinculo-a.net/english_site/text_prada.html [accessed 9 June 2009].

17 Lefebvre, *Everyday Life*, 56.

18 Deleuze and Guattari have pointed out that capitalism produces a very special kind of delirium that has '… its extreme cases, i.e. schizophrenics who decode and de-territorialize themselves to the limit' (*Anti-Oedipus*, 121).

19 Jack Abecassis, 'The Eclipse of Desire': L'Affaire Houellebecq,' *Modern Language Notes*, 115.4 (2000), 801–26, 811, 13.

20 Pierre Bourdieu, 'Utopia of endless exploitation' in *Le Monde Diplomatique*, December 1998, http://mondediplo.com/1998/12/08bourdieu [accessed 17 April 2011].

21 Pierre Bourdieu, *Distinction: A Social Critique of the Judgment of Taste,* trans. Richard Nice (Cambridge: Harvard University Press, 1984), 66.

22 Bourdieu, 'Utopia of endless exploitation'.

23 Le Flunch is a cafeteria-style restaurant chain in France offering reasonably priced fast food in brightly coloured dining rooms. Houellebecq's characters are often devotees of *la malbouffe*, that is, 'fast' and pre-packaged food.

24 Martin Crowley, 'Low Resistance', 150–1.

25 See Biron, 27–41.

26 Adorno and Horkheimer, *Dialectic of Enlightenment*, 167.

27 Svend Brinkmann, 'Literature as Qualitative Inquiry: The Novelist as Researcher', *Qualitative Inquiry*, 15,8 (2009), 1376–94, 1379–80.

28 John Banville, 'Futile Attraction: Michel Houellebecq's Lovecraft', Bookforum (April/May 2005), http://www.bookforum.com/archive/apr_05/banville.html [accessed 18 March 2012].

29 *Interventions*, 79, my translation.

30 Adorno, *Minima Moralia: Reflections on A Damaged Life* (London: Verso, 2005, originally pub. 1951), 63.

31 Abecassis, 807.

32 Nikolas Rose, *Powers of Freedom* (Cambridge: Cambridge University Press, 1999), 178.

33 Each of the streets in this area, Marcel-Sembat, Marcel-Dassault, Émile-Landrin and Ferdinand-Buisson, is named after a prominent figure in the Third Republic.

34 On the image of the *flâneur* in Houellebecq's writing see Katherine Gantz, 'Strolling with Houellebecq: The Textual Terrain of Postmodern Flânerie', *Journal of Modern Literature* 28.3 (2005), 149–61, 2.

35 *Empire*, 293.

36 *Platform*, 53, 55.

37 *Empire*, 293.

38 *Atomised*, 242.

39 *Platform*, 225. The gradual immaterialization of labour is the focus of Jed Martin's artistic work in *The Map and the Territory* (2010). As a student at the École de Beaux Arts de Paris, Martin notes 'from what he had been able to observe, the existence of men was organised around work, which occupied most of life, and took place in organisations of variable dimension' (65). He sees that the 'long historical phase of increased productivity' is reaching an end in the West and begins taking photographs of the world's entire stock of manufactured objects, including 'handguns, forks, printer cartridges, diaries and suspension files' with the aim of compiling an objective and encyclopaedic catalogue of these 'objects that formed the backbone of Europe's industrial success' in the nineteenth and twentieth centuries (70). The project lasts a full six years and produces more than eleven thousand photographs, all of which fit into a hard disk weighing 'a little under 200 grams' (21). The virtual weightlessness of these products, the result of over two hundred years of manufacturing, leads on to his next project in which he takes close-up photographs of a series of Michelin maps of provincial France for an exhibition titled 'THE MAP IS MORE INTERESTING THAN THE TERRITORY'.

40 *Empire*, 289.

41 Ibid., 289–94.

42 Ibid., 295.

43 Lyotard, *The Postmodern Condition*, 27.

44 Baudrillard (1998), 131.

45 Zygmunt Bauman, *Postmodernity and Its Discontents* (New York: NYU Press, 1997), 14.

4

Liquidating the Sixties

Poor imbeciles. You thought you were acting in conflict against capitalism, but [...] your efforts were a – if not the – key step in accomplishing the peaceful synthesis of all social relations, be they economic, political, or cultural, under the aegis of the market.[1]

Kristin Ross

Temporarily released from a psychiatric institution in which he had been confined following an incident of gross sexual impropriety in a *lycée* classroom, failed libertine and disgraced teacher, Bruno, sits by his estranged mother's death-bed and whispers into her ear: 'You're just an old whore [...] You deserve to die [...] I'll make sure they incinerate you. I'll put what's left of you in a little pot and every morning when I get up, I'll piss on your ashes' (*A*, 307). Mental illness notwithstanding, Bruno's macabre fantasy envisages a symbolically apposite gesture for the denigration of both his mother's body and the generational values that she represented. Using his omega-grade phallus to degrade his hippy mother's remains in this grotesque act expresses a profound sense of both bodily and moral abjection which encapsulates the intense antipathy expressed in Houellebecq's work towards the 'spirit' of 1968, in particular, towards its sexual spirit and the perceived effects of this on women. Houellebecq's writing is compulsively focused on the damaging extension of 'capitalist ethics into the erstwhile sheltered domain of sexual intimacy' with *Whatever*, *Atomised* and *Platform* all variations on this thematic.[2]

In many ways representative of a reactionary view of 1968 that began in earnest in France in the 1980s, Houellebecq's writing suggests, indeed asserts, that May '68 was not primarily an emancipatory and political moment but one of damaging antinomianism that emphasized transgressive desire and egotistical individualism. Arguing that 1968 marked the point at which France began its slide into moral and political decline, Houellebecq's view of '68 is unwaveringly negative and antagonistic, arguing at every turn that it produced nothing but selfishness and egotism and further, that it ushered in the first murmurings of neoliberal cultural capitalism which began to erode many spiritual and symbolic dimensions of everyday life. For Houellebecq, then, '68 was the consolidation of a disenchanting, materialistic ethos that would come to define the late twentieth century, reducing everything to what Marx called the 'universal venality' of the market.[3] Blithely disregarding any social or cultural advancements gained by the demands of the *soixante-huitards* and there were of course very many, he presents 1968 as *l'année maudite* and views its encouragement of sexual and personal liberation, far from 'unblocking' human subjects, as a precursor to a selfish individualism that encouraged the separation of sexuality from the confines of marriage and the family, resulting, in turn, in societal breakdown:

> It is interesting to note that the 'sexual revolution' is usually portrayed as a communist utopia, whereas in fact it was simply another stage in the rise of the individual. As the lovely phrase 'heart and home' suggests, the couple and the family were to be the last bastion of primitive communism in a liberal society. The sexual revolution was to destroy the last unit separating the individual from the market. The destruction continues to this day. (*A*, 135–6)

Dating the beginning of this sexual revolution very precisely to 14 December 1967 and the passing of the Neuwirth Act's legislation of the contraceptive pill which was to be freely available to all, *Atomised* points up that this 'offered a whole section of society access to the sexual revolution' and access to a life of pleasure previously available only to 'professionals, artists and senior management – and some small businessmen'. In short, the liberalization and democratization of sexual relations were, according to Houellebecq's thesis repeated throughout all of his work, the crumbling of the one of the last moral defences against the 'free market' (*A*).

If it is something of a truism to assert that 1968 inhabits an equally conse-crated and contested position in French history, eliciting a long trajectory of detraction and support since the *événements* themselves took place, it is never-theless important to remember its central, if somewhat occluded, importance in French cultural and intellectual history; indeed, Philippe Sollers has suggested that '68 remains 'one of three poorly resolved "closets" in French politics', the others being Vichy and Algeria .[4] It is generally agreed, that the 1980s saw the emergence and consolidation of a recognisably anti-'68 rhetoric typified in many ways by the arguments in Alain Renaut and Luc Ferry's denunciation of '68's 'anti-humanism' in *La Pensée '68* (1985) (*French Philosophy of the Sixties; an Essay on Anti-Humanism*) (1990). Laying many contemporary social and

moral ills at the feckless feet of the *soixante-huitards*, Renaut and Ferry's sentiments are clearly discernible in a speech given during the second round of the
presidential elections at Bercy, Paris, more than 20 years later, on 29 April 2007,
by Presidential candidate, Nicolas Sarkozy. Taking on this holy cow of French
political culture before a 20,000 strong crowd, Sarkozy declared; 'It is a question
of whether the heritage of May '68 should be perpetuated or should be liquidated
once and for all. I want to turn the page on 1968'. Accusing the *soixante-huitards*
of paving the way for not only a pervasive atmosphere of moral relativism, a
climate of 'anything goes', and the 'end of authority, politeness, and respect',
but also for weakening the 'morality of capitalism', Sarkozy claimed further
that they had prepared the ground for an 'unscrupulous capitalism', a position
ironized by Kristin Ross in this chapter's opening epigraph. With a rhetorical
fervour drawing on the ideological language of the left to frame his centre-
right agenda, Sarkozy forwarded a rather confused political position veering
between seemingly incompatible ethical and ideological positions demanding
the 'restoration of morality to capitalism', claiming that the idea of morality 'had
disappeared from the political vocabulary' in a tidal wave of relativism unleashed
in 1968. Stating his abhorrence for 'the left's apology for communitarianism' and
tapping into a rhetoric of national decline and moral dissolution, he continued
that 'the true heirs of the events of May 1968' had initiated an ethical disaster
resulting in a pervasive 'hatred for the family, society, state, nation and republic'
and had 'paved the way for scavengers and speculators to triumph over honest
businessmen and workers'. In ways that are strongly reminiscent of the *rouge-
brun* demeanour seen in much of Houellebecq's work, Sarkozy's cataloguing of
the ills of '68 drew from the left and right in an ideological concoction typical of
neoliberalism with its ideologically promiscuous appeal to both libertarianism
and communitarianism. Sarkozy's appeal was, as one journalist put it, 'intended
to prepare voters for [neo] liberal shock treatment and a break with the past'.[5]

Trickles of anti-'68 sentiment had begun to emerge very quickly after the
events themselves, slowly gathering momentum over the ensuing years, growing
ever more robust with each decennial anniversary, so by the time Sarkozy made
this Bercy speech the parameters of *la pensée anti-'68* were well-established in
a set of reactionary discourses holding the era culpable for the breakdown of
authority and the family, as well as for the spread of moral relativism and anti-
rationalism. The thrust of Sarkozy's homily had strong continuities with one
of the most voluble purveyors of anti-1968 rhetoric, Gilles Lipovetsky, whose
Tocquevillean approach suggested that May '68 was a '"soft" revolution' that
had at its heart the 'gradual softening of social mores'. With scant regard for any

of its serious radical politics, Lipovetsky regarded '68 as primarily a ludic event 'emphasizing permissiveness, humor, and fun'; 'the spirit of May recaptured what had historically been the central tenet of consumer society: *hedonism*' and was characterized by the 'very thing that it denounced in politics' and that was the 'euphoria of the consumer age'.[6] The sentiments expressed in this essay are similar to, indeed in very many places identical with, a preoccupation with the negative consequences of '68 so evident in *Atomised* and *Platform*. In Houellebecq's work the fixation on the deleterious effects of May '68 centres for the most part on sex and desire, targeting most vehemently feminism and its politicization of sex. These accusations situate Houellebecq within, if not the generation of new reactionaries as Lindenberg claims, then certainly on the *rouge-brun* spectrum, part of the ideologically nebulous 'moral re-arming' of French politics that took place from the 1980s onwards and rekindled in Sarkozy's speech.[7]

Houellebecq's virulent and sustained attack on the legacy of '68 not only exemplifies Lipovetsky's anti-'68 stance, it is part of a more pervasive *droitisation* in French intellectual culture, a rightwards ideological shift that began around the middle of the 1980s. Renaut and Ferry's work, then, joined a steadily growing body of writing bemoaning the perceived decline of Western civilization and incriminating, to a greater or lesser degree, May '68.[8] According to François Noudlemann, this turn to the right has been 'twenty-five years in the making' and forms part of a wider 'paradigm shift' in French political culture that involves not only an ideological reorientation but a tension 'at the heart of French society between a conservative penchant for continuity and a new mode of becoming that threatens national identities'.[9] However, as the editors of a special issue of *Yale French Studies* on *droitisation* point up, it is important to distinguish between two outwardly identical gestures: one is 'the yearning of conservative or reactionary discourses' and the other a 'melancholic opposition to the "neoliberal, capitalistic status quo"' that originates from a disillusioned leftist context.[10] The broad-range appeal of Houellebecq's work is that it may be read on both of these ideological levels simultaneously; that is, both conservatively and progressively. Thus, when we read his novels we experience a sharp jolt of recognition, finding ourselves, even perhaps if we are female readers, empathizing with the beleaguered anti-heroes battling away against the odds to get laid and find love in a world that values only the most crass signifiers of physical and personal worth. We might even be persuaded to recognize the extremities of his critique of neoliberal capitalism, but then we are pulled up short as, on closer view, his satire is tinged with the moral idealism characteristic, not of a disappointed leftism, but of a profoundly conservative vision. The difficulty is, of course, that these two positions appear, from the outside at least, almost indistinguishable.

Published in 1998, the year of the thirtieth anniversary of *les événements*, *Atomised* explicitly attacks much, if not all, of what both Houellebecq and Lipovetsky regard as its lasting legacies: individualism, sexual narcissism and social anomie all of which first became apparent in France in 1974–5, the real beginning, according to the novel, of the 'atomised society' (*A*, 184). This chapter, then, considers *la pensée anti-'68* rehearsed in *Atomised* and *Platform* and suggests that Houellebecq's work forms part of what might be called a 'backlash' generation; writers who may once have had broadly leftist political sympathies, *ex-gauchistes*, but who moved from the left to the right between the 1970s and the 1990s.

Houellebecq's assault on '68 begins with the breakdown of moral and social authority and the promotion of sexual liberation which is, he thinks, but a short step to sadism and finally leads to something darker and altogether more brutal at its Sadean extremes: 'A subtle but definitive change had occurred in Western society during 1974 and 1975 [...] Western society had tipped towards something dangerous [...] the supreme manifestation of this focus on the individual, was once again about to flare up in the West' (*A*, 184). Houellebecq's attack on '68 has another target of contempt: that of a perceived harmful moral relativism imposed by the Nietzschean critical establishment of 'high' French theory, chief among whom were Deleuze, Lacan, Derrida and Foucault, and on the German side Marx, Heidegger and Freud. Ferry and Renaut argue that in the 1960s the 'pure' domain of philosophy was replaced by the irrationalism of literary 'theory', described by them as a 'hyperbolic repetition of German philosophy', centred on the destruction of the idea of truth, reason and universality. As they state:

> ... French philosophy of the '68 period resolutely chose the antihumanist position. From Foucault's declaration of the 'death of man' at the end of *The Order of Things* to Lacan's affirmation of the radically antihumanist nature of psychoanalysis since 'Freud's discovery' that 'the true center of the human being is no longer in the same place assigned to it by whole humanist tradition,' the same conviction is upheld: the autonomy of the subject is an illusion.[11]

Part of this anti-humanist programme was, according to Houellebecq's work at least, the systematic separation of women from the idea of the 'natural', a task carried out by the feminist movement as they began to unpick the cultural construction of gender identity. In Houellebecq's novels, feminism has robbed women of a 'natural' sensuality and coerced them into doctrinaire positions on sexual difference and equality thereby producing a generation of self-centred women unwilling and unable to care for their children and who treat sexuality as they might a business transaction. Ignoring the momentous legal, social and cultural progress that feminism brought for women, not least of which was effective contraception, access to safe medical abortion and political parity, in *Atomised* and *Platform* feminism is presented as simply an egotistical outcrop of a kind of sexual neoliberalism, a form of sexual privatization, and merely 'another stage in the rise of the individual', sweeping way older kinship relations (*A*, 135–6). While the antipathy directed towards 1968 in *Atomised* is frequently humorous in the caricature of the New Age camps with their chakra chanting and so on, when the novel's attention is directed towards feminism the tone becomes positively vicious. Women who discovered sexual and personal liberation in the sixties are represented as pitiful and deluded leftovers of sexual liberation; victims of their own feminist rhetoric of self-realization and empowerment, they now find themselves unwanted in the sexual marketplace, destined to live out their middle-age 'ugly', 'ageing' and 'alone' with 'cobwebs in their cunts' (*A*, 174, 184). Feminism, then, is blamed unconditionally for ushering in the commodification of sexuality and for making the conditions required for love, altruism and compassion, impossible.

La pensée anti-'68

That critical opinions in France have been divided over the legacies and meanings of May 1968 is incontrovertible and demonstrable by the large number of works analysing, defending, attacking and rehabilitating the events.[12] In the 40 or so years that have passed since the barricades went up in the Quartier Latin, critical opinion has resolved itself into a complex affair crossing back and forth over ideological boundaries.[13] Noting these ideological crossings, Serge Audier observes quite correctly that 'On both the right and the left you often hear a similar paradoxical theory – that the '68 generation played a key role in the development of capitalism at the end of the 1970s, by lifting the last barrier to unfettered commercialism: traditional values …'. It is precisely this indictment – that is to say, that the libertarian aspects of '68 paved the way for a newly energized version of capitalism drawing upon hedonism, individualism and particularly on sexual liberation – that concerns me here. The perceived nihilism, hedonism, disdain for state and family as well as the focus on play and pleasure, is summed up in one of the more famous of the numerous slogans of the time, '*Vivre sans contraintes et jouer sans entraves*' (Live without limits and enjoy without restraint). It is precisely this idea of untrammelled desire that has been blamed for the 'perversion' of the French society by destroying, according to Sarkozy, the boundaries between binary terms; good and evil, truth and lies, beauty and ugliness. In short, then, the anti-'68 view holds that the destruction of all hierarchies that had kept society in check in de Gaulle's Fifth Republic started to collapse irretrievably in 1968.

In his survey of the body of anti-'68 thought, *La Pensée anti-'68* (2008), Audier itemizes the charges levelled against '68 which include narcissism, debauchery, the destruction of authority, the desecration of the family and the education system, relativism, a destructive egalitarianism and postmodernism.[14] Elsewhere, and from a quite different standpoint, Jean-Pierre Le Goff states that May '68 was the end of important social and cultural boundaries that had hitherto marked human life: gone were the 'distinctions between rationality and irrationality', as well as the 'distinctions between public and private' and 'normal and pathological'.[15] Unequivocal in his admiration for Lipovetsky's *L'ère du vide*, whose ideas bear a striking similarity to those in *Atomised,* Le Goff based his own arguments on Lipovetsky's central hypothesis which asserted that May '68 was 'the wellspring of modern individualism'. Encouraged by what Lipovetsky calls the 'narcissistic cult of the Ego', the spirit of May '68 very quickly began to contradict its own revolutionary rhetoric and became marked, not only by an erosion of 'collective engagement' but also more generally by a disaffection for any real sense of the political.[16] In his 'Modest Contribution to the Tenth Anniversary' (1978), Régis Debray argued that the libertarian nature of the uprising was the 'the cradle of a new bourgeois society' that would replace 'The France of stone and rye, of *apéritif* and the institution, of *oui papa, oui patron, oui cherie*, was ordered out of the way so that the France of software and super-markets, of news and planning, of know-how and brain-storming could show off its vitality to the full'.[17]

By the time the twentieth and thirtieth anniversaries came around the characterization of '68 as the catalyst for a new, more affectively nuanced capitalism was well-established. As Ross notes in *May '68 and its Afterlives*, the trajectory of thinking, what she calls the 'narrative labor', on '68 has 'in the last 30 years has been buried, raked over the coals, trivialized, or represented as a monstrosity'[18] to the point that the charge that 'some of May's more radical ideas and practices came to be recuperated or recycled in the service of Capital' has become something of an orthodoxy in the 'official story'.[19] This narrative of '68 as an essentially libertarian moment reached its apogee in the 1980s, at a point where Houellebecq would have been very conscious of its circulation and currency in intellectual thought. Arguing against the increasingly 'deterritorialized' 1980s version of '68, Ross resists a reading which understands it as devoid of meaningful political import and at 'one with a stage of capitalism that itself denies any succeeding historical stages'.[20] Boltanski and Chiapello take up a similar, if differently focused, view when they argue that the iconoclastic cultural and ethical concerns of May 1968, what they term 'artistic critique', have undergone a 'well-nigh reversal' and, in some cases have morphed into their direct antithesis.[21] This reversal is not, they argue, due to any particular failure of the internal mechanisms of the critique itself but rather to the fact that many of the ideals promulgated by the artistic critique, as opposed to the social critique, were actually used to disarm and diffuse the very opposition to capitalism thrown up by '68's anti-establishment stance. This artistic critique criticized capitalism for its rigidity and repression of the individual at the level of creativity and authenticity. The demand was for more feeling, less standardization and above all, for an expansion of individual freedom. The ways in which capitalism recuperated this artistic critique is summed up in the following:

> Capitalism [...] has always relied on critiques of the status quo to alert it to dangers in any untrammelled development of its current forms, and to discover the antidotes required to neutralize opposition to the system and increase the level of profitability within it. Ready to take advantage of hospitable conditions, firms began to reorganize the production process and wage contracts. systems, sub-contracting, team-working, multi-tasking and multi-skilling, 'flat' management – all the features of a so-called 'lean capitalism' or 'post-Fordism' – were the result. For Boltanski and Chiapello, these molecular changes were not simply reactions to a crisis of authority within the enterprise, and of profitability within the economy, although they were that too. They were also responses to demands implicit in the artistic critique of the system, incorporating them in ways compatible with accumulation, and disarming a potentially subversive challenge that had touched even a younger generation of managers who had imbibed elements of the 'spirit of '68'.[22]

In many ways, Boltanski and Chiapello's arguments elaborate upon earlier discussions of capitalism's unerring ability to absorb its opponent's discourses and to use them to make itself stronger and more palatable, examined most memorably by Henri Lefebvre in the final volume of *Critique de la vie quotidienne* (1981).

Thus, the very criticisms levelled against society in 1968 have been subsumed and assimilated by an economic system that learned from and strengthened itself out of that very critique that 'appealed to creativity, to pleasure, the power of the imagination' a liberation, Boltanski and Chiapello note, 'affecting every dimension of existence' was stolen away from under the eyes of the '68ers and deployed in the service of the old order, in fact, often made the buying and selling, the whole process of accumulation a great deal easier. They say: 'The price paid by critique for being listened to, at least in part, is to see some of the values it had mobilized to oppose the form taken by the accumulation process being placed at the service of accumulation ...'.[23] In short, capitalism, in all its cunning, found ways of not only surviving the downturn of the 1970s, but actually fortified itself by incorporating the rebellious energies of its enemies and finding new, mostly cultural and aesthetic, routes to its survival. Drawing renewed vigour from its detractors, capitalism thus absorbed the potency of the left's anti-normative critique that looked for unassimilated creative life 'under the paving stones', packaged it up and sold it on the open market. As Boltanski and Chiapello note, when capitalism is 'obliged to respond' to the critique levelled against it, it must work hard to 'maintain the support of the troops', who are in danger of listening to its denunciations and so '*incorporates some of the values in whose name it was criticized*'.[24] The question they pose regarding the participation, often leadership, of the 'class of '68' is crucial; what is it that made this group of radicals feel 'so at ease in the emerging new society that they made themselves its spokesmen and egged on the transformation'?[25] The answer seems to be that the '68ers have found it unproblematic to accept the spirit of the 'new' capitalism because the demands of their generation – for authenticity, self-determination and freedom – have been recuperated to give it an attractive veneer of liberalism and non-standardization (see the niche marketing of sex tourism in *Platform*); thus capitalism itself is presented as an antidote to alienation.

Freedom and self-realization, cornerstones of the youthful demands of the *soixante-huitards*, become the highly differentiated package holidays meticu-lously tailored to the individual tastes of a niche demographic in *Platform* and in *Whatever* as 'the ability to order a hot meal online at any time of the day'. One of the crop of ex-*gauchiste* 'new philosophers', Lipovetsky is unequivocal in his opinion that 'not only is the spirit of May individualist, but in its way it contributed [...] to the acceleration of the arrival of contemporary narcissistic individualism, largely indifferent to grand social ends and mass combat'.[26] It was a 'cool' and 'soft' revolution lacking in any proper historical programme and in this way was ripe to be assimilated into the artistic critique. Raoul Vaneigem provides an inkling of how this manoeuvre might operate, although from a different ideological perspective, when he notes:

> Power, State, religion, ideology, army, morality, Left, the Right – that so many abominations should have been sent one after another to the wrecker's yard by the imperialism of the market, for which there is no black and no white, might seem at first glance good reason to rejoice; but no sooner does the slightest suspicion enter one's mind that it becomes obvious that all these forces have been redeployed, and are now waging war under different colours.[27]

Outside of a specifically French context, David Harvey offers a very similar analysis: '... the counter-cultural movements of the 1960s created an environment of unfulfilled needs and repressed desires that postmodernist popular cultural production has merely set out to satisfy the best it can in commodity form ...'[28] Many Houellebecq scholars have, of course, identified the significance of the virulent attack on '68 in much of his writing. One of the most compelling commentators on this aspect of Houellebecq's work is Martin Crowley, who argues that for Houellebecq the sixties 'resulted in hypocritically pro-capitalist forms of individualism'.[29] Another important Houellebecq critic is Ruth Cruickshank who, while largely agreeing with Crowley's position on Houellebecq and May '68, defends him, at least to some degree, against accusations of uniformly 'discrediting the generation of 1968' by situating his work in a more historically specific *fin de siècle* context. His work, she says, is 'less an attack on *soixante-huitards* than a reductive attribution of the ills of turn-of-the-millennium France to the model of American liberalism adopted by the youth of the 1960s'.[30]

I examine now the anti-'68 offensive in Houellebecq's novels, specifically its condemnation of sexual liberation which has, according to almost all of his work, been a wretched failure and has simply succeeded in delivering sexuality into an ever more transgressive hedonism leading either to a destructive Sadean excess that reinstates a savage Darwinist struggle between humans or directly into the hands of commercial interests. Houellebecq's work is inhabited, as Abecassis puts it, by the restricted binary logic of the *Moraliste*: 'We are condemned to choose between two bleak options; repression (the Pauline regime) or self-destruction (the Sadean racism) and nothing in between.'[31] The rush to a voluptuary Sadean existence leads to death, destruction and, perhaps more importantly, straight back into the very conditions that the radicals of the 1960s sought to escape; the overweening imperial power of the market. Sexual liberation is emphatically *not* the holy grail of political emancipation here; in fact, it is quite the opposite as it is seen to interpellate the subject more fully into Marcuse's 'one-dimensional society'. Further, I argue that Houellebecq's work suggests that '68 has led us back to a sexual primitivism in which the violent hierarchies of alpha and omega masculinity battle it out for the attention of ever-younger females in a primal scene of antagonistic sexual competition. In a sense, Michel Djerzinski's biogenetic project, the Movement for Human Potential, is an attempt, however improbably madcap, to counter such a sexual primitivism by restoring an 'absolute morality' to a genetically feminized humanity. By implanting erogenous zones all over each and every human body, *all* humans are permitted to participate in and enjoy Freud's 'polymorphous perversity'; thus, the emancipatory goal of sexual egalitarianism is achieved through science and technology rather than by any ideological or philosophical means. This purifying project is achieved not through human struggle but through über-rationalist methodologies which can be seen as the final liquidation of the legacy of '68 and the death of its ideology and ethics, both of which have been superseded by the positivism of the scientific solution, itself a logical progression of a rationalized world view.

From Rousseau to Sade

A thesis leads this novel by the nose, and the thesis, still startling France, is that the libertarian advances of the post-'68 generations have led to a sinkhole of violence and despair: that materialism and sexual liberation end inevitably in misery, violence, and hopelessness ...[32]

In *Atomised*, Bruno's appalling sexual torture at the hands of the older boys at his boarding school in Meaux functions metonymically as an example of the beginnings of the breakdown of authority in the sixties allowing institutions to revert to a 'state of savagery' (*A*, 40). One night in March 1968, eleven-year-old Bruno, discarded by his parents and on his third boarding school, finds himself 'naked and covered in shit' lying on the bathroom floor after an attack by some of the older pupils who are already brutish alpha males. In the absence of the authority of either family or school, the supremacy of the most obviously powerful phallic presence is central to the establishment of the masculine hierarchy; Brasseur, the oldest boy at 14, 'takes out his prick, which seems huge to Bruno. He stands over the boy and pisses on his face' (*A*, 49). This encounter is a meaningful one, not least for its prefiguring of Bruno's later desire to urinate on his mother's ashes but also for the insight it provides as to why Bruno strives so assiduously to become a libertine alpha male in later life. In keeping with Houellebecq's aversion to psychoanalysis detailed in *Public Enemies* that is based on a belief that to confess is utterly futile as it will never 'change anything about one's personality', Bruno is not permitted a chance to articulate this trauma until it is far too late and he is incarcerated in a mental institution. Thus, the harrowing experience of sexual brutality is wholly glossed over, submerged in the past, never to be examined, just like the incident in which Bruno dashes out the brains of a nearby cat after masturbating over his mother's vagina as she sleeps naked on a bed next to her young lover (*A*, 35).[33] Inappropriate pissing, masturbating, vomiting, dreams of castration, putrefying bodies and self-blinding, are the disturbing reactions to trauma for the Houellebecquian male, all of which take place in a wider context of the explicit and vehement denunciation of the validity of any therapeutic use of psychoanalysis despite the fact that we are told that Bruno's experiences at the hands of Michel Brasseur, an incipient Nietzschean *übermensch*, likely will leave him 'psychologically scarred for life' (*A*, 52). Beginning with urination, the encounter ends with the threat of castration as a razor blade is held to the terrified Bruno's genitals, and is the last in a long line of a stream of sadistic assaults by older pupils on the younger ones, almost always sexual in nature but all predicated on staking out a crude pecking order among the boys.

The contempt for psychoanalysis is in keeping with the *pensée anti-'68* comportment of *Atomised* and Bruno's suffering here is presented as a direct result of '68, in particular the demands for more freedom in the French educational system resulting in the system of *autogestion* being installed in many educational establishments. *Autogestion* is, as historian Pierre Rosanvallon explains, 'the refusal and contestation of all centralized and hierarchical systems' integral to the 'emergence of a new conception of democracy' in 1970's France and worked on three principal levels, the first of which 'suggested the generalized extension of democratic procedures to the governance of all of the different spheres of social life'. More generally *autogestion* searched for a 'way of transcending the procedural limits of traditional representative democracy'; and 'finally, it corresponded to a new perception of the relation between public and private life, "self-management" looking as if it were the corollary, at once legitimate and necessary, of more specifically institutional reforms [...] People began speaking, in a general manner, of the self-management of everyday life [*autogestion du quotidien*].'[34] Described in *Atomised* as a 'ministerial directive taken after the riots of 1968', *autogestion* is applied to Bruno's school with negative and violent consequences and rapidly degenerates into the undemo-cratic violence of the natural world. As a result of the relaxation of any external authority controlling the boys, it now 'became easier for pupils to move around at night and soon the bullies took to staging raids on the younger boys' dormi-tories as least once a week' (*A*, 50). A 'natural' hierarchy of the young boys is thus restored, reasserting the naked Darwinian struggle of the survival of fittest in the school. This is the occasion for one of Houellebecq's trademark semi-sociological interventions underscoring the moral message where Bruno's housemaster Cohen takes up close to two pages detailing the 'strict hierarchy', the alpha, beta males and so on, of animal societies in which 'rank relates directly to the physical strength of each member' and the brutish, bestial rituals of dominance and submission in which the 'weakest' suffer 'acts of gratuitous cruelty'. Cohen's beliefs in the righteousness of Nietzsche's 'rejection of passion' and the 'triumph of the will', demonstrates a particularly morose spin on the use of Nietzsche in the 'theory'-driven anti-humanism of 1968 (*A*, 51, 52). Just as boys will, *Lord of the Flies*-like, return to a 'natural', which is to say, primitive and murderous way of organizing their social structure, sexuality too cannot be left to the self-determining mode of *autogestion* as it will degenerate into a series of mechanical orgiastic performances which simply replicate the 'survival of the fittest' dynamic which in turn leads to unbridled sadism and even murder.

With a significantly wider historical scope than *Whatever*, *Atomised* permits a broader canvas on which the effects and consequences of 1968 can be examined and held to account. Much of the novel is concerned with sex, and in particular with the loosening of the repressive and authoritarian binds on human sexuality freeing it from its associations with sin and dirt. This leads, however, not to erotic fulfilment and contentment but to a pervasive and, for many, lifelong sexual misery and impoverishment. As Foucault's repressive hypothesis is reconfigured, post-'68 sexuality leads to 'an unlimited right of all-powerful monstrosity [...] which itself knows no other law but its own'.[35] Houellebecq's work argues in the strongest terms that the sexual liberation demanded by the *soixante-huitards* led to sadism and violence as they relentlessly promoted a society 'where the link between sex and procreation has been broken' and human interaction is motivated by '... individuation, narcissism, malice and desire' (*A*, 191). The liberation of sexuality does not lead to the democratic Rousseauesque eroticism of the hippy flower-children but to ever-more trans-gressive models of a Dionysian/Sadean sexuality incarnated in its popular form by the diabolical but seductive figure of 'rich, adored, cynical' Mick Jagger, described as 'the image of evil unpunished'. Jagger, it is suggested, represents a softer version of the sexual 'evil' that culminates in the demented actions of Charles Manson who was not, according to *Atomised*, 'some monstrous aberration in the hippy movement, but its logical conclusion ...' (*A*, 248, 253). One of Houellebecq's paramount concerns, one might even call it an obsession, is how the ideals of free love and sexual liberation central to the alternative cultures of the 1960s succeeded only in reinforcing a more exclusive sexual marketplace now dominated by the commercial discourses of mainstream hard core pornography. Sexual liberation has resulted in the direction of sexuality into an increasingly transgressive 'sexual abandon' that is 'an empty experience' in its 'intellectual and moral' vacuity, exacting a heavy physical toll upon bodies (particularly those of women) which sooner or later begin to gape from multiple rough penetrations, their genitals losing any erogenous sensations through over-rough use; 'their cunts had all the sensitivity of blocks of lard' (*A*, 294). This trajectory from Rousseau to Sade begins with the Californian hippy commune of Francesco di Meola, Bruno's mother's erstwhile lover, and ends in the satanic sexual rituals of his son, David, a failed-Jagger figure who turns to the sadism of snuff films and finally, to sexual murder.

At the beginning of the 1970s Francesco di Meola, the son of an Italian anarchist emigrant, anticipates that the kind of utopian space attempted by the *Lieu de Changement* would form a crucial part of a new, leisure-rich post-war economy and sets out to profit from the aftermath of 1968 that had released a 'time bomb of resentment suffocated under the legacy of Gaullist patriarchy'. Di Meola speculates that, in the West, economic activity will broaden to encompass ever-expanding opportunities for consumption linked to both a rise in disposable income and the growing demands for self-authentication. He also predicts that 'the idea of leisure' and 'free time' will become 'radically different' with many activities and pursuits previously 'considered marginal or elitist' becoming 'economically important' (*A*, 93). The stimulation and expansion of the mind as well as of the body will proliferate into a myriad of profitable activities to occupy those now used to the idea of their right to pleasure ostensibly espoused by '68's demands for personal autonomy and self-determination. Riding the wave of the anti-establishment sentiment released in the immediate post-'68 years, di Meola brings the 'flower power' ideas of California to France and sets up an ersatz hippy commune in Haute-Provence, a copy of one in the Big Sur where he had once entertained countercultural figures like Carl Rogers and Aldous Huxley. In theory, the commune offers a spiritual refuge from the materialistic vulgarities of the modern world, a 'sweeping away of Western civilisation in its entirety', but is, in reality, a place where di Meola can get high with 'very young girls' whom he thinks of as 'stupid little WASP bitches' then 'fuck[s] them among the mandalas and the smell of incense' (*A*, 94). This is strongly reminiscent, of course, of many feminist accounts that the sixties, while bringing sexual liberation for women, also meant that they were increasingly duped by men using an idealistic 'free love' agenda to further their own, sometimes exploitative, sexual promiscuity.[36]

Another version of this is the *Lieu de Changement* which, as Ben Jeffery notes, functions as a 'microcosm for one of Houellebecq's central concerns'.[37] Founded in 1975 by a group of young '68 veterans (more in spirit than in action), the year that France began to first show the effects of the permissive society, this 'haven of humanist and democratic feeling [...] inspired by the liberal values of the early Seventies' was an attempt to 'create an authentic utopia', a place where the principle of self-government, respect for individual freedom and true democracy could be practised in the 'here and now'. The *Lieu* is a New Age camp complete with chanting, crystal healing, angel workshops and naked Gestalt massage. With splenetic humour, Bruno attempts to join in these activities with inevitably limited success as he is really there, of course, in the hope of finding a sexually permissive atmosphere in which he can pursue his own concupiscent interests. Not strictly speaking a commune, the *Lieu* began as a place where like-minded people could spend their summer holidays in an atmosphere that 'would create synergies' and 'facilitate the meeting of minds' and, with a ratio of two females for every male in the camp, provide 'an opportunity to "get your rocks off"', at least for the men (*A*, 113, 114). Naturally, one of the first things Bruno does on arrival is to rummage through a plastic bin under a condom machine to see for himself if this promised sexual activity is actually taking place. In the event, he spends his first night alone, masturbating over a copy of *Swing* magazine, reading its small ads and realizing, not for the first time, that 'he did not come close to the minimum size' required by those seeking sex. Hopefully, he muses, the hippies would be more forgiving of his phallic inadequacy (*A*, 118).

As the 1970s wore on into the 80s, the *Lieu* did not fare well. As its clientele grew older the 'anarchic' spirit guiding its management did not lend itself to an easy financial situation and its rudimentary hippy accommodations failed to measure up to 'the standards of package holidays'. So in 1984, to the dismay of its more left-wing founders, it dramatically remodelled itself along corporate lines as a venue offering alternative therapies, workshops and 'residential courses aimed at businesses' soon counting IBM, the Banque Nationale de Paris and the

RATP among its multinational clientele. Dropping its cooperative association status, the *Lieu* duly floated itself on the stock market and continued to intensify its aggressive marketing techniques in ways wholly antithetical to its '68 anti-establishment ideals. By the time of Bruno's sexually optimistic visit to the *Lieu* at the end of the 1990s, although initially 'dedicated exclusively to sexual liberation and desire', the *Lieu* had '*naturally* became a place of depression and bitterness' (my emphasis) and had started to reveal the raw sexual competition behind the 'cult of the body' (*A*, 126). The veterans of '68 continued to visit the *Lieu* but increasingly found themselves excluded from the sexual activities that they had once enthusiastically promoted 30 years earlier; their ageing, sagging and decaying bodies with their 'flaccid pricks and fleshy tits' now only 'filled them with disgust', a 'disgust they could see mirrored in the gaze of others' (*A*, 126). Bruno asks a grizzled veteran of '68, Paul Le Dantec, about his memories of the sexual abandon that he suspects must have taken place every night in the early days of the *Lieu*: 'Liberation my arse', replies the old hippy '... take it from me nothing much has changed ...' Here, Bruno prompts the man to confirm his own partisan position; 'So, what you are saying [...] is that there was never any real sexual liberation – just another form of seduction' (*A*, 161, 162). In this way, it is suggested that 1968 was a sham; merely the excuse for nothing more radical than sexual predation.

More upmarket in accordance with the unabashed commercialism of its time, the nudist resort in the Cap d'Agde offers sexual freedom with distinctly less mysticism, a place where 'very correct, very middle-class' Dutch, Scandinavians and Germans can be trusted to enjoy a 'sexual "social" democracy' in a permissive sexual environment that is close to some of the utopian ideals of the sixties. In addition to sexual freedom, there is a range of activities for the holidaymakers who can sign up for yoga, silk painting and oriental exercises. The resort is based upon a highly exclusive sexual permissiveness based on an extremely strict ethical contract in which 'sexual pleasure is recognized as an important commodity' (*A*, 260). Enjoying strenuous and pleasurable group sex with Rudi and Hannelore from Hamburg, Bruno and Christiane are, for a while at least, bathed in the warm glow of erotic fulfilment: 'It was nice to know that there would be no problems, that all the sexual issues had been resolved: it was good to know that each of them would do their best to bring pleasure to the others'. In this quasi-idyllic space sexuality is brought 'back to its original form' and is, above all, 'based on the notion of goodwill' (*A*, 262, 263). Although sexual differentiation still occurs between the old and the ugly and the young and beautiful, masturbatory voyeurism is 'looked on with kindly compassion', and in this way no-one is fully excluded and there 'is not so much as an undertone of violence' (*A*, 264). This sexual utopia is not, however, as 'free' as it first appears. Structured by strict, if unwritten, regulations and rules, the sexual contract of the resort is only workable due to its homogenous class demographic made up of almost entirely liberal, middle class professionals who are 'an uncommon example of the qualities of discipline and respect for the social contract' (*A*, 264). But even this kind of orderly erotic democracy cannot endure and just as all romantic and sexual relationships end in death in Houellebecq's novels, sexual contentment is forever compelled to degenerate into its depraved opposite as the polite reciprocity of the Cap d'Agde metamorphoses into the harsher environment of the Parisian sex clubs.

The sex clubs, revisited in *Platform* as S & M clubs, 'can only exist among cultured cerebral people for whom sex has lost all attraction' and, as such, represent the next logical step of this journey to the Sadean system and are initially enticing for the would-be philanderer Bruno (*P*, 244–5). At first, he finds the offer of all the 'cunts and mouths open to him' unbearably exciting, almost swooning with the variety of pleasure on offer, but very quickly realizes that, even in this ostensibly liberated erotic environment, 'there was no escape' from the exacting standards of the market; his 'five-inch cock' is indisputably too small and many of the women he encounters are 'somewhat disappointed' when they see his penis (*A*, 292, 293). Far from being a utopian erotic space however, the laws of the commercial marketplace are even more strictly applied in these clubs as they are revealed to be exaggerated mirrors of the 'dominant culture'. The 'teeming and bestial' atmosphere takes its cue from the reductive and standardizing discourses of contemporary pornography with a strict homogeneity imposed on the size and shape of sexual signifiers; 'cocks are invariably enormous and rock hard', 'breasts are enhanced' and 'cunts wet and shaven' (*A*, 293). Erotic pleasure which requires 'time, finesse and sensitivity' is overtaken by the 'empty experience' of 'prodigal sexual abandon' in which, against a background of techno music, participants ape sexual techniques learned from mainstream porn films: 'Imitating the frenetic rhythm of porn actresses, they brutally jerked his cock in a ridiculous piston motion as though it was a piece of dead meat' (*A*, 294). This, then, is the heart of the Sadean-libertine system for which a strong sense of authorial distaste is shown through a marked preference in these passages for a more sensual approach to sexual activity defined by words such as like 'deftness', softness', 'gently' and 'delicately', starkly contrasting with the more brutal descriptions of the women habitués of the clubs, their bodies 'gaping from multiple penetrations' (*A*, 292). Effectively sacrificed to this evermore transgressive Sadean system, Christiane is killed by sexual dissipation – 'five men had fucked her without Christiane even glancing at them'. She then begins her rapid descent into illness then death, a process that starts with Bruno's penis in her mouth and a succession of anonymous men penetrating her and ends with her paralysis then suicide. Unfettered by moral or kinship constraints and underwritten by a commercial rather than affective or spontaneous drive, sexual desire will always, it is suggested, revert to the Sadean system which is 'governed by the principle of adventure' and 'seduction'. Such a system flows only one way; towards destruction. The sex clubs Bruno and Christiane visit are a step away from the degenerate sexual trajectory that reaches its apotheosis in the figure of David di Meola whose actions bear out Michel's theory that sexuality is 'a useless, dangerous and regressive function' and as such must be done away with (*A*, 320).

If the wretched Bruno remains at heart the chubby, pasty and victimized omega male, then Francesco di Meola's son, David, with his raw animal beauty, his 'long, thick phallus' and 'big, hairy balls' is the definitive alpha male. An increasingly monstrous figure who progresses from seduction to sexual sadism of the most depraved kind, di Meola is a modern Neanderthal who 'had done nothing more than to extend and to put into practice the principles of individual freedom advocated by his father' (*A*, 249, 263). A paradigmatic figure of Jameson's famous aphorism the 'sixties gone toxic', di Meola's brand of gladiatorial masculinity fares well in the new sexual marketplace of the 1960s and '70s. Despite brief but ecstatic moments of erotic fulfilment, none of Houellebecq's protagonists can ever hope to match up to di Meola, a sexual athlete who has slept with more than five hundred women and who represents the 'logical conclusion' of his father's sexual conquests among the incense sticks and Afghan rugs. In characteristic Houellebecquian style that reads more like a sociological treatise than a novel, we learn that di Meola's sexual degeneration evolves from a relatively innocuous serial promiscuity into monstrously sadistic sex acts and eventually the production of pornographic 'snuff' films. It is a 'really disgusting story' but no more that the 'logical conclusion' of 'the principles of individual freedom advocated by his father' (*A*, 253). The façade of hippy spirituality now dropped, sexuality reverts to an orgiastic savagery that confirms the novel's thesis that the sixties prompted a 'return to the true nature of desire' which inevitably leads to murderous violence against the weak (*A*, 125). A biographical study of David di Meola, *From Lust to Murder: A Generation* (published in French as *Génération meurtre*), clearly explicates this message lest it not be already sufficiently clear: '… like their master, the Marquis de Sade, they were pure materialists – libertines forever in search of new and more violent sensations' and 'the destruction of the moral values in the Sixties, Seventies, Eighties, and Nineties was a logical, almost inevitable, process' (*A*, 252).

Anti-feminism

For women in Houellebecq's fiction, the legacy of '68 is decidedly more destructive as feminism has made them 'complicit with the individualistic ethos of capitalism' in ways that differ from their male contemporaries. For the feminists of '68, ageing involves not only the trials of physical decay but also the recognition that they brought their sexual obsolescence upon themselves and thus must accept 'their own inevitable defeat: for the market will move on, no product can dominate indefinitely'.[38] The most unpleasant denunciation is reserved for older women; feminists of 'the old school', who are the subject of a volley of derision and for whom '… their mature years brought only failure, masturbation and shame' (*A*, 126). Described as 'deranged old lefties who were probably all HIV positive', they are 'intolerable at breakfast, but by the early evening the mystical morons were hopelessly vying with their daughters' (*A*, 121, 150). Sexual competition between generations, particularly between parents and children, is a recurring thematic in Houellebecq's meditations on sexuality and there are long passages devoted to a detailed explication of this thesis: 'Sexual desire is preoccupied with youth, and the tendency to regard ever-younger girls as fair game was simply a return to the norm; a return to the true nature of desire, comparable to the return of stock prices to their true values after a run on the exchange'. (*A*, 125) In *Platform*, Michel sees the time coming when he and his son will compete over the same females, a situation that Aldous Huxley envisages in *Brave New World* where advances in pharmacology will 'break down the distinction between youth and age' (*A*, 187). The *soixante-huitards* have 'endorsed a cult of youth over age …' and sexually liberated women in particular have 'shot themselves in the foot' as by the time 'they hit 40' feminists find themselves in a 'difficult position' and 'could hardly claim to be surprised when they, in their turn, were dismissed by succeeding generations'. 'As their flesh begins to age, the cult of the body, which they had done so much to promote, simply filled them with disgust for their own bodies' (*A*, 125). Men, on the other hand, can get away with ageing and could continue to enjoy the comparative sexual advantage in this Darwinist scenario as their period of physical attraction could be extended by successful public performance; those 'who had attained a certain intellectual, financial or social position fared much better in their pursuit of young women' (*A*, 126). To suggest that women had been the main promoters of the 'cult of the body beautiful' is a patently unfair and inaccurate observation but it is in accordance with the pervasive anti-feminism inhabiting all of Houellebecq's novels discussed here. This anti-feminism is countered by an over-idealized portrayal of women as naturally 'compassionate' and tender beings that inspires the slogan for Michel's biogenetic revolution: 'The future will be feminine' a take on the only slightly more clichéd advertising slogan employed by Monoprix 'The future is female'.

Houellebecq's representation of feminism in his novels is at best prejudiced and, in very many cases, defiantly fallacious. Always understood pejoratively as the destroyer of 'natural' sexual relations, feminism is depicted as little more than a new opportunity for the reification of sexuality that has resulted in widespread erotic dysfunction by destabilizing the categories of both masculinity and femininity, the weakening of the 'conjugal bond' and the wrecking of the 'personal domain' by an insistence on politicizing the personal. A staple feature across Houellebecq's oeuvre, anti-feminism reaches its apotheosis in *Platform* which builds upon the earlier mood of *Whatever* and *Atomised*, offering a more elaborately articulated anti-feminist invective through its narrative structuring conceit that proposes the 'solution' of Third World sex tourism for men unhappy with the demands of Western women 'who do not appreciate men'. But is this not a satirical suggestion in the mould of Jonathan Swift's modest proposal? How seriously can we take such an outrageous proposition? Before examining the particulars of anti-feminism in *Platform*, the question regarding the satirical (or not) nature of this proposition must be tackled.

It has now become something of a critical orthodoxy in Houellebecq scholarship to align oneself broadly for or against the seemingly reactionary agenda in his novels, or more precisely, to take a decisive critical position in relation to the narrative techniques employed to express controversial content. On one side of this critical debate, critics such as Dominique Noguez (2003) and Fernando Arrabal (2005) assert that Houellebecq's agenda is clearly a satirical one and thus any offence expressed along the way cannot be taken at face value.[39] Others see Houellebecq's writing as an 'insistent and acerbic critique of capitalism' that boldly offers a political agenda eclipsing all other concerns.[40] Those on the other side of this critical divide argue that satirical or otherwise, 'his texts express an unvarying and unambiguous stance on women, Islam, blacks, homosexuals, ecologists, Americans, etc. …' and despite his humorous agility in prodding the hallowed convictions of right and left alike, Houellebecq does so 'only to reveal an intellectual myopia of his own'.[41] In her essay 'La Barbarie postmoderne', Marie Redonnet acknowledges the interpretative dilemma posed by Houellebecq's ideologically double-voiced writing position and vigorously lambasts him for a 'hypocritical double-crossing'. His writing is, Redonnet claims, ideologically duplicitous as he '... can turn precisely the kind of objections made by readers considered too critical back against them: the reader who dares express a critical opinion is nothing more than a blinkered sheep, a censor, or an interrogator who wants to cast literature in the name of political correctness and right thinking'.[42] This 'damned if we do and don't' ideological impasse discourages us from speaking directly about difficult material, a critical stalemate recognized by Crowley as a 'pre-emptive closing down of the space of critical dialogue'.[43] Houellebecq's fiction, he suggests, both anticipates and deflects charges of being reactionary by a process, however inconsistent, of disavowal that seems to forestall critical positions: 'To criticize Houellebecq for the insistent presence of such material in his texts is, however, to already situate oneself in a position which these texts themselves criticize'.[44] The slippery ideological territory of Houellebecq's writing, then, requires more than a simple identification or censure of his 'modest proposal', rather it necessitates a direct engagement with what Crowley calls the prose's 'insulating frame'.[45] It is possible, however, to obtain some critical purchase, and even dare to 'express a critical opinion' on the anti-feminism in the novel, by examining how the ideological manoeuvres of *Platform* set up this anticipatory critical silencing. The novel's ostensibly satirical proposal of sex tourism, in many ways a logical conclusion of '68's call for sexual liberation, dissimulates a troubling gender politics. Rehearsing another obsessive concern of Houellebecq's, that of the 'ludicrous over-rating' of critical theory, in particular the work of Foucault, Lacan, Derrida and Deleuze, *Platform* invokes the figure of the un-socialized 'natural' woman in a quasi-primitivist sexual discourse that returns women to a pre-Foucauldian biological essence where they function as the site of solace from the wreck of culture (*A*, 376).

The most ubiquitous of Houellebecq's framing techniques is a somewhat crudely executed narrative ventriloquism in which potentially controversial material is thrown somewhere other than in the authorial voice; a strategy of disowning that 'disallows any authoritative meta-discourse' while simultaneously refusing 'the singularity of any one discourse'.[46] The following extract from *Atomised* in which a female character articulates a deep abhorrence of feminism perfectly exemplifies such a technique:

"Never could abide feminists …," continued Christiane when they were halfway up the hill. "Stupid bitches always going on about the washing up and the division of labour; they could never shut up about the washing up. Oh, sometimes they'd talk about cooking or vacuuming, but their favourite topic was the washing up. In a few short years, they managed to turn every man they knew into an impotent, whinging neurotic. Once they'd done that, it was always the same story – they started going on about how there were no real men anymore. They usually ended up ditching their boyfriend for a quick fuck with some macho idiot [...] Anyway, they fuck their way through a couple of bastards, maybe more if they're really pretty, and wind up with a kid. Then they're off making jam and collecting recipe cards from *Marie Claire*. It's always the same story." (*A*, 173–4)

This use of free indirect speech, what Douglas Morrey calls a 'facile device to evade responsibility' diverts the omniscience of the narrator into refocalized essayistic asides giving the impression that the ideas expressed are those of the characters and not of the author.[47] A similar technique is employed to deliver anti-Islamic comments though the voices of Arab characters who rather implausibly, but conveniently for the novel, express their disdain for Islam: 'Islam could only have been born in a stupid desert, among filthy Bedouins who had nothing better to do [...] than bugger their camels' (*P*, 251). This technique of narrative displacement is secondary, however, to the wider ideological framing of a critique of Western capitalism which forms a central element of the 'double-crossing' to which Redonnet refers.

Houellebecq's view of feminism is that it functions as an apolitical affective outcrop of neoliberal capitalism, and as such confirms his thesis of modern life as a process of '… setting into place of multiple relational exchanges that can be quickly renewed (between consumers and producers, between employers and businesses, between lovers), so as to promote a fluidity of consumption based on an ethic of responsibility, transparency and choice' (*P*, 63). This critique could, on the face of it, seem like a genuine criticism of neoliberal capitalism whereas in fact it is an attack on feminism couched as admiration for 'naturally' sensual women. Feminism is set up as a case study of Houellebecq's anti-'68 agenda, and in *Platform* a Manichean opposition is constructed between the 'good-natural' non-feminist woman versus the 'bad-unnatural' feminist woman, that is, the kind of woman who espouses even the most basic principles of feminism. An authentic, non-feminist femininity, represented by the Thai sex workers, 'a gift from heaven', and the main female character, Valérie, is represented as a sensual and sexual sanctuary from a ruinous capitalism and set in distinction to a 'bad' and inauthentic feminist femininity which is mercenary and emasculating, the very embodiment of capitalism (*P*, 316). Clearly, such a crudely drawn opposition is a profoundly regressive move against over 50 years of intellectual reflection on the complexities of sex, gender and sexuality and, in one sweeping gesture, the distinction between nature and culture is collapsed, reinstating a biological essentialism that audaciously ignores most, if not all, modern theories of gender as a social and cultural construction. At every turn then, *Platform* reverts to a regressive patriarchal discourse of a kind of sexual primitivism, a crude phallogocentrism that wipes out any trace of feminism from the face of the earth. In the novel, women exist as either harridans whose demands for sexual equality and help with the washing up drive men into the arms of non-feminist 'natural' women who are effortlessly affectionate, passive and, most important of all, sexually obedient, precisely the kind of self-sacrificing femininity that is the inspiration for Michel's biogenetic ideal. Such women, Kristeva argues, must be kept 'separate from and thus untainted by the social sphere', their subjectivity 'separated from reason, language and the symbolicity that [...] alters, socializes, and sexualizes it'.[48]

Houellebecq's female characters are there to seduce and seduction is their only real power. In this way they all enact Baudrillard's faintly whimsical suggestion that 'only by the power of seduction does woman master the symbolic universe'.[49] This seductive power is never permitted to come close to the messy business of life (none of his women, for example, have any friends) or to be involved in any wider social or cultural socialization that might threaten to politicize their sexual and gender identity. Exquisite, blank ciphers, Valérie and the Thai women function as conduits to an imagined sexual Eden where femininity is ontologized as nature itself. It is crucial that non-feminist women are emphatically not consumers of sexuality themselves but skilled practitioners in the lost art of sensuality. They know how to 'make' love in the real sense of making, pointing up a persistent anxiety, discussed earlier, in Houellebecq's work around the disappearance of physical skills and the spectre of a useless masculinity: 'Meanwhile people were working making useful commodities. They were productive. What had I produced in the forty years of my existence? To tell the truth, not very much' (*P*, 86). Once again, *Platform* portrays modern masculinity as more or less bewildered by its new role in the immaterial economy. Performing a kind of labour that is both intangible and indefinable, the narrator's job in the novel is abstract, even mysterious, even to him: 'I managed information, facilitated access to it and disseminated it; sometimes, too I carried out bank transfers ...' (*P*, 8). As we have seen, in a neoliberal and post-Fordist immaterial economy, the worker's role is no longer primarily the maker of things, but as an enabler and facilitator for the intensification of the possibilities of differentiated consumption which he must himself, as a consumer, learn to negotiate in all its variations. Young, beautiful and erotically generous, women function as the exact opposite of this; they are somehow *real*, authentic and above all, embodied in the present. A primitivized essential femininity functions as a compensation for the disappearance of traditional labour and gender roles as sexually abundant young female bodies and their 'small, strange, cleft organs' offer an abundant 'realness', even a quasi-spiritual deliverance, from a sense of masculine uselessness and unreality (*P,* 61). Tender, generous and sensually beguiling, the bodies of these 'natural' women, specifically their perfect genitals, are interpellated as a site of a lost immediacy and 'realness', functioning as what Fredric Jameson has called, albeit in a different context, utopian objects of compensation.[50] Simple, yet transformative auratic spaces, these 'strange cleft organs' are sites where every social and cultural tension and contradiction is reconciled within the gently welcoming folds of accommodating flesh. In a postmodern economy of signs characterized by the disappearance of the real, the female body, in its fleetingly youthful prime, offers a return to the natural and the lost purity of the thing itself. Michel's hobbyist enthusiasm for gazing mesmerized at young women's vaginas is, he says, one of his 'few remaining recognisable truly human qualities'; 'Watching pussy in motion cleared my head. The contradictory trends of contemporary video art, balancing the conservation of national heritage with support for living creativity [...] all of that quickly evaporated before the facile magic of a moving pussy' (*P,* 17, 62). Such sexual magic is nowhere more keenly demonstrated than in the tender erotic expertise of the Thai sex workers. At the moment of an implausibly mutual orgasm with Thai bar girl no. 47, Michel hugs her to him and feels profoundly 'reconciled' by the purity of the sexual experience (*P,* 118). Moreover, this reconciliation extends beyond the purely genital. Perfect examples of non-feminist femininity, Thai women desire a highly traditional domestic life with a strictly gendered division of labour that Western women have largely rejected as limiting and oppressive. Writing in *Phuket Weekly*, the owner of the Heart to Heart marriage agency in Bangkok, Mr Sawasanee, (another good example of Houellebecq's ideological ventriloquism) concludes his article by claiming to be helping 'modern Western women to avoid what they despise':

> There seems to be [...] a near perfect match between the Western men, who are
> unappreciated and get no respect in their own countries, and the Thai women,

who would be happy to find someone who simply does his job and hopes to come home to a pleasant family life after work. Most Western women do not want such a boring husband [...] [they] want someone who looks a certain way, and who has certain social 'skills', such as dancing and clever conversation, someone who is interesting and seductive. (*P*, 125)

In contrast, 'bad' femininity is one fatally corrupted by feminism's encouragement of women to put their own interests before that of their husbands and children, and to demand the right to autonomy and pleasure. Destroyed rather than emancipated by their newly liberated sexuality, women influenced by feminism find it difficult to experience real desire or pleasure as one character in *Platform* opines nostalgically: 'It's very rare now to find a woman who feels pleasure and who wants to give pleasure [...] you won't find a white woman with a soft, submissive muscular pussy anymore, that's all gone now' (*P*, 112, 145). The possibility of the submissive female is gradually disappearing in the West, compelling men to travel to Thailand to be present at the 'gentle and constant roll-call of Asian pussy' that offers them a natural, real sexuality (*P*, 108). The 'little Thai whores' then, are 'a godsend', a 'gift from heaven, nothing less' to men worn out trying to please difficult and un-sensual Western women who immodestly flaunt a commodified sexuality, one unworthy even, we are told, of his two French travelling companions Babette and Léa, of being Thai prostitutes (*P*, 316). The satirical intent, such as it is, seems to have worn off completely at this stage of the novel as every woman who is not a sex worker or Valérie is unpleasantly denounced for her failure to possess a gentle and 'natural' willingness to give sexual pleasure to men.

This attack on feminism is equally explicit in the opening pages of *Whatever* where, at an office leaving party, a woman described as a 'stupid bitch' performs a striptease to the indifference of the assembled partygoers. More ironic than earnest, the woman's performance underscores the ruination of a natural female eroticism and just before he passes out in a drunken stupor, the narrator mutters to himself, 'The last dismaying dregs of the collapse of feminism'. (*W*, 3–4) In his drunken sleep he dreams of two women from his office singing the following ditty: 'If I go around bare-assed/It isn't to seduce you/If I show my hairy legs/It's because I want to' (*W*, 4). This ode to exhibitionist self-empowerment and the dismally received striptease crudely suggests feminism is responsible for rendering women virtually asexual in their refusal of the male gaze. Compare that scene, then, to the display of Thai women in a Bangkok bar whose acceptance of the male gaze is central to their appeal:

On the dance floor a dozen girls swayed gently to some sort of retro disco beat. Some of them wore white bikinis, others had taken their tops off and were wearing only G-strings. They were all about twenty, they all had golden brown skin, supple exciting bodies. An elderly German was sitting in front of a Carlsberg at the table on my left [...] He stared at the bodies moving before his eyes, completely hypnotized ... the girls left the stage, to be replaced by a dozen others wearing garlands of flowers around their hips and busts. Slowly, they turned around, the garlands occasionally revealing a breast or the top of the buttocks. The old German still stared at the stage [...] He was in paradise. (*P*, 106)

In this bucolic scene of sexual intoxication, the male customer is overwhelmed with the possibility of the proffered female bodies, all of them smooth and unresisting with little sense of any agency beyond the simple financial trans-action around sexual intercourse. It is important to note here that the economic dynamics of sexual exchange for which feminism is blamed, that is the opening up of sex to the forces of demand and supply, do not apply to the sexual economy of Thai prostitution, which is praised unconditionally for its cheerfully tender sale of sex. The heavily romanticized nudity of the bar display and the subsequent sexual intercourse with sex workers Ôon and Sin form part of a kind of sexual pastoral in which labouring brown (Third World) bodies are rendered as uncom-plicated sites of pleasure. Easily readable non-Western bodies possessing neither subtext or context, the Thai women offer life-affirming sex to Western men with an expertise and tenderness that combines the maternal – some tenderly bathe and dry their customers after sex – and the sexually compliant 'slut' (*P*, 115).

Any ethical complications of the sex industry have erased by the women's blissfully transformative sensuality which elevates the sex workers to a quasi-sublime realm of sensual and undemanding idealized femininity long since destroyed by Western feminism: 'In Thailand [...] everyone can have what they desire, and everyone can have something good' (*P*, 74). It is left to the 'plump, shrewd faced' feminist, Josiane, to articulate any ethical concerns around prostitution. Described in surpassingly offensive terms as 'exactly the kind of bitch who'd made me give up studying literature many years before', Josiane embodies feminist censoriousness 'trotting out tired political positions' (*P*, 48, 78). Compared to the writers of the *Guide du Routard* as one of those 'Protestant humanitarian cunts' with 'nasty little faces', Josiane exists only to reproach and condemn in her exaggeratedly anti-sex utterances (*P*, 51). A cartoon version of a 'sex-negative' 1980s feminism, her disapproval of sex tourism represents a feminist sexual politics that is distinct from the 'bare-assed' sexual exhibitionism more characteristic of post-feminism. Disregarding any historical specificity or cultural or ideological complexity, feminism is reduced to two exceptionally simple caricatures of its second and third waves, both held in equal contempt. In their timely examination of the individualist and consumerist turn in 1990s post-feminism, Yvonne Tasker and Diane Negra describe the ways in which criticisms of earlier feminist politics of the 1970s and 1980s make use of an 'invented social memory of feminist language' that characterizes feminist critique as 'shrill, bellicose and parsimonious' sex-negative ranting.[51] This is precisely the purpose of the character Josiane whose only function in the novel is to articulate the 'unsexy' griping of an imagined feminist sexual politics. The character of Valérie, on the other hand, expresses the possibility of an essential and 'natural' femininity, untouched by any social or cultural change.

On their first meeting, Michel's initial impression of Valérie is striking for its immediate appreciation of her passivity: 'she wasn't demanding, she really was a nice girl' with a pleasing 'canine docility', who is 'just submissive in general, and maybe ready to look for a new master' (*P*, 43, 45). Valérie's sexual charms are subtle, even demure; thus, it is only on closer inspection that Michel notices that she has a 'pretty hot mouth' that is 'just ready to swallow the spunk of a true friend', which of course she will do regularly just before serving Michel his morning coffee in bed before going off to work her 'insane hours' (*P*, 43, 45). Lecturing Valérie on how she possesses the real sensuality of a non-feminist woman, Michel commands her 'Suck me' ... 'You see', he says, 'I say "suck me" and you suck me. When actually, you didn't feel the desire to do so [...] Offering your body as an object of pleasure, giving pleasure unselfishly; that's what Westerners don't know how to do anymore' (*P*, 244). She is praised, above all, for possessing the most clichéd attribute of femininity '... one of those creatures who are capable of devoting their lives to someone else's happiness' (*P*, 360). Sexually adventurous, Valérie is, however, crucially not visibly 'sluttish' like her travelling companions Babette and Léa, or the Russian teenage girls who, Michel scornfully notes, 'had attained the pinnacle of sluttishness [...] the sleazy little cocksuckers' (*P*, 353). Like the Thai women, Valérie is outwardly modest in her sexuality; even when performing the most audacious of sexual acts she possesses a 'simple joy, innocent and eternally blessed' (*P*, 276). Thus, the Thai sex workers have their exact romantic counterpart in the sexually obliging and industrious Valérie who cheerfully works twelve hour days to promote sex tourism in South East Asia, Africa and South America in between episodes of uninhibited sex with Michel and an assortment of sexual partners. In fact, Valérie is given the dubious accolade of being almost as sexually skilled as a prostitute: '… before Valérie I had never met a single girl who could come close to a Thai prostitute' (*P*, 206). With her perky breasts and supple vagina, at 28 Valérie has the body of a 17-year-old (the optimum age of sexual attractiveness in Houellebecq's fiction), with 'breasts as firm as ever […] arse amazingly round too, without a trace of fat' (*P*, 58). Passive but boldly bi-sexual, devoted to her 'master' and younger looking than her years, Valérie is the incarnation of the phallonarcissistic imagination; the ideal Houellebecquian woman. However, while she is endlessly sexually accommodating, she is crucially (and wholly implausibly) lacking in any previous significant sexual experience which prevents her from being classified as 'an old slag', like the Russian teenagers. It is imperative that 'good' women have not participated in long term sexual promiscuity as this, just like psychoanalysis, destroys a capacity for romantic love and sensual innocence. This idea of sexual innocence is subject to a typical Houellebecquian double-standard. Sexual promiscuity is inherently ruinous for European women for whom 'Love as a kind of innocence and as a capacity for illusion, as an aptitude for epitomizing the whole of the other sex in a single loved being rarely resists a year of sexual immorality, and never two'; but this is not the case, however, for Thai sex workers or for the men who pay for their sexual services (*W*, 113).

Depicted as psychologically and intellectually blank, Valérie crucially does not recognize or realize her exchange value in the sexual marketplace and is completely disengaged from consumption, sexual and otherwise: 'No doubt she could have made a bit more of herself …' (*P*, 58). Protected from the vicissitudes of the sexual open market by her long working hours, she is unlike most Lilith-like Western women who are focused on the highly commodified processes of seduction. This is the *Sex and the City* 'high–maintenance' version of liberal feminism that increasingly came to define feminism in popular culture in the 1990s.[52] Michel describes Parisian women in precisely these terms, depicting sexual encounters with them as little more than sexual pantomimes consisting of an 'élitist, trashy, bizarre seduction that was not the least bit erotic' (*P*, 206). In this way, then, third-wave feminism is charged with producing sexually calculating women, the foot soldiers of neoliberal capitalism, who approach love and sex with the deadening spirit of consumption as if they were shopping for shoes. In complete contrast, Valérie is uninterested in material or sexual consumption, manifesting '… a complete indifference to Kenzo blouses and Prada handbags …' (*P*, 271). 'By the time she sat her *bac*, she had more or less given up (on sex)' and for ten years before she meets our narrator 'what she was lacking, essentially, was the desire to seduce' (*P*, 271). Concurring with the narrator's characterization of modern women, Valérie happily agrees that Western men need the restorative and tenderly expert touch of sex workers who seem not only willing but cheerful in their work unlike, the 'sexy, cool' Parisian women who need to be dined and talked to before the serious job of sex can begin (*P*, 362):

> It's rare now to find a woman who feels pleasure and who wants to give pleasure. On the whole, seducing a woman you don't know, fucking her, has become a source of irritations and problems. When you think of all the tedious conversation you have to put up with just to get a girl into bed, only to find out she's a second-rate lover who bores you to fuck with her problems, goes on at you about her exes – incidentally giving you the impression that you're not exactly up to scratch […] it's easy to see why men might prefer to save themselves the trouble by paying a small fee […] they find it easier just to go and find a whore. Actually, not a Western whore, they're not worth the effort, they're real human debris. (*P*, 145–6)

Presented as the age of no return for female sexuality and beauty, Houellebecq's novels systematically condemn women over 40, particularly those who have grown up with the feminist movement, to a de-sexualized decrepitude. Charged with having brought this sexual obsolescence on themselves by their allegiance to feminism, such women are depicted as pitiful losers in the new libidinal economy, living out their remaining years in isolation and unrequited sexual longing. While the male clientele of the Thai brothel bars are described in sympathetic, even tender terms, middle-aged women who seek similar paid sexual encounters are described as repugnant and wretched figures. Sitting in a Cuban bar, a group of 'fifty-something *québécoises*' with their 'aged, worn-out bodies' are seen as grotesque, even lethal, in their hideous sexuality: '… they were thickset and tough, all teeth and blubber, talking incredibly loudly; it wasn't difficult to understand how they had buried their husbands so quickly […] As the ageing hunk approached the table, they shot him amorous glances, almost becoming women again in the process' (*P*, 215).

Far from liberating individuals from the dynamics of consumer capitalism, Houellebecq suggests that '68 merely intensified the opportunities for the commodification of sexuality. While *Platform* does offer a compellingly splenetic, and at times fiercely original, account of the affects of neoliberal consumerism on sexuality, it is one finally compromised by its failure to achieve real complexity in both its logic and range. In short, the novel fails as critique as its vision of gender politics is finally too limited, resorting to an intellectually spurious concept of the 'natural' to articulate the concerns of culture. Standing metonymically for a more general sense of what Houellebecq has called the 'spineless political correctness' of culture, feminism can only be argued away back to the natural by a facile process of gender re-essentialization.[53] It may well be, however, as many have argued, that this failure of ideological complexity in the novel is precisely the point and that Houellebecq's writing points up the collapse of meaningful critique in a system so totally reified that no speaking position exists outside of its contaminated heart. Such a textuality would require a narrative and ideological balancing-act in which the text is simultaneously complicit with, and critical of, its own subject. The enthusiasm with which the idea of the 'natural' woman is evoked in *Platform* effectively compromises the novel's satirical intentions and points up the lack of any ideological distance from the subject matter which is essential for the production of real critique.

If, in Houellebecq's view, '68 destroyed the possibility of a natural, essential femininity, replacing it with a calculating economic subject, then in a broader sense sex has also been destroyed as it was encouraged to move increasingly away from its traditional moral and emotional constraints. Thus, we read in *Atomised* it is only natural that 'having exhausted the possibilities of sexual pleasure, it was reasonable that individuals, liberated from the constraints of ordinary morality, should turn their attentions to the wider pleasures of cruelty …' (*A*, 252–3). It is to that downward trajectory of post-'68 sexuality that I now turn.

Notes

1 Kristin Ross, *May '68 and its Afterlives* (Chicago: University of Chicago Press, 2002), 184–5.

2 Michallat, 314.

3 Karl Marx, *Poverty of Philosophy* (Chicago: Charles H. Kerr and Company, 1920, orig. pub 1847), 33.

4 Philippe Sollers, *Éloge de l'infini* (Paris: Gallimard, 2001), 902. See also Armine K. Mortimer, 'The Third Closet: Sollers's War', *Yale French Studies* 'Turns to the Right?', 16, 117 (2009) 169–82.

5 Serge Halimi, 'France: Sarkozy's Old Familiar Song', *Le Monde diplomatique*, http://mondediplo.com/2007/06/02france [accessed 8 July 2012]. On the use of '68 in French politics, see Daniel A. Gordon, 'Liquidating May '68? Generational

Trajectories of the 2007 Presidential Candidates', *Modern and Contemporary France*, 16,2 (2008), 143–59.

6   Gilles Lipovetsky, 'May '68, or The Rise of Transpolitical Individualism', in *A New French Thought Political Philosophy*, ed. Mark Lilla (New Jersey: Princeton University Press, 1994), 216).

7   See Nina Power and Alberto Toscano, 'The Philosophy of Restoration: Alain Badiou and the Enemies of May', *Boundary 2*, 36, 1 (2009), 27–46, 29.

8   François Noudelmann and Andre Piggott, 'A Turn to the Right: "Genealogy" in France since the 1980s', *Yale French Studies*, 116/117 (2009), 7-19, 9.

9   Noudelmann, 8.

10   'Turns to the Right?', *Yale French Studies*, Michael Johnson and Lawrence Schehr (eds), 116/117 (2009), 1–4, 2.

11   Luc Ferry and Alain Renaut, *French Philosophy of the Sixties: An Essay on Antihumanism*, trans. Mary Schakenber Cattap (Amherst: University of Massachusetts Press, 1990), xxxiii, 19. See also Alain Minc's *L'Avenir en face* (Paris: Seuil, 1984) and his notion of '*le capitalisme soixante-huitard*'.

12   Works on the meaning and legacy of May 1968, particularly around its fortieth anniversary in 2008, are too numerous to be listed in full here. On the specific connections between Sade and May 1968 in Houellebecq's writing see Liza Steiner, *Sade-Houellebecq, du boudoir au sex-shop* (Paris: Éditions L'Harmattan, 2009), (36–6); Robert Gildea, 'Forty years on: French writing on 1968 in 2008', *French History*, 23, 1 (2009), 109–18; '*68, Une Histoire collective*, Philippe Artières and Michel Zancarini-Fournel (eds) (Paris: La Découverte, 2008); Julian Bourg, *From Revolution to Ethics: May '68 and Contemporary French Thought* (Montreal & Kingston: McGill-Queen's University Press, 2007); *Mai-Juin '68*, Dominique Dammam et al. (eds) (Paris: Editions de l'Atelier, 2008); and Michael Seidman, *The Imaginary Revolution: Parisian Students and Workers in 1968* (New York and Oxford: Berghahn Books, 2004). For a perspective on '68 as primarily a youth revolt see Edgar Morin, 'Mai '68: Complexité et ambiguïté', *Pouvoirs*, 39 (1986), 71–80, and Raymond Aron's seminal reactionary reading in *The Elusive Revolution*, trans. Gordon Clough (New York: Praeger, 1969). See also processes of a conference 'Mai '68 en quarantaine' by Boris Gobille et al., http://colloque-mai68.ens-lsh.fr/ [accessed 15 May 2008]; and Keith Reader (with Khursheed Wadia), *The May 1968 Events in France: Reproductions and Interpretations* (New York: St Martin's Press, 1993).

13   It is important to note that the for and against '68 involves a complex set of debates that ranges right across the ideological spectrum. Just as there was no such thing as a unique and singular '*pensée '68*' there really cannot be said to be a unified 'anti-'68 thought'. Serge Audier notes that many of the intellectuals who have been dubbed as adherents of *la pensée '68* have varying responses to

it. 'Pierre Bourdieu', Audier notes, 'spoke of a "failed revolution" that sparked a reactionary counter-attack [...] As for Jacques Derrida, he was wary of spontaneity. As he put it in an interview: "I was not a sixty-eighter". Roland Barthes was critical of the riots and Claude Lévi-Strauss literally detested them. One exception was Gilles Deleuze in Lyon.' http://www.france24.com/en/20080427-may-%E2%80%9968-multitude-ideas-essay-philosophy [accessed 14 August 2012].

14 Serge Audier, *La pensée anti-'68: Essai sur une restauration intellectuelle* (Paris: Editions La Découverte, 2008), 21.

15 Jean-Pierre Le Goff, *Mai '68, ou l'héritage impossible* (Paris: La Découverte, 2006) 20.

16 Le Goff, 457.

17 Régis Debray, 'A Modest Contribution to the Rites and Ceremonies of the Tenth Anniversary', trans. John Howe, *New Left Review*. 115 (1979), 46.

18 Ross, *Afterlives*, 3. Her notion of the 'afterlives' of '68 attempts to reinvest the moment with some of its original progressive intentionality that has been lost, she believes, in a general rightwards turn in French culture.

19 Ross, *Afterlives*, 6.

20 Kristin Ross, 'Establishing Consensus: May '68 in France as Seen from the 1980s', *Critical Inquiry*, 28, 3 (2002), 650–76, 652.

21 Boltanski and Chiapello, xxxv.

22 Sebastian Budgen, A New 'Spirit of Capitalism', *New Left Review* (Jan–Feb 2000), http://newleftreview.org/II/1/sebastian-budgen-a-new-spirit-of-capitalism [accessed 30 July 2011].

23 Boltanski and Chiapello, 29.

24 Ibid., 28.

25 Boltanski and Chiapello, xxxvi. Houellebecq's example of this is seen in the figure of the *soixante-huitard* Jacques Maillot, the founder of Nouvelles Frontières who made an effortless switch from barricade to boardroom.

26 Gilles Lipovetsky, '"Changer la vie" ou l'irruption de l'individualisme transpolitique', *Pouvoirs*, 39 (1986), 99, 98.

27 Raoul Vaneigem, *The Revolution of Everyday Life* (London: Rebel Press, 2010), 114.

28 Harvey, *The Condition of Postmodernity*, 63.

29 Crowley, 'Wreckage', 18.

30 Cruickshank, 141.

31 Abecassis, 284.

32 Gopnik, 61.

33 *Public Enemies*, 41. Houellebecq adds that his hatred of psychoanalysis is based upon an 'extraordinary overestimation' of his own character 'which leads me

to believe that no confession can ever exhaust the indefinite richness of my personality, that one could draw endlessly on the ocean of my possibilities'.

34 Pierre Rosanvallon, *La démocratie inachevée: Histoire de la souveraineté du peuple en France* (Paris: Gallimard, 2000, 2003), 386–87.

35 Michel Foucault, *The History of Sexuality, Volume 1: An Introduction*, trans. Robert Hurley (New York: Vintage Books, 1980), 149.

36 See Sheila Rowbotham's remark on the 'prevailing culture of masculinity' in most of the counterculture until the middle of the 1970s in *Promise of a Dream: A Memoir of the 1960s* (London: Allen Lane, 2000).

37 Ben Jeffery, *Anti-Matter: Michel Houellebecq and Depressive Realism* (Winchester: Zero Books, 2011), 9.

38 Crowley, 'Wreckage', 21.

39 Dominique Noguez, *Houellebecq, en fait* (Paris: Editions Fayard, 2003) and Fernando Arrabal, *Houellebecq* (Paris: Cherche Midi, 2005). See also Gavin Bowd, 'Michel Houellebecq and the Pursuit of Happiness', *Nottingham French Studies*, 42 (2002), 28–39.

40 Jerry Varsava, 'The Dialectics of Self and Community in Toni Morrison and Thomas Pynchon', *Contemporary Literature*, 4 (2002), 794–803, 803.

41 Ralph Schoolcraft and Richard Golsan, 'Paradoxes of the Postmodern Reactionary: Michel Rio and Michel Houellebecq', *Journal of European Studies*, 37 (2007), 349–71, 365, 366. On the question of Houellebecq's ideological complicity with his subject matter see also Michel Waldberg, *La Parole putanisée* (Paris: La Différence, 2002) and Nancy Huston, 'Writers and Writing: Michel Houellebecq: The Ecstasy of Disgust', *Salmagundi*, (2006), 20–39.

42 Marie Redonnet, 'La Barbarie postmoderne', *Art Press*, 244 (1999), 60–4, 62.

43 Crowley, 'Wreckage', 19.

44 Ibid., 20.

45 Ibid., 22.

46 Schoolcraft and Golsan, 365.

47 Morrey, 'Sex and the Single Male', 110.

48 Julia Kristeva, *Powers of Horror* (New York: Columbia University Press, 1982), 162–3.

49 Jean Baudrillard, 'The Ecliptic of Sex', in *Seduction*, trans. Brian Singer (London: Macmillan, 1988), 8.

50 Fredric Jameson, *Marxism and Form* (New Jersey: Princeton University Press, 1974), 59.

51 *Yvonne Tasker and Diane Negra, Interrogating Postfeminism: Gender and the Politics of Popular Culture* (Durham, NC: Duke University Press, 2007), 3.

52 On post-ideological feminism deploying consumption as a strategy and the depoliticization of feminism in the 1990s see Angela McRobbie, *The Aftermath*

of Feminism (London: Sage, 2009); Rosemary Hennessy, *Profit and Pleasure: Sexual Identities in Late Capitalism* (New York, Routledge, 2000); Tania Modleski, *Feminism Without Women* (London: Routledge, 1991); and J. Baumgardner and A. Richards, 'Feminism and femininity: Or how we learned to stop worrying and love the thong' in *All About the Girl*, A. Harris and M. Fine (eds) (London: Routledge, 2004), 59–69. See also Nancy Fraser's 'Heterosexism, Misrecognition, and Capitalism: A Response to Judith Butler', *New Left Review*, 1/228, (March–April 1998), 140–9.

53 *Interventions*, 75.

5

Sex: 'a second system'

On every floor, human beings were improving, or trying to improve, their
social, sexual or professional skills or find their place within the cosmos.

(*Atomised*, 154)

With a take-no-prisoners declaration in the prologue that the 'latter half of the
twentieth century' was a 'miserable and troubled' age, *Atomised* wrestles with
what Julian Barnes has called, in perhaps in a somewhat overstated way, 'big
game'. Moving at a substantial narrative clip through the last hundred years or
so of French history, the novel takes in a broad chronological palette, at times
reading like an extended, if somewhat partisan, philosophical–sociological
essay on late twentieth-century history. Its starting point is the grandparental
generation of late nineteenth-century France, then hastens on to the first two
post-World War Two decades, particularly attending to the major cultural,
economic and social changes that took place between the 1950s and the 1990s;
the post-industrial decline in manufacturing and agriculture; the post-'68 'sexual
revolution'; New Age 'philosophy'; the decline of organized religion; the concept
of the 'body beautiful' and the subsequent rise in the popularity of cosmetic
surgery; the collapse of the nuclear family and rise of single person living; Max
Planck's theory of quantum energy; the rise of Minitel and the advent of the
internet. Leaping forward in great chronological jolts, the narrative concludes
in the near future, 2079, where technical advances in biogenetics have solved
the 'problem' of human sexuality as cloned human beings are able to fully auto-
eroticize. Thus, they are rid of the troubling vicissitudes of sexual desire and the
need to engage with other bodies for either pleasure or reproduction.

Written in what one critic describes as 'overwrought declinist rhetoric',
Atomised presents the history of the West (exemplified here by France) as one
of deterioration, an unstoppable downward movement towards social and
ontological disintegration that inexorably moves towards its eschatological
conclusion in the novel where the last human beings have vanished from the

face of the earth.[1] As noted earlier, the discourse of *déclinisme*, a particularly although not uniquely French phenomenon, holds that France is in terminal cultural and social decline, living in the shadow of its faded national glory, and in danger of losing its much-cherished exceptional status.[2] The France of *Atomised*, and indeed of all Houellebecq's novels, is a culturally and intellectually diminished space; a politically troubled nation state staring down its own reactionary nature in the reluctant knowledge that it has not fully addressed its colonial past and post-colonial present. No longer the nation of Racine, Molière and Proust, France is a country, as Houellebecq mischievously points out, more culturally influenced by the rap of Snoop Dog than by the Duchess of Guermantes. *Atomised* registers France's ineluctable sliding, whether imagined or real, into the 'ranks of the less developed countries' and into what Emily Apter describes as a kind of cultural and socio-economic 'neo-Medievalism', a regressive social and geographic segregation that is, she claims, incipient in many Northern European countries which are fast becoming spaces of 'abrogated sovereignty, atrophied national consciousness, and barbaric cultural atavisms'. Apter regards the *déclinisme* of Houellebecq's writing '... with its images of existential bleakness and anarchic regionalism' and 'Dark Age version of global culture' as one of the most striking contemporary articulations of this 'new medievalism'.[3]

The most significant part of this declinist discourse in *Atomised* and elsewhere in Houellebecq's work coheres, however, not around national identity or cultural disintegration but around sex; specifically, the changed nature of sexual desire as it becomes liberated from repressive societal strictures and religious interdiction and floated on the free market in an 'authentic free enterprise culture' of neoliberalism (*W*, 15). Most of Houellebecq's male characters spend their lives maneuvering themselves towards some sort of sexual inclusion. Alternately thinking about, looking for and paying for sex, they are all, however, finally expelled from this sexual domain into a desireless, monadic isolation that is without sexual difference or social distinction. Houellebecq's frequently quoted declaration on the 'strictly equivalent' relationship between sex and commerce in *Whatever* is central to his thesis that sexual liberalism unleashed a 'violently hierarchical' logic dividing people into either sexual paupers or princes. This thesis is, as we have seen, rehearsed in all of his novels but nowhere so strikingly as in *Atomised*.[4] Sex, the narrator muses, operates 'as a second system of differentiation' that can produce the 'phenomena of *absolute pauperization*. Some men make love every day; others five or six times in their life, or never [...] It's what's known as "the law of the market"' (*W*, 99). The thesis that 'economic liberalism' is the 'extension of the domain of the struggle' to 'all ages and classes of society' extends most agonizingly into the sexual domain, and is explored in *Atomised* through the antithetical responses of Bruno and Michel to the commodifed sexual economy that exists around them. Tracing the effects of the liberalization of sexuality in post-'68 France, examined in detail in the previous chapter, *Atomised* describes a culture in which sex, far from being either an ecstatic erotic union or a meaningful human connection, has become simply another product to be obtained and consumed. In this way, then, sex is little more than an onanistic gesture of individuation and narcissism, consonant with the entrepreneurial view of the self as human capital that makes any engagement with another individual part of a calculated transaction rather than an organic relation. Sex becomes, then, part of the desublimated *monde houellebecquien* in which imitate relations between humans are another type of currency and investment under the new biopolitical conditions of neoliberalism, a proposition illuminated for the reader in one of Houellebecq's helpful explanatory aside: 'Pleasure and desire, [which] as cultural, anthropological, and secondary phenomena, explain little about sexuality itself; far from being a determining factor, they are in fact themselves sociologically determined' (*A*, 292).

In the years immediately following 1968, sexual liberalization led to what Houellebecq calls, rather over-simplistically, a 'totally liberated sexual system' in which he suggests there exists a directly isomorphic relationship between economics and sexuality.[5] As we saw in the previous chapter, one of the prevailing anti-'68 views that has developed since the 1980s has characterized the countercultural opposition to a technocratic and authoritarian society as a 'psychodrama', a 'soft' revolution that was merely the precursor to individualism and the incursion of a commercial ethos into the affective domain. Every decennial anniversary of May '68 was accompanied by an upsurge in its interpretation which can be broadly speaking summarized, as Julian Bourg notes in *From Revolution to Ethics* (2007), as gathered around either positive or negative poles, viewing 'May 1968 as either the sign of a marvellous new beginning, or, with increasing frequency after the mid-1970s, as the sign of nihilistic, individualistic and anti-political tendencies'.[6] The compulsion to sexual pleasure is blamed, then, on the hedonism of the *soixante-huitards*. The demand for pleasure was part of '68's insistence on notions of authenticity for the masses long denied to them by the bourgeoisie, as libertinage had historically been the exclusive prerogative of the aristocracy. As Guillebaud notes, 'in the leaflets, slogans, and proclamations disseminated during and after May 1968, one may find this insistent denunciation of the "fascistic", "bourgeois" and "commercial" order, which prohibits the free sexuality of the masses in order to better exploit their productive force. One finds, in parallel, the denunciation of the *principle of authority*, presented as the principal instrument of this oppression'.[7] In these terms then, sexual freedom was part of an anti-commercialism and a rejection of bourgeois capitalism – a way of cocking a snook at the 'straights' and the 'squares'. According to Houellebecq, taking his cue from a substantial body of anti-'68 thought in France, this countercultural impulse gets quickly swallowed up by capitalism and becomes coterminous with the very same capitalism it had been trying to resist. Moreover 'free sexual consumption', as Guillebaud argues, 'far from being prejudicial to the new established order, meets its needs and satisfies its interests'.[8]

In *Atomised*, as elsewhere in his writing, it is very clear to which of these two camps Houellebecq belongs. He unequivocally presents sexuality as an area of human life ruined by what he sees as the indisputably harmful effects of sexual liberation. This is, of course, in itself not entirely without some mileage as a proposition and, of course, many feminist and queer theorists have noted that sexuality is an affective zone in the life-world where the 'cultural is grafted onto the economic' in some plainly visible ways and as such emerges as 'a highly contested and conflicted zone'.[9] What Houellebecq does is intensify the relationship between culture and commerce, to conjoin, as Cruickshank notes, 'the private crisis of failure in sexual competition to the public struggle of neoliberal economic competition'.[10] Houellebecq's oft-quoted passage cited above that posits a homological relationship between sex and economics in which the 'sexual system stands as a perfect analogue to the economic' is, as I have been arguing, one of the recurring premises of Houellebecq's work, and in fact may be *the* most important thematic. Although independent of money *per se*, sexuality is profoundly affected by the economic and at every turn in the novels considered here it is depicted as a perpetual hierarchical struggle subject to the 'law of the market' that creates a clear division between winners and losers.[11]

Sex and sexual desire are not only subject to the laws of the free and deregulated market, they become an integral part of the speculative entrepreneurial project of the self. The sexual subject of neoliberalism, as Shannon Winnubust argues, is encouraged to be an 'endlessly self-enhancing circuit of interest'; a self-sufficient space of inwardness for whom 'the notion of "freedom" is severed from any concern with the other—much less, the Other—as a meaningful site of relationality'. The logic of the neoliberal free-market is one, Winnubust continues, that permeates all intimate relations: 'Turned wholly towards the pleasure of maximizing one's interests, the neoliberal subject only registers a concern with others who are "outside" of oneself insofar as they present opportunities or obstacles to that endless self-enhancement'.[12] *Atomised*, then, turns a quasi-ethnographic gaze on the changing nature of the body as it becomes more fully interpellated as sexual capital. Once again, however, Houellebecq's position seems to straddle two seemingly incompatible ideological poles as his critique of post-'68 sexual liberation swings from right to left, coming to rest in some indeterminate space in between. Pointing up this ideological slipperiness, James Woods notes that Houellebecq's writing is 'right-wing, in that unrestrained sexuality is pinned on the degradations of the 1960s and on American self-indulgence; left-wing, in that unrestrained sexuality is likened, in Marxist fashion, to the ravages of the capitalist market'.[13] This indeterminancy, then, is the *rouge-brun* or greyish ideological timbre of *Atomised* that is as intriguing as it is infuriating.

The shift in France's middle-class attitudes towards sexuality is considered at length in Hervé Juvin's *The Coming of the Body* (2010) in which he describes the radical changes that have occurred in the space of 'less than two generations', a time during which there has been an 'abrupt abandonment of the world of dues and bonds for the world of the self and rights'. For a large part of France's middle class, argues Juvin, the lines of inheritance and patrimony have disappeared as vast tranches of 'business workers' do not live to accumulate wealth and pass it on but rather to consume and to pursue pleasure for its own sake. As the 'morality of satisfaction' gradually replaces the morality of repression and self-denial we move closer, Juvin says, to a scenario in which pleasure becomes a duty.[14] When this is the case, the body is put to work to fulfil the criteria that accompany that duty; it is worked out, made smooth, depilated, injected and filled until it is fit for sexual purpose and able to compete in a sexual marketplace where commodification produces a greatly weakened *jouissance*. This is a very profitable point of convergence for capital. By realizing that 'the desire to spend, for its own sake, could itself be marketed', as David Bennett notes, the cultural energies of advertising and marketing in the post-'68 years began to challenge 'the orthodoxies of neoclassical economics and its premise of *homo œconomicus*' with its rational calculations of utility versus cost, and produced a subject he calls '*homo desiderans*' or '*homo sexualis*' in 'whom desire exceeds reason and is always in excess of any potential object'.[15] As sexuality loses its subversive allure of transgression, it becomes democratized, almost ubiquitous; a product in a market where everything has an approximately equal value but where, in the flattening drone of consumption culture, everything becomes equally value-less. Assiduously targeted by the niche marketing tactics of a post-'68 sexual liberation, Bennett goes on, '… "dropping out" and "turning on" became the recreational route to full integration with consumer capitalism for the middle classes, who were finally bidden to abandon their self-definition as more repressed, more self-denying, more self-disciplining than the so-called "working masses"'.[16]

New social divisions are thus initiated by this idea of the body as sexual, as well as cultural, capital. In the hierarchies of inclusion and exclusion produced by liberalization of sexuality, Juvin suggests that a gap opens up in which those 'who lack the good fortune or the means to form stable, exclusive and unpaid […] relationships' have to make do with a second-hand or borrowed sexuality that is 'virtual, onanistic and paid for …'.[17] It is within this 'gap' that Bruno Clément and Michel Djerzinski live, surrounded by ever more urgent exhortations to find personal fulfilment through sex, an environment in which pleasure and desire 'must be constantly heightened, tweaked, and intensified by ever more finely tuned tools' and the pursuit of sexual pleasure, no longer belonging to the space of the carnivalesque or the festival, is a fundamentally commercial one that is central to the 'distinguishing promise of neoliberalism'. In such a scenario, then, sexuality is, as Winnubust argues:

> … no longer something to be feared, avoided, moderated or domesticated. In previous ontologies of Christianity, liberalism and even Marxism, pleasures were conceptualized as tied to desire, which was driven by a lack. In the social rationality of neoliberalism, these pleasures are unhinged from fulfilling any need or lack or desire: they are detached from any register of evaluation other than that of endless self-enhancement […] Compulsive repetition, indifferent to the object, becomes the meaning of 'enjoyment' for the neoliberal subject, displacing any teleological story of a subject fulfilling a need.[18]

In this way, then, sexuality is an integral part of the self-interested struggle at the heart of affective neoliberalism, an important part of its psychological ability to produce a certain type of subjectivity, or, as Dany-Robert Dufour puts it, to 'shrink heads'.[19] Viewed through Lyotard's idea of a libidinal economy, the yoking of sex to neoliberal economics is, as Morrey notes, to see that the workings of sexual desire are really 'contiguous to, and often overlapping with, the flow of capital and, as such, just as impersonal …'.[20] It is worth recalling again here that this is by no means a new insight. This link between the external economic order and the sexual one has long been noted by feminism; indeed, one of feminism's most valuable exposés has been the uncovering of the patriarchal basis of capitalism.

As I have discussed earlier, one of the most significant manoeuvres of neoliberalism is the conflation of the private and the public spheres so that gradually the personal and private domain is thoroughly occupied by what was previously external, nominally at least, to the self, that is, the economic sphere. Thus, the outside becomes inside and vice versa, a transformation that has some serious repercussions on sexuality. As Abecassis notes, every 'detail of the private and personal occupies a place within an erotic-consumer sphere [...] each detail is labelled and thus the whole fabric of the personal becomes integrated into the generalized economy driven by erotic marketing'.[21] This reduction of sexual desire to a mercantile transaction, 'an ideal trading opportunity',[22] produces very different effects on Michel and Bruno, eliciting paradigmatically contradictory responses; Michel withdraws altogether from the body into a virtually sexless world of scientific rationalism that seeks to surmount the problem of the body and sexuality through the promise of mechanical certainty while Bruno valiantly, but ineffectively, attempts to inhabit the overblown sexual system ruled over by 'Eros-driven marketing'. Both responses end, not only in a retreat from the contingent sensuality of everyday, but also in tragedy. Michel takes his own life driving over a cliff in Ireland; Bruno ends his days locked away in a psychiatric hospital, still visiting prostitutes but wholly incapable of feeling any sexual pleasure; the Michel of *Platform* ends his days alone in a sweltering, seedy room on Naklua Road after his lover, Valérie, is killed by terrorist bomb. This, then, is the arc of sensual withdrawal tracing the retreat from both desire and affect, and finally from life itself. This chapter examines the trajectory of that withdrawal through the antithetical 'solutions' Houellebecq offers to the problem of sex; either libertine participation or a stoic acceptance of failure and subsequent withdrawal, both of which, I argue, have the same end point – a kind of pure space in which the body and its libidinal energies are silenced and stilled.

A (very) brief history of sexuality

Adumbrated in a chapter of little more than nine pages, chapter four of *Atomised* offers a brief overview of some the key socio-economic changes of early twentieth-century France that provides a context for the emotional and sexual difficulties of the ill-fated half-siblings Michel and Bruno. The chapter opens with a description of the life of Michel's maternal grandfather, Martin

Ceccaldi. Born in 1882 in Corsica to 'illiterate peasants', Ceccaldi's movement away from the rigours of agricultural labour is used as a sociological case study; his life was to become 'entirely symptomatic of the role played by secularism throughout the Third Republic'(*A*, 24–5). Ceccaldi is a 'symptomatic individual': 'Carried forward by the sweep of history and their determination to be a part of it, *symptomatic* individuals lead lives, which are, in the main part, happy and uncomplicated'. Crucially, these types of individuals are more or less content with their levels of sexual activity within and occasionally outside of marriage. Encouraged by a sympathetic teacher who recognized the boy's aptitude for 'abstract thought' and who saw that he was gifted with a 'singular destiny', Ceccaldi is educated out of his social class, moving from the rural labouring classes into a career in engineering via the prestigious corridors of the École Polytechnique.

Giving a set of snapshots of certain '*symptomatic* individuals' rather than a detailed account of twentieth-century history, Houellebecq adopts a somewhat idiosyncratic, often scattershot, way of ordering these social groups: he sets the lives of particular individuals against those of another group designated as 'precursors'. This latter group are 'merely catalysts' rather than 'revolutionaries' or 'prophets' whose lives are linked to 'some form of social breakdown' and are thus are more 'torturous and confused' (*A*, 26). Michel and Bruno's wayward mother, Janine, belongs to this category. Unrestricted by loosening religious interdictions or moral prohibitions, she pursues a sexual trajectory which would have been unthinkable for the previous generation. Dancing *le bebop* in Paris with a dazzlingly ugly Sartre 'during the existential years', consorting with celebrities on the Riviera and enjoying a wide assortment of lovers, Janine's sexual attitudes and behaviour prefigure the imminent sexual revolution of the 1960s. Meeting the 'somewhat hirsute' young surgeon Serge Clément they become a prototypical 'modern couple', producing Bruno in 1956 (*A*, 28). Very quickly, however, they realize that 'the burden of caring for a small child was incompatible with their personal freedom' and before long separate (*A*, 28). Returning from a filming trip in China to their house in St Maxime, Serge encounters evidence of shocking maternal neglect when he finds their house full of naked, drunk people and the abandoned toddler Bruno whimpering wretchedly and crawling around alone in 'pools of urine or excrement' (*A*, 31). The child is sent off to live in Algeria with his maternal grandmother. Janine's relationship with the filmmaker Marc Djerzinski produces Michel in 1958 who is soon packed off to *his* grandmother as the couple go their separate ways. Not long after, she meets Francesco di Meola, the Italian–American co-founder of the Esalen hippie commune in Big Sur California, and moves to America to join this commune. She does not see her children for 15 years. Rejected and abandoned by their different sets of parents, Michel Djerzinski and Bruno Clément each grow up with the values of the grandparental rather than the parental generation.

Born at the tail end of the post-war Baby Boom in the 1950s, crucially, both boys are too young to experience the events of 1968, coming to sexual maturity in the decade of the 1970s at the end of the post-war spike in the birth rate when sexual liberalism has reached a certain apogee, in France at least, in terms of a so-called cultural permissiveness.[23] The 1970s occupy an important place in *Atomised*. In particular, 1974 is singled out as the year in which the growing 'moral relativism' reaches a critical point in French culture and society, an opinion borne out to some extent by the juridical events of that year: the Veil Act legalized abortion, adultery was removed from the penal code paving the way for divorce by mutual consent and the age of consent was lowered (*A*, 80). Culturally, there was a discernible escalation in the importance of the 'cult of the body', a new idea of the body as a perfectible product that could be improved by exercise and cosmetics. The popularity of 'exotic' foreign locales prevalent in magazines, on television and in the cinema was bound up into an eroticized discourse epitomized in films such as *Emmanuelle*, Just Jaeckin's 1974 soft porn film – 'a manifesto for the leisure industry'. This is a moment at which the idea of 'lifestyle' becomes a marketable product, part of a context of an increasingly hedonistic sense of freedom, particularly sexual freedom, catalysed undoubtedly by the decline in the influence of Catholicism in France. Under the 'law of the market' in a 'totally liberal economic system' a materialist way of life is established in which any idea of religious or spiritual transcendence is replaced by the ascendancy of 'determinist anthropology' which is 'more moderate in its ethical counsel' than the religious beliefs of the previous two centuries (*A*, 80–1).

Like many of their contemporaries, the brothers belong to what Houellebecq calls a 'sacrificed generation', one whose destiny lies not in the kinship relations of family and its attendant duties, affiliations and inheritances, but in an almost obligatory hedonism and sexual promiscuity that leaves little to pass on to future generations, something Bruno realizes in relation to his son: 'I work for someone else, I rent my apartment from someone else, there's nothing for my son to inherit. I have no craft to teach him [...] By the time he grows up, the rules I live by will be meaningless—the world will be completely different' (*A*, 201). Bruno attempts to join in the over-fired sexualized atmosphere in which he reaches adolescence. However, lacking the necessary physical allure to compete successfully in this new sexual marketplace, he spends most of his time watching enviously from the sidelines. While Bruno obsesses over getting women to have sex with him, Michel lies alone in his bed, staring at the radiator and thinking, not about sex but about the particle composition of the universe, his world view growing increasingly 'pitiless and mechanical'. Freed from erotic distraction, he can reflect on what his brother's sexual obsessions might mean in sociological and philosophical terms. Michel recognizes that Bruno is representative of his generation; 'his hedonistic world view and the forces that shaped his consciousness and his desires were common to an entire generation' (*A*, 212). It is, however, a hedonism devoid of much real pleasure.

Sharing a mother and united by the experience of parental abandonment, Michel and Bruno represent two opposing 'solutions' to the sexual predicament thrown up by the 'unrestrained economic liberalism' of their times and the saturation of culture by the 'compulsive, almost fetishistic desire for prepackaged pleasures' marking the era of sustained material prosperity in France spanning the years 1945–75: *Les Trente Glorieueses* (*A*, 27). This period saw major economic transformations in which France changed from being a largely rural, Catholic country into an industrialized and secular modern nation state. Noting that during this time there was a discernible ideological 'movement inward', Ross points out that the processes of modernization were regarded by some contemporary critics, such as Cornelius Castoriadis and Lefebvre, as encouraging an increasing 'privatization' that originated in the ideologically deadening energies of *la société de consommation*. This inward movement, suggests Ross, was 'echoed on the level of everyday life by the withdrawal of the new middle classes to their newly comfortable domestic interiors ... '; from this tastefully decorated life there developed a depoliticized 'ideology of happiness built around the new unit of middle-class consumption'.[24] *Atomised* articulates something similar, suggesting that the private space of the 'heart and home' was the last remaining fortification, a private bulwark, against the market: 'It is interesting to note that the "sexual revolution" is usually portrayed as a communist utopia whereas in fact it was simply another stage in the rise of the individual [...] the couple, and the family were to be the last bastion of primitive communism in a liberal society. The sexual revolution was to destroy the last unit separating the individual from the market. The destruction continues to this day' (*A*, 136).

The Manichean *weltanshuung* of *Atomised* entertains only two, equally unsatisfactory, rejoinders to this 'merciless' sexual marketplace: complete withdrawal into isolated rationalism or a self-indulgent and self-destructive, libertine participation. As noted above, either way these two responses lead to monadic solitude; death or madness. As the unhappy progeny of the first post-'68 generation, Bruno's and Michel's lives, then, are representative of the two, equally unappealing, ways in which to respond to sexual liberation. Should one simply profit from the availability of all forms of transgression on offer and fully participate in the sexual carnival? Or should one, in a gesture of complete asceticism, withdraw wholly and refuse the proliferation of desire in all its forms? These two alternatives are regarded by some critics as consistent with the 'either/or' moral universe of the seventeenth-century *moralistes*.[25] The opposition has been insightfully glossed by a number of the more perceptive Houellebecq critics. Jack Abecassis holds that Houellebecq is suggesting an antithetical opposition of St Paul against the Marquis de Sade, an idea taken up by Jerry Varsava who develops the idea of the Pauline/Sadean binary in an argument on contrasting ideological types of communitarianism.[26] Reformulated in more philosophical terms, Gerald Moore regards the opposing tendencies in Houellebecq's work as that of Nietzsche versus Schopenhauer. The lack of any position between these two equally dismal choices leads us finally to a feeling of despair. What is to be done? If both paths lead to the same end, that of complete deprivation of sensual and bodily life, are we with Bruno or Michel?

On the one hand, then, there is Michel, the monkish scientist whose legacy is the eradication of sexual desire through biotechnical means leading to the creation of a new asexual species. In many ways like a prototype of the affectless clones that his biogenetic work will eventually create, Michel becomes increasingly defined throughout his life by his inability to interact in any meaningful way with his fellow human beings: 'emotion would pass him by, sometimes tantalizingly close; others would experience happiness, and despair, but such things would be unknown to him, they would not touch him' (*A*, 99). Growing up in the small village of Charnay in the Yonne, Michel spends an idyllic, if lonely childhood, generously and lovingly raised by his grandmother. In December 1968, after the tumult of that year had passed by the villagers in Charnay, Michel and his grandmother move to just outside of Paris to Crécy-en-Brie. An introverted child, Michel's tastes tend early on towards moral and epistemological curiosity and as a small boy he 'feeds on knowledge', spending long hours reading *The Universe Explained*, a scientific journal aimed at children, and comics like *Pif gadget*, in which he identifies very closely with 'Black Wolf, the Lone Indian', the romantic hero-savage who 'instinctively came to the aid of the weak' and the figure who could always be counted on to explain the 'transcendent ethic which underpinned his actions' (*A*, 37).[27] Graduating to natural history television programmes, Michel watches transfixed by scenes of natural selection in action, a pitiless round of the strong against the weak in which gazelles and antelopes spend their days in 'abject terror' of the lions and panthers who 'lived out their lives in listless imbecility punctuated by explosive bursts of cruelty'. His intellectual imagination and moral indignation developing apace, he is given a chemistry set and begins his experiments examining the 'mysterious and strange science' that seemed to offer an escape from the 'repulsive cesspit' of the natural world (*A*, 38, 40). Missing out on love with his childhood sweetheart, the beautiful Annabelle, he becomes more profoundly isolated and withdrawn during his student years, often taking to his bed for weeks at a time to ponder how society can function without religion. Without 'Christian notions of grace and redemption', Michel sees the human spirit, and his own, turning cold and mechanical. Over dinner one night in a Chinese restaurant with Bruno, Michel puts down his chopsticks and holds forth on the role played by sexual desire in a world where the link between sex and reproduction has been broken, a society no longer driven by material lack and physical danger:

> ... any philosopher worthy of the name knows that, in itself, desire – unlike pleasure – is a source of suffering, pain and hatred. The Utopian solution – from Plato to Huxley by way of Fourier – is to do away with desire and the suffering it causes by satisfying it immediately. The opposite is true of the sex-and-shopping society we live in, where desire is marshalled and organized and blown up out of all proportion. For society to function, for competition to continue, people have to want more and more until it fills up their lives and finally devours them ... (*A*, 191–2)

For Michel, any utopian vision must be one that is free from desire and, by extension, from its regressive human expression, sexuality.

While Bruno throws himself with abandon into trying to access the spoils of an overblown and brash sexual marketplace, losing weight and working out to improve his physical appearance, Michel grows increasingly indifferent to the possibility of any sensual experience and, despite a late and fleetingly brief sexual reunion with Annabelle that ends with her death from ovarian cancer, he is happy to retreat into isolation in the rarefied, predictably rational world of bio-molecular science. Following Annabelle's death, he moves to the Galway Centre on the remote West coast of Ireland where he begins working obsessively on his biogenetic project, soon thereafter withdrawing permanently from any social contact. Seeking a technical 'cure' for desire and the suffering that it causes, Michel finally creates a new species of beings who have surpassed individuality and separation. Bioengineered asexual clones are Michel's answer to this 'sex and shopping' (or sex *as* shopping) society and 'doing away with desire' is precisely what he attempts in his biogenetic experiments. No longer characterized by any sexual difference or sexual reproduction, the clones are freed from the commercialization of desire and no longer need any other body to fulfil sexual desire. This 'cure' for sex comes far too late, however, for Bruno who goes through a series of painful and humiliating sexual encounters leading him, like the narrator of *Whatever*, to the confines of a psychiatric clinic.

The 'omega' male

The complete opposite of Michel, Bruno is wholly defined by his society's excessive emphasis on desire and, as such, he is characteristic of his generation in that his sexual destiny is closely linked to economic conditions: 'While he was a teenager, the fierce economic pressures which France had suffered for two hundred years had abated'. With the decline of material scarcity in the 'great middle-class of labourers and office workers' sex became 'a new sport in which to compete' (*A*, 73, 74). Michel observes that most of the middle-class people he knows are broadly similar to Bruno; affluent, professionally and creatively fulfilled, they see life as kind of shopping mall where, as one desire leads to another, they need never be without what they desire. Such people, notes Houellebecq in *Interventions*, are governed by the 'logic of the supermarket' that inevitably leads to 'a dissipation of desires'. Should sexual appetite wane, however, one could just as easily channel this ever-consuming desire into 'gourmet food and wines' (*A*, 211).[28] In contrast to his quietly bookish half-brother, Bruno's early childhood in Algiers demonstrates an inclination towards more fleshly pursuits. While Michel 'feeds on knowledge', Bruno's appetites as a young boy are already gravitating towards the more sensual pursuits of food and girls. 'If Michel has given up on individuation through desire and satisfaction', Abecassis notes, 'his brother Bruno seems to have invested himself completely in individuation through sex.'[29]

Also bought up by his grandmother but then sent to a boarding school, Bruno experiences a more traumatic childhood than that of Michel. More profoundly and somatically affected by maternal rejection, his earliest memory is one of intense humiliation at nursery school where he fails to complete making a necklace to present to the girls: 'How could he tell them that he too needed love?' (*A*, 41). As previously detailed, Bruno suffers sexual assaults at the hands of the other boys who, beneficiaries of the post-'68 policy of *autogestion* and more relaxed disciplinary educational regimes, are effectively given the run of the school. Turning to food to sate his early libidinal urges, Bruno feasts daily on his grandmother's lavish cooking; saddle of hare with olives, stuffed aubergines and a plate of *hors d'oeuvres* for main courses before finishing off the meal with boxes of pastries and sticky-sweet confectionery. Unsurprisingly, he soon becomes a 'fat, fearful child' who experiences episodic bouts of bulimia often brought on by trauma and overwhelming feelings of lovelessness; he confesses 'I wanted to be a sinner, but I just couldn't do it. I felt like I'd been robbed of my childhood' (*A*, 45, 210).[30] On reaching adolescence, his bulimia transfers into obsessive masturbation as he realizes that he occupies a lowly rank in the male sexual hierarchy; he is an 'omega male' and will be a loser in the equally ferocious sexual economy outside of boarding school. Constantly comparing his sexual success with other males. Bruno sees his omega sexual status reinforced at every turn. On a school holiday, Bruno experiences one of his earliest episodes of desperate sexual exhibitionism. Jealously noting that on the holiday '... Patrick Castelli, a young French boy in his class, succeeded in fucking thirty-seven girls in the space of three weeks. Over the same period, Bruno managed to score zero. In the end he flashed his prick at a shop assistant in a supermarket; luckily, the girl broke out laughing and did not press charges' (*A*, 77).

Overweight, physically unattractive and devoid of anything resembling charm, Bruno is a more fully realized version of the hapless Tisserand in *Whatever*, who is 'so ugly that his appearance repels women, and he never gets to sleep with them. He tries though, he tries with all his might, but it doesn't work. They simply want nothing to do with him' (*W*, 53–4). Bruno understands that he is not going to get very far in this 'strict hierarchy' and very early on in his adolescence begins to feel the intense sexual *ressentiment* that will shape him into the 'embittered, middle-aged cynic' he will eventually become (*A*, 42, 51). 'Bruno jerked off at least three times a day […] he was surrounded by the vulvas of young women, sometimes less than three feet away, but Bruno realized that they were closed to him: other boys were bigger, stronger, more tanned' (*A*, 69). As an omega male he is forced to watch from the excluded sidelines as the alphas have their fill of the available women, a Darwinist scenario reminiscent of nothing so much as one of Michel's wildlife programmes. Unable to get any girls to go out with him, Bruno begins an adolescence of frenzied masturbation over any vaguely erotic scenario or object, including a Kafka novel and, in one memorably disturbing scene, his sleeping mother's vagina. Although he does later have a wife and a son, neither play much part in his life as he continues to lust after every woman that crosses his path. As not one of these women reciprocates his feelings, he resorts to paying regularly for sex. In an unsettling scene that replays his own childhood of parental abandonment, Bruno is left in charge of his son one night. He puts sedative drugs into some jam and feeds it to the child in order that he may slip out of the flat to have sex with a prostitute in a room above an all-night bar. After some sneeringly cruel comments on his wife's post-natal body in erotic lingerie, Bruno divorces her and continues to pay for sex until he meets Christiane at the New Age camp, the *Lieu de Changement*.

The relationship between Bruno and Christiane takes place at a historical point in the West where there are few restrictions on erotic behaviour; they have several outlets for the satisfaction of their sexual pleasure and for a time enjoy their participation in this new middle-class 'sport' where 'pleasure is a right' (*A*, 118).

> In the liberal system which Bruno and Christiane had joined, the sexual model proposed by the dominant culture [...] was governed by the principle of adventure: in such a system, pleasure and desire become part of the process of *seduction*, and favour originality, passion and individual creativity (all qualities required of employees in their professional capacities). In concentrating on the physical aspects of seduction to the exclusion of the intellectual and moral considerations, regulars at such clubs were led to a fantasy version of the dominant culture: the *Sadean* system. (*A*, 293)

As their sexual passion wanes, Christiane and Bruno venture into the sex clubs of Paris. In these *clubs échangistes* (swingers' clubs), 'adventurous' Sadean couples diligently work their way through a whole gamut of sexual permutations on offer, but Bruno is not a popular a choice of partner as what he has to offer in the visually overdetermined world of the pornographic gaze is a penis which simply does not measure up to industry standards. The laws of the sexual market place prove even more exacting and ruthless than the economic one and Bruno is regularly passed over in orgies as potential sexual partners quickly note that 'he did not come close to the minimum size they required' (*A*, 118). To Bruno's dismay, these new sexual outlets are based more on seduction, which has, Houellebecq argues, replaced 'natural' desire and pleasure and requires sustained effort rather than sensuality or eroticism. The techniques and discourses of seduction in the sex clubs are comparable to those of the workplace; indeed, as Morrey observes, the 'discourses of work and sexuality appear increasingly inseparable, each borrowing and re-employing the key terms of the other'.[31]

The Sadean system to which Bruno desperately wants to belong, one that Houellebecq views as the logical outcome of a commodified sexuality, requires that its participants view sexual experience as a purely mechanical exchange of bodies and sensations. When sex becomes another market transition, it responds to precisely the same demand and supply dynamics as any other commodity and it is crucial that 'the narcissistic gratification that accrues to the individual is a function of the desirability of the partner'.[32] Therefore the delivery of quantity becomes paramount, something that Bruno observes in the sex clubs: 'couples quickly abandoned their search for pleasure (which required time, finesse and sensitivity) in favour of prodigal sexual abandon' (*A*, 292). His relationship is not to be a lasting one with Christiane, and, like so many sexual relationships in Houellebecq's work, ends in tragedy when she kills herself when she becomes paralysed after a sexual orgy.

If sex is only a commodity among others and is stripped of any sense of erotic *jouissance*, sexual relations are subject to the same commercial ethos as the wider market and become as banal as any other commercial exchange. This proposition is taken to its logical, if satirical, conclusion in Houellebecq's next novel *Platform*. If sex is a commodity and youth is the 'most precious of all worldly goods', *Platform* controversially, some say satirically, explores Bruno's assertion that in this kind of sexual marketplace he did not have to have sex with women his own age (42) but was prepared to go 'to the end of the earth' (to Bangkok, in fact) for 'young pussy wrapped in a mini-skirt' (*A*, 124).

Platform: Women on the market

Prostitution is ubiquitous in Houellebecq's work. In many instances, it is only a stop-gap measure for the rejected or unattractive male who cannot find a willing partner rather than a complete substitute for sexual relations, which it becomes for Jed Martin in *The Map and the Territory*, a novel less about sex than his previous work. In *Whatever*, Tisserand is at first far too proud to consider paying for sex, but soon comes to see this as his only choice, calculating that he has sufficient money from his wages to put by for a weekly visit to a prostitute. In *Atomised* Bruno spends a substantial portion of his income on peep shows and prostitutes, and in a grisly Oedipal scene one day recognizes the client next to him in the 'massage' parlour as his own father. Later, driving up to the *Lieu de Changement* he contemplates how, from a 'sexual point of view', his year had begun well as an 'influx of girls from Eastern Europe had meant that prices had dropped. For 200 francs you could get a little personal relaxation, down from 400 francs some months earlier' (*A*, 121). In *Platform*, the focus on prostitution is intensified. Functioning paradigmatically as the next 'extension of the struggle', namely, the supply of 'Third World' sex to Westerners who can afford to travel to purchase sexual services, a literalised sexual marketplace becomes the novel's central preoccupation.

The narrative begins with another isolated and disgruntled middle-aged male protagonist, another Michel – a different one to that of *Atomised*, this one is a composite of both Bruno and Michel – happily ready to adopt his role as a 'lonely pot-bellied European' on holiday to Thailand where he enjoys and greatly admires the 'natural' eroticism and sexual services of the Thai sex workers (*P*, 101). Observing the comfortable, even congenial, erotic commingling of tourists and Thai women, Michel realizes how 'important sex tourism would be to the future of the world' and thus, the quasi-Swiftian proposal is set in place suggesting the legitimate sale of sex by 'Third World' sex workers to Western men (and some women) as a rational 'solution' to the problem of the availability or accessibility of sex, a problem that has afflicted the characters in the previous two novels (*P*, 106). A perfectly rational and utilitarian solution to a simple problem of demand and supply, this is the *reductio ad absurdum* set in motion in the novel that takes as its starting point the increasingly unfettered market forces of neoliberal capitalism. On holiday in Thailand, Michel meets Valérie, a successful businesswoman who works for the French travel company Nouvelles Frontières. Intrigued by the sexual appeal that Thai prostitutes hold for their satisfied customers, Valérie sees a business opportunity for the niche marketing of luxury sex tourism catering for the jaded libidos of Western men. Along with her partner, she embarks upon a new business enterprise setting up discreet sex tourism in a number of Third World venues. This new venture debuts in Thailand just as Valérie is killed on Patpong beach during a terrorist attack by Islamic fundamentalists.

Prostitution, or to use the less pejorative term, sex work, is at base a very simple relationship of exchange. Predicated on the demand and supply of sexual activity, it is not the body that is a commodity in this transaction, but rather the sexual services offered by that individual. There is no good reason then, or so *Platform* would have us believe, that those who possess the ability to pay for these sexual services should not be permitted to purchase them from willing suppliers who can maximize their income as a result of such a transaction. Under the terms of this implicit contract, once the services have been delivered the sex worker is free to sell those services to another buyer. Crucially, the body of the sex worker is not owned by the buyer after the expenditure of the sexual act and, therefore, as Shannon Bell puts it up: 'the prostitute does not behave like any other commodity' but is precariously positioned at '... the centre of an extraordinary and nefarious economic system. She is able to represent all the terms within capitalist production; she is the human labour, the object of exchange and the seller at once. She stands as worker, commodity and capitalist and blurs the categories of bourgeois economics in the same way as she tests the boundaries of bourgeois morality ... '.[33] Thus, the sex worker is simultaneously both use and exchange value. A liberal outlook on sex work argues that workers are free to sell their services and equally free not to sell these same services. On the other hand, many others argue that this 'freedom' is nothing of the sort and in very many cases, exchanging sex for money is simply the last resort of women in an economic system that does not provide adequately paid alternatives.[34] This is certainly true in the case of Thailand. We learn in *Platform* that when the country became part of the global 'market economy' it was the first real tragedy to strike the country for more than two centuries and brought the country to the 'brink of ruin'; now the country is economically 'deep in shit' (*P*, 81, 310).

In an essayistic aside on the relationship between beauty, money and sex, Michel muses upon the residual *droits de seigneur* of the twentieth-century European male inherited from his imperial ancestors who conquered the world not solely out of 'economic self-interest' but also in a belief of the 'superiority of their civilisation' (*P*, 298–9). This assumption of a 'natural right' to 'dominate the world' endures in the present stripped of its moral civilizing mission (the old colonial *mission civilisatrice*) but continues because European men with relatively modest incomes now have the financial means to travel halfway around the world to buy 'superior' sexual services: 'As a wealthy European, I could obtain food and the services of women more cheaply in other countries ...' (*P*, 298). The locale of the Thai sex trade is constructed so that the mechanical, commercial nature of the transaction is concealed within a more general scenario of luxury and abundance, in which food, drink and accommodation are as cheap and as pleasurable as the wide variety of sexual services on offer. The perception of Oriental females as more subservient and sexually compliant than their European counterparts lends, to what is essentially a purely commercial transaction, a veneer of romantic fantasy in which the sex worker seems to be not simply serving but caring for her 'companion' who they look upon with 'an attitude of loving expectancy' (*P*, 108). 'This is all a part of the fantasy' says one researcher on Thai sex tourism, 'in the land where the sex tourist advertisements say "Come to Thailand where all your fantasies will be made to come true".[35] The Thai fantasy is, then, as much concerned with a more general subordination of women, where the woman 'serves' the man in every possible respect, as it is with actual sexual activity. Of course, feminist critics have had much to say about the trafficking of women, not only in the sex trade but also in more structurally anthropological ways as part of primitive kinship relations in which females are the equivalent of money or land for the men trading them as commodities in the most basic sense. Gayle Rubin suggests that the 'exchange of women' is a consolidation of certain aspects of the social relations of sex and gender, 'a systematic social apparatus' that uses women as raw materials and establishes hierarchy from sexual difference.[36] Linking the sexual economy with the 'real' one, in a broader sense, Luce Irigaray has force-fully argued that 'Whether they be considered as origin, practice, or reflection, sexual relations clearly cannot be disassociated from the general economy in which they operate'.[37] In the case of Cuba the general economy is not looking good; 'The poor people of Cuba', says one old man at a hotel in Baracoa, have 'nothing left to sell but their bodies' (*P*, 235). The economic law of demand and supply is applied here to sexual transactions thus making explicit what has been more or less implicit in Western sexual relationships; once this is accepted, it is simply a case of turning the sale of sex into a legitimate part of the leisure industry.

A 'passionate liberal' and an exemplary figure of a post-'68 creative turned entrepreneur, Jacques Maillot went from manning the barricades to setting up the travel company Nouvelles Frontières. Regarded as 'a symbol of the new face of modern capitalism', the idea for the company was conceived 'at the dawn of the leisure society', and thrived in the booming years of the 70s and 80s when, at its peak, in 2000, tourism became 'the biggest economic activity in the world' (*P*, 29).[38] Dependent on a notion of leisure as a consumer product that entails the purchase of experiences within some strictly defined parameters, tourism is the transplantation of one's indigenous rights and liberties as a Westerner to reside in a locale in which a certain degree of licence, often involving alcohol, drugs and sexual promiscuity, may be granted to you for the period of your stay. In the case of the package holiday it is often a relatively simple financial trans-action; one reads the description of the 'package' in the brochure and decides if it is sufficiently tailored to one's own particular desires. Leafing through the travel literature ahead of his Thai holiday, Michel admires the abstraction of the language in the brochures and is equally impressed by the star-ratings system that 'indicated the intensity of the pleasure one was entitled to hope for' (*P*, 15). Mischievously listing the kinds of models of consumer satisfaction used by economists he tells us, 'According to the Marshall model, the buyer is a rational individual seeking to maximize his satisfaction while taking price into consideration; Veblen's model on the other hand analyses the effect of peer pressure on the buying process' (*P*, 14). He cites other models of demand and supply, such as the Baudrillard and Becker model and that of Copeland before deciding that the Marshall model best suits the particular conditions of sexual tourism.

In order to drive down costs, companies provide holidays that would have the broadest appeal to the largest number of customers, and this requires a certain level of standardization that was the mark of the earliest incarnation of the package holiday. While phenomenally successful for a while in the 1970s and 80s, sales in the travel industry, particularly package holidays, began to flag in the 1990s. The standard '4 Ss' model of vacation, 'Sea, Sun, Sand and Sex', was far less popular in the new post-Fordist world as it relied 'too heavily on standardization' and the things to offer on a holiday now more clearly pertained to the 'affective topography of individualism and personal development; authenticity, discovery, a sense of sharing ...' (*P*, 168). The language of advertising in the travel industry needed to reflect the change to niche marketing; that is, the micro-tailoring of the tourist experience to a society which, as noted, increasingly understood individual freedom as the widest possible choice of goods and services. This is the mission of the modern travel industry:

> The Spirit of Aurore is the art of marrying know-how, tradition and innovation with rigour, imagination and humanism, to attain a certain form of excellence. The men and women of Aurore are repositories of a unique cultural heritage: the art of welcoming. They know the rituals that transform life in to the art of living, and the simplest of service into a privileged moment. It is a profession, it is an art: it is their gift. Creating the best in order to share it, getting in touch with the essential through hospitality, devising spaces of pleasures ... (*P*, 263)

While this piece of advertising copy was not originally intended to promote sex tourism it is remarkable, notices Valérie, that the notion of the 'spirit' described in here could just as easily describe the 'skills' of the Thai sex workers. Reading a journal, *Tourisme Hebdo*, she happens upon an article analysing the affective composition of the 'new consumer'. The author is using the newer Holbrook and Hirschman model of affective consumption 'which focuses on the emotion the consumer feels when faced with a new product or service'; in a pointed and incisive piece of writing, Houellebecq describes this new form of cultural capitalism and its 'new consumers'. More ethically concerned about authenticity, they are:

> ... less predictable, more eclectic, more sophisticated, more concerned with humanitarian issues. They no longer consume to 'seem', but to 'be'. These new cultural consumers wanted less entertainment, *more serenity*. They had balanced diets, were careful about their health: they were slightly fearful of others and of the future. They demanded the right to be unfaithful out of curiosity, out of eclecticism; they favoured things that were solid, durable, authentic. (*P*, 202)

Lest we think the case is being is overstated here, consider the example of 'cultural capitalism' that Žižek gives in the form of Starbucks' advertising copy: '... when you buy Starbucks [...] you're buying into something bigger than a cup of coffee. You're buying into a coffee ethic [...] When you choose Starbucks, you are buying a cup of coffee from a company who cares'.[39] The same logic is applied to setting up a travel company dedicated to providing access to paid sexual encounters; discretion and attention to luxury details bring cheerful and apparently unforced erotic experience to sex-starved and lonely Westerners. This model works as '... we were living in a mixed economy which was slowly evolving towards a more pronounced liberalism, slowly overcoming the prejudice against usury—and in more general terms, against money—which persists in traditionally Catholic countries' (*P*, 165).

In *Platform*, we read that the criteria for selling sex are 'unduly simple'; no longer linked to reproduction or to the transmission of property and wealth down genetic blood-lines, female beauty and youth is 'now something marketable, narcissistic' and enters into the 'category of tradable commodities', thus 'the best solution was probably to involve money, that universal mediator which already made it possible to assure an exact equivalence between intelligence, talent and technical competence; which had already made it possible to assure a perfect standardization of opinions, tastes and lifestyles ...' (*P*, 297–8). It is then but a small step to transcribe this commercial business model, replete with its affective lexicon drawn from traditional holiday pastimes of sightseeing, sunbathing and yoga classes, onto a sexual bill of fare. 'The ruthless competition and demand for excellence that drive the labour market and economic relations', says Morrey, 'have gradually encroached upon the private sphere in such a way that personal relationships and sexual practices are now subject to the same pressure'.[40] Houellebecq is referring here, satirically we assume, to the theory of comparative advantage applied to sexual services.[41]

As noted earlier, the sexual domain in *Platform* reverts to an unashamedly phallocentric, or more precisely what Bourdieu calls a 'phallonarcissistic vision of the world' where the space of the Thai brothels and bars is determined, very literally, by the 'big dicks' of patriarchal culture in which the feminine exists *solely* to mutely service in every possible way the presence of the masculine.[42] The Thai sex workers are not represented as merely prostitutes but as erotic practitioners in the lost art of sensuality, 'natural' women who still know how to 'make' love. Untainted by the consumer logic of Western culture that has turned sex into shopping, these 'natural' women are venerated with what Kristeva describes as a 'pagan enthusiasm' central to 'the phallic idealization of Woman', where they become not only sexual objects but havens of existential solace, they are invoked as an 'idealized fantasy-fulfilment' for the incurable emotional lack caused by separation from the mother'.[43] The narrator's sexual transactions with Ôon and Sin form part of a kind of romanticized sexual pastoral, one which exists in a state of suspended separation from any moral or ethical considerations. Concealing the weight of colonial history, their labouring exoticized bodies render them as uncomplicated sites of pleasure. Smiling and acquiescent, the Thai women's bodies possess neither subtext nor context and exist only to offer life-affirming sex to disenchanted Western men with an expertise and tenderness that combines a maternal tenderness with the advanced sexual techniques of the whore. This then, is the ultimate 'girlfriend experience'. The allure of the Thai sex worker is that they seem to offer what all Houellebecq's male protagonists seek – intimacy and feeling, and above all an affective experience of the other that has been destroyed, as we have seen, by Western feminism. The 'natural' erotic experience with the Thai sex workers is untouched by demands for equality or agency or any sense of reciprocity and, as such, can reconnect men with some sense of sublimity or enchantment, something that Michel will find in his relationship with Valérie. But again this is a short-lived happiness as she is killed in a terrorist attack, leaving Michel to live out his days in his room on Naklua Road where, although he still visits the prostitutes, his penance for living is to be deprived forever of any real sexual pleasure. Thus, the order of the Houellebecquian universe has been restored; the protagonist is left alone, about to die, still railing against the West: 'I know only that every single one of us reeks of selfishness, masochism and death. We have created a system in which it has simply become impossible to live; and what's more, we continue to export it' (*P*, 361).

In the closed circuit of Houellebecq's reasoning in his novels, it is inevitable that the logical extension of the struggle, what Crowley describes as the 'reductive, materialistic anthropology he sees as responsible for the hegemony of the free market, both economically and sexually', *must* extend to selling sex, as anything less than this would not adequately demonstrate his hypothesis that suggests a correlation between the economic and the sexual.[44] But the problem of sex, how to get it in a 'deregulated' libidinal economy, how to make it last, and what to do when it is no longer freely available is, however, not finally the real preoccupation of Houellebecq's work; rather it is an alibi, a decoy for an examination of the disappearance of love, compassion and the possibility of intimate communion. Love, in Houellebecq's work, is 'immense and admirable' and 'in the absence of love nothing can be sanctified', says Daniel 1. When the creative energies necessary for the apprehension of otherness and for love are destroyed by the reifying forces of commerce, then the affective human body is in danger of obliteration. It is to this obliteration of affect to which I now turn.

Notes

1 Jerry Varsava, 'Utopian Yearnings: Dystopian Thoughts: Houellebecq's *The Elementary Particles* and the Problem of Scientific Communitarianism', *College Literature*, 32, 4 (2005), 145–67, 155.

2 Amelia Gentleman defines *déclinisme* as a pervasive sense of 'nostalgia for a lost era of French greatness', and more specifically, '… France's loss of its position as a global power, its weakening role within Europe, its failure to integrate its immigrant population, its exhausted public services and its stumbling industry …' in 'Summertime, and living is not easy for French racked with self-doubt', *The Guardian*, 10 August 2004, http://www.guardian.co.uk/world/2004/aug/10/france. ameliagentleman [accessed 1 July 2012]. See also Perry Anderson, 'Dégringolade', *London Review of Books*, 26, 2 (2004), 3–9; Donald Morrison and Antoine Compagnon, *Que reste-t-il de la culture française?*, suivi du *Le souci de la grandeur* (Paris, Éditions Denoël, 2008), and *France is Falling, The Great Waste, The War of the Two Frances* and *The Middle Class Adrift*; and Nicolas Baverez, *La France qui tombe* (Paris: Perrin, 2004). For a counterpoint to this rhetoric of *déclinisme*, see Michel Wieviorka, *Le printemps du politique: Pour en finir avec le déclinisme* (Paris: Robert Laffont, 2007).

3 Emily Apter, 'Mobile Citizens, Media States', *PMLA*, 117,1 (2002), 79–83, 82.

4 Crowley, 18.

5 See Keith Reader, *The Abject Object*, 106.

6 Bourg, 30.

7 Guillebaud, Jean-Claude, *La tyrannie du plaisir* (Paris: Seuil, 1998), 69.

8 Ibid., 71.

9 Margot Weiss, 'Gay Shame and BDSM Pride: Neoliberalism, Privacy, and Sexual Politics', *Radical History Review,* 100 (2008), 86–101, 89.

10 Cruickshank, 123.

11 Varsava, 149.

12 Shannon Winnubust, 'The Queer Thing about Neoliberal Pleasure: A Foucauldian Warning', *Foucault Studies*, 14 (2012), 79–97, 92.

13 James Wood, 'Love Actually', *The New Republic Online*, 14 September 2006, http://www.powells.com/review/2006_09_14 [accessed 18 April 2012].

14 Hervé Juvin, *The Coming of the Body* (London: Verso, 2010), 35, 37.

15 David Bennett, 'Libidinal Economy, Prostitution and Consumer Culture', *Textual Practice*, 24, 1 (2010), 93–121, 110, 112.

16 Ibid., 112.

17 Juvin, 82.

18 Winnubust, 92.

19 Dany-Robert Dufour, trans. David Macey, *The Art of Shrinking Heads: On the New Servitude of the Liberated in the Age of Total Capitalism* (London: Polity Press, 2008).

20 Morrey, 2004, 5.

21 Abecassis, 812.

22 Houellebecq, 2001, 234; 2003, 242.

23 It is significant, of course, that contraception for women became widely available in France during this time. Introduced in December 1967, the Neuwirth Law legalized all forms of contraception in France. The law was amended in December 1974, removing the requirement for parental consent to provide contraception to minors. The Veil law legalizing abortion was passed soon thereafter in January 1975.

24 Kristin Ross, *Fast Cars, Clean Bodies: Decolonization and the Reordering of French Culture* (London and Cambridge, MA: MIT Press, 1996), 11.

25 See both Abecassis and Varsava on the resonance with the *moralistes* in Houellebecq's writing. See also Bruno Viard who insists that Houellebecq is not so much a misogynist as a moralist: *Houellebecq au laser: La faute à Mai 68* (Nice: Editions Ovadia, 2008), 83.

26 See also Liza Steiner, *Sade-Houellebecq, du boudoir au sex-shop.*

27 On Houellebecq's reference to comic books (*bandes dessinées*) in *Atomised*, see Wendy Michallat, 'Modern Life is Still Rubbish: Houellebecq and the Refiguring of "reactionary" Retro', *Journal of European Studies*, 37, 3, 313–31.

28 *Interventions*, 72, my translation.

29 Abecassis, 809.

30 It is striking that despite their traumatic experiences of their childhoods,

Houellebecq has little time for psychoanalytical explanations of either Bruno's or Michel's unhappiness.

31 Morrey, 'Sex and the Single Male', 145–6.

32 Ibid., 142.

33 Shannon Bell, *Reading, Writing, and Rewriting the Prostitute Body* (Bloomington: Indiana University Press, 1994), 11.

34 There is a complex ongoing debate across several disciplines on the question of sex work. See Kathleen Barry, *The Prostitution of Sexuality* (New York and London: New York University Press, 1995); Ursula Biemann, 'Remotely Sensed: A Topography of the Global Sex Trade', *Feminist Review*, 70, 1 (2002), 75–88; Jo Doezema, 'Ouch! Western Feminists' "wounded attachment" to the "third world prostitute"', *Feminist Review*, 67, 1 (2001), 16–38; Charlotte Hooper, *Manly States: Masculinities, International Relations, and Gender Politics* (New York: Columbia University Press, 2001); Christa Wichterch, *The Globalized Woman: Reports from a Future of Inequality*, trans. Patrick Camiller (London: Zed Books, 2000); Jan Jindy Pettman, 'Body Politics: International Sex Tourism', *Third World Quarterly*, 18, 1 (1997), 93–108; and J. Seabrook, *Travels in the Skin Trade – Tourism and the Sex Industry* (London: Pluto Press, 1996). In *Sex and Social Justice* Martha Nussbaum makes the case for sex work to be treated as a job like any other and, as such, not be stigmatized (Oxford: Oxford University Press, 1999).

35 Patricia Green, 'Thailand: Tourism and the Sex Industry', *Women*, 54 (2001), 20.

36 Gayle Rubin, 'The Traffic in Women: Notes on the Political Economy of Sex' in *Toward an Anthropology of Women*, ed. Rayna R. Reiter (New York and London: Monthly Review Press, 1975), 158.

37 Luce Irigaray, *Speculum of the Other Woman,* trans. Gillian C. Gill (New York: Cornell University Press, 1985), 120.

38 For a detailed discussion of the representation of travel and tourism in *Platform* see Aedín Ní Loingsigh's 'Tourist Traps Confounding Expectations in Michel Houellebecq's *Plateforme*', *French Cultural Studies,* 16, 1 (2005), 73–90, which argues that the novel has 'something vital to tell us about modern-day France, the legacy of colonialism in contemporary global travel practices and the uneven nature of cultural exchange in the modern world', 87.

39 Žižek, 53. This is quoted from an advert in *USA Today*, 4 May 2009, 9.

40 Morrey, 'Sex and the Single Male', 143

41 See Stefan Mann, 'From Friendly Turns Toward Trade – On the Interplay Between Cooperation and Markets', *International Journal of Social Ethics*, 35, 5 (2008), 326–37.

42 Pierre Bourdieu, 'La Domination Masculine', *Actes de la recherche en sciences sociales*, 84 (1990), 2–31, 30. It is no accident that the most highly venerated sexual skill in Houellebecq's novels is fellatio where women, sex workers and

lovers, worship tenderly at the temple of phallus. This female worship has its obverse, as Keith Reader has pointed up, in scenes of phallic revulsion and the private abjection of the phallus (*The Abject Object*, 122–3).

43 Julia Kristeva, *Powers of Horror* (New York: Columbia University Press, 1982), 166.

44 Crowley, 'The Wreckage of Liberation', 23.

6

The End of Affect

... deep down, I am with the utopians, people who think that the movement of History must conclude in an absence of movement. An end to History seems desirable to me.

Michel Houellebecq

Planning the extinction of desire in Buddhist-like terms, the [Elohimites] had banked on the maintenance of a weakened, non-tragic energy, purely conservative in nature, which would have continued to able the functioning of thought [...] This phenomenon had been only produced in insignificant proportions, and it was, on the contrary, sadness, melancholia, languid and finally mortal apathy that had submerged our disincarnated generations. The most patent indicator of our failure was that I ended up envying the destiny of Daniel1, his violent and contradictory journey, the amorous passions that had shaken him ...

(*The Possibility of an Island*, 313)

A precious and elusive experience, love is a 'scarce, artificial and belated phenomenon' in Houellebecq's work. Possessed of an 'ontological fragility' and a 'prodigious operative energy', love can only 'flower under certain historical conditions' which are 'absolutely opposed to the freedom of morals' characterizing 'the modern era' (*W*, 93, 113). Houellebecq's characters struggle to find love in a world where, in his view, sex has become the only signifier for *all* human interaction and where desire has been so comprehensively marshalled by commercial interests that it now brings only suffering. In such a world then, 'human relationships become progressively impossible' (*W*, 14). All of his writing describes in one way or another the failure of generational transmission, what might be called the disintegration of patrimony. There are no children or parents to speak of in Houellebecq's work, thus love can only be experienced in the context of romantic or erotic relationships which are underwritten by the dynamics of commercial exchange in which attraction becomes '... a simple numerical calculation that involves attractiveness, novelty and value for money'; love and intimacy become, therefore, virtually impossible in contemporary society.[1] In the wake of sexual liberation, the body has become an important, even crucial, part of social capital, a commodity among others and desire has become so comprehensively reified that it has irreparably damaged our ability to form intimate human bonds and has thus made impossible the conditions in which love, based on altruism and compassion rather than exchange and transaction, might flourish. Therefore, after a brief but finally doomed attempt at love, each of the male protagonists in *Whatever*, *Atomised* and *Platform* continue their lives, in different ways, in a state of unrelenting atomized misery and affective deprivation. In their reflection on the difficulty of human relations, and in particular sexual ones, these three novels remain open to the possibility, however slight, of some kind of human or social 'solution' to the problem of affective alienation. Whether by sexual murder in *Whatever*, sex tourism in *Platform* or the biogenetic extension of the body's erogenous zones in *Atomised*, these novels still attach themselves to the idea of human striving even in the context of increasing depressive isolation. Indeed, right up to the last few pages of *Atomised* there is the hope of love, or something like it. *The Possibility of an Island* is the death of this hope.[2]

Beginning where *Atomised* leaves off, *Possibility* ponders at first the problem of sex but it has become clear that it is not sex that is at issue but the difficulty of all human affective attachment and, in particular, love. Sex is overdetermined in Houellebecq's work. Being a meaningful human is almost always defined as being successfully bound into networks of sexual belonging in one way or another and when sex fails, as it does in all of these novels, this failure represents not only the failure but also the impossibility of *all* human relations under neoliberal capitalism. As Christian Moraru notes, sexuality is the most stubbornly *embodied* of all affective dimensions and remains 'the only dimension in which our bodies still need and seek out relationships, remains something to contend with, nudging us toward each other'.[3] The problem of sexuality, and by extension all human affect, has not been 'fixed' by the provocative, but still recognizably human, solution of sex tourism in *Platform* so it is science to which *Atomised* and *Possibility* turn to find a cure for an anomie which is as much emotional as it is sexual. Love, a 'skill for epitomizing the whole of the opposite sex in a single loved one', had been possible only under 'certain historical conditions' (*W*, 14). With the absolute hegemony of capitalism, these conditions have passed away, and now only science can help us.

Simultaneous with the incitement to define oneself by sexual desire, have more sex, with more partners, all the time, is the drastic falling away of active social bonds and of affective relations. Defining affect as a capacity for bodily and emotional potential, that is, 'a body's *capacity* to affect and to be affected' that extends into a continuum of encounter and belonging, Gregory Seigworth and Melissa Gregg observe that 'affect marks a body's belonging to a world of encounters or; a world's belonging to a body of encounters but also, in non-belonging, through all those far sadder (de) compositions of mutual in-compossibilities'.[4] Elsewhere, Bruno Latour has essayed a definition of the affective body: '... to have a body is to learn to be affected, meaning "effectuated", moved, put into motion by other entities, humans or nonhumans'.[5] Houellebecq's characters struggle to find a place in a society in which the logic of exchange is extended to the affective body; where the entire communicative world of the neoliberal subject is defined by the ethos of production; more specifically, where the relations of labour reproduce themselves in personal and affective sexual relations. Assailed at every turn by the libidinal energies of pornography and popular culture, Houellebecq's characters move around in their diminishing atomized spaces in a 'miserable and troubled' age in which people live out 'lonely, bitter lives' and where feelings of 'love, tenderness and human fellowship have all but disappeared ...' (*A*, 3). Abandoning any possibility of either social or political intercession, both *Atomised* and *Possibility*, then, suggest a post-political, biotechnical solution to the problem; a solution that is inherently apocalyptic: 'If there is to be breakthrough, it will be apocalyptic or not at all'.[6] The solution to the disenchantment of capitalism is the eradication of the hope for affective renewal or regeneration.

Posthumanity

After a swift diversion via the markedly less accomplished work *Lanzarote* (2000, 2002), an unconvincing and largely unnecessary reiteration of *Atomised*, Houellebecq turns to the question of posthumanity. If sexual murder was not the answer in *Whatever*, and neither was the sexual tourism of *Platform*, then in *Atomised* and *Possibility* it is the discourses of science in the form of a 'third metaphysical mutation' that might be able to 'restore the practical possibility of human relationships' (*A*, 249). Science is humanity's only hope for an 'ontological overhaul' of human nature and for finding a cure for its anomic 'suffering of being'. Thus, in *Possibility*, the bioengineered neohumans Daniel 24 and 25 have been 'cured' of the vexing irregularities of all human emotion. For them, feelings of happiness, love and sadness remain only as something to read about, a nostalgic story of the old human species, recorded in the book of the original Daniel that the cloned Daniels are reading. While the neohuman bodies in *Possibility* are still recognizably organic entities, they have been purged of any eating, excreting and reproductive functions, in short, of their entire human corporeality. Perfectly self-sufficient organisms with no need for a social whole or indeed any sense of outside to the self, their environment is devoid of any sense of otherness as they exist in pristine technical contentment in their disconnected monads. The predictable and regulated affect-free lives of the neohumans represent the end of what Raymond Williams has called the 'structures of feeling', the lived quality of life, the 'affective elements of consciousness and relationships' embodying the fluctuations, the ebbs and flows of '... a particular sense of life, a particular community of experience'.[7] Such a movement away from the contingency of everyday life with its continual possibility and potentiality of otherness towards a posthumanism characterized by ontological homogeneity and stasis is, of course, deeply antithetical to the intellectual legacy of '68 thought that privileged multiplicity, heterogeneity, difference and desire. In *Atomised* desire is technically exterminated through the rearrangement of molecular genetic matter – the eponymous elementary particles – in order that there might be a restoration of a 'world of feelings' (*A.* 360). In *The Possibility of an Island*, however, this 'world of feelings' is also eradicated. What are we to make, then, of a proposition that suggests that there is no hope for a different world; one that suggests that the only hope for humanity is in cloned 'happiness'? Is this a dystopian warning of what might happen if we fail to staunch the march of materialism and the concomitant collapse of the political and civil sphere?[8] Or is it, perhaps, a kind of utopian suggestion?

Moving more decisively into the territory of science encountered at the end of *Atomised*, *The Possibility of an Island* effectively discards any human solution to this loss of poignancy produced by 'capitalism's web of suffering'. If there is no longer any hope of an ethical, philosophical or political way out of this situation then the solution is a wholly technical one, achieved through the positivist, über-rational phenomenon of eugenic science. The neo-humans exist in a bio-engineered existential 'web of joy' in which life is wholly pain-free but affectless, indistinct and undifferentiated. In this posthuman vision, all humans are cloned multiples, exact genetic replicas of the same; neither identity nor difference has survived the great 'paradigm shift' with which *Atomised* concludes. In such a bio-technically managed totality defined by genetic similitude and asexual reproduction, there is no longer any need for the somatic presence of the body or *any* encounter with other bodies. Both

Atomised and *Possibility*, then, propose that the only cure for ruined human affect is a biotechnical one: that is, the creation of new species of posthuman with 'a radically new biological constitution' in whom the organic desire for physical sexual relations is bioengineered out of their genetic schema. This new neohuman species has sidestepped the long, and occasionally unreliable, processes of Darwinian evolution through wholly technical means, which permits the eradication of the destructive egotism of erotic competition, thereby restoring 'the possibility of love' (*A*, 363). The 'passing away' of the old human order allows a new species to be created that is no longer hostage to the capricious mechanisms of either affect or desire. As Richard Bauckham sardonically notes, love is now genetically 'rooted in the post-human DNA' and therefore '... now comes naturally'.[9]

Houellebecq's solution to the problem of sex and love, in fact to that of all human affect, that he has been exploring in all of his work is a definitively post-anthropological view of humanity. If, as he has suggested, capitalism has made human affective relations entirely unworkable the only solution must be to re-make humans as entities free from the unpredictable contingencies of desire and love. In short, he has given up wholly, politically, ethically and philosophically, on *how to be human now* and thrown his hand in with the technicians and the scientific solution. This chapter, then, considers this scientific solution presented as the cure for the metaphysical problem of human suffering caused by the disappearance of love in a commodifed world. As noted, the solution involves the elimination of desire, and all forms of difference from the human schema and, as such, can be regarded as a continuation of Houellebecq's ongoing attack on '68 thought, especially on the intellectual sovereignty of post-structuralist theory. The 'global ridicule' heaped upon the works of Foucault, Lacan, Derrida Deleuze and other philosophers of difference whose work has suddenly 'foundered after decades of inane reverence' is the starting point for a discussion of the 'dominance of the scientific community' and, what might be tentatively called, a post-political notion of identity and difference (*A*, 376–7). Examining both *Atomised* and *The Possibility of an Island*, I consider here this scientific solution as a riposte to an era in which philosophy and ethics have an increasingly limited influence.

In *Atomised*, Michel Djerzinski's 'biophysical work' produces a radical change in the genetic make-up of the human being that evacuates the 'useless' and 'regressive' function of sexuality out of the human body. This is described as a bioethical 'paradigm shift' in which twentieth-century humanism, already in its ontological death throes, is superseded by the technocratic supremacy of biotechnology that opens up 'a new era in world history' (*A*, 4). This 'new rational species' of posthumans has 'outgrown individuality, individuation and progress' and, with the ability to self-eroticize, no longer needs the presence of others for the fulfilment of desire (*A*, 214, 371). Possessing no genetic distinctiveness and, more importantly for Houellebecq's recurring thesis, no sexual differentiation or real sense of desire, these clones are no longer dependent upon the serendipity of sexual encounters for the fulfilment of affective life as they are now able to fully auto-eroticize and thus, are no longer tied into the 'Darwinian struggle of sex.' All of this may facilitate, Michel hopes, the possibility of love. While such a proposition may seem somewhat outlandish in the context of a 'literary' novel, when situated in the tradition of utopian and science fiction writing, this proposition seems somewhat less incongruous. As noted in *Atomised*, 'the Utopian solution from Plato to Huxley' has consistently regarded human desire as the stumbling block to utopia and, over the centuries, writers have envisaged a myriad of solutions to 'do away with desire and the suffering it causes' (*A*, 192).

Before the 'paradigm shift' of cloning, desire had long since left the realm of the 'natural' (as much as it ever really resided there) and become bound into the mechanisms of commodity exchange. No longer transgressive or sacred in the way that Bataille might view it, desire is easy to satisfy through prostitution, pornography or promiscuity; as Lacanain psychoanalytic critic Charles Melman puts it, 'it is no longer a psychic economy centered on the lost object and its representatives that is being legitimized [by our society]. Quite the opposite – it's a psychic economy organized by the presentation of an accessible object and by the ultimate accomplishment of *jouissance*'.[10] In Houellebecq's work, only the most mechanical and perfunctory sense of *jouissance* is now available as sexuality has become part of a rationalized system of investment and exchange. Given Houellebecq's near-compulsive working over of the idea of contemporary sexuality as a corollary to the neoliberal modality of late capitalism, one might plausibly expect the erasure of sexual difference and the ability to self-eroticize to produce a perfect technical solution to the problem of commodification, and this is indeed the case in *Atomised* where the clones live peacefully and happily, free from the attachment to otherness hitherto required to fulfil desire (*A*, 32). However, such a solution is taken much further in *Possibility* in which the cloned neohumans do not even possess all-over erogenous zones with which they can auto-eroticize and have been deprived of any actual ability to desire and thus to feel.

Send in the clones

Around the time Houellebecq began writing *Atomised* there was much intellectual interest in posthumanism and the idea of a post-theological world. If, as
Feuerbach argued, 'the task of the modern era was the realization and humani-
zation of God', a movement which effected 'the transformation and dissolution
of theology into anthropology', then it might be said that one the main tasks
of the postmodern era (a term used here with all the usual caveats) has been,
and continues to be, the technological transformation of anthropology into the
post-anthropological.[11] Rapid developments in biotechnologies, in particular
genomic sciences, have nudged the twenty-first century ever closer to what
might plausibly be called a posthuman or post-biological era.[12] Certainly, it is
clear from the extensive body of critical work in this area, most of it produced
in the humanities the 1990s, that the moment of the posthuman is no longer the
future vision of science fiction but has already begun.

As one might expect, both within the academy and without, posthumanism is
a prospect welcomed by some, dreaded by others and approached with a mixture
of guarded optimism by still others. Some thinkers regard the dissolution of the
boundaries between the human and the non-human as a move towards an
emancipatory anti-essentialism, greeting the possibilities of extending, altering
and adapting the physical limits of the human body as a new opportunity to
circumvent restrictive notions of the 'natural'. In contrast, fearing a kind of
unchecked Frankensteinism over both the creation and destruction of human
life, others have warned against any premature celebration of posthumanism.
Counselling a politically vigilant approach that is mindful of the potentially
hazardous effects of the artificial acceleration of human evolution, these critics
have warned of the consequences involved in the human assumption of
messianic powers and of the coercive commercial pressures that inevitably
surround the issue of biotechnology.[13] Of these critics, Steven Best and Douglas
Kellner offer one of the most persuasive critical surveys of the intellectual
landscape of posthumanism marked by profound disagreements between pro-
and anti-humanists over its merits and menaces in *The Postmodern Adventure*
(2001), which counsels a non-sectarian, politically cautious approach using a
'supradisciplinary critical philosophy' capable of addressing the vast field of
bioethics and particularly that of transgeneticism and molecular nanotechnology.[14] No longer the fantasy so beloved by science fiction writers but now
a scientific reality (at least in theory), the question of human cloning assumes

a central position in many of these debates. Cloning is fascinating for many reasons. Not only would it allow the thwarting of the biological sweepstake and its 'random shuffling of genes', it also raises the possibility of 'a return to asexual reproduction', throwing into radical doubt the idea of human character itself. In the next few decades of the twenty-first century, Best and Kellner argue, the ability to replicate humanity through genetic engineering will represent as immense a change as the invention of the Gutenberg press: 'Rather, much as the printing press replaced the scribe, cloning allows mass reproduction of a devised type, and thus opens genetic engineering to vast fields of commercial possibilities.'[15]

Creator of the figure of the cyborg, biologist turned philosopher of science Donna Haraway was among the first critics, and remains the most well-known, to offer a systematic examination of the posthuman subject. Initially conceptualized in 'A Cyborg Manifesto' (1985), Haraway's ideas were developed in more detail in *Simians, Cyborgs, and Women* (1991), which rapidly became a seminal work with widespread cross-disciplinary influence.[16] Interestingly, however, at no point in either of these works does she use the term posthuman; rather, the arguments consider the implications of breaching the nature and culture binary by cloning or otherwise. Elsewhere, Katherine Hayles (1999), Eugene Hacker (2003), Judith Halberstam and Ira Livingstone (1995), Rosi Braidotti (1993), Bruno Latour (1999) and Keith Ansell-Pearson (1997) have all contributed to the rich seam of critical inquiry on what constitutes, in cybernetic, AI and pharmacological terms, the subject and limits of the posthuman.[17] Outside of the academy, the debates around the biotechnical posthuman have assumed a vaguely apocalyptic tone, warning of immense, possibly disastrous, social, sexual and ethical changes. Economist, political commentator and prolific chronicler of the biotechnological revolution, Jeremy Rifkin, typifies this strain of commentary when he outlines what he sees as the reach of biotechnology into every facet of human life:

> The biotech revolution will affect every aspect of our lives. The way we eat; the way we date and marry; the way we have our babies, the way our children are raised and educated; the way we work; the way we engage in politics; the way we express our faith; the way we perceive the world around us and our place in it [...] each of us [will be forced] to put a mirror to our most deeply held values, making us ponder the ultimate question of the purpose and meaning of existence.[18]

A persistent and largely understandable anxiety over the threat posed to the idea of a core or essence to human subjectivity features in many of these discussions;

what happens to the idea of humanity under, what Paul Rabinow and Nikolas Rose have called, the 'molecular gaze' of biotechnologies?[19] This 'gaze', already active in many areas of life sciences and medical research, is a rather startling prospect for those outside of the techno-scientific industries, particularly for those who see the advent of the biotechnically enhanced or engineered posthuman as a threat to an often hard-won twentieth-century humanism: 'Over the last thirty or forty years, we have invested an enormous amount of thought, emotion, treasure and blood in what we call human values, human rights, the defence of human dignity and of human life. Over the same period, quietly but devastatingly, science and philosophy have combined to undermine our traditional concept of humankind.'[20]

In *Our Posthuman Future* (2002), a follow-up to his highly contentious work *The End of History and the Last Man* (1992), Francis Fukuyama has expressed similar worries, although from a different ideological perspective: 'What is ultimately at stake with biotechnology is the very grounding of the human moral sense', arguing that human nature remains a powerfully meaningful concept which along with religion 'defines our most basic values.'[21] Citing *Brave New World* (1932), a text that haunts Houellebecq's *Possibility*, Fukuyama believes that Huxley was correct to satirize the slavish chemical 'happiness' of the clones. We must remain vigilant, he says, of the dangers of human cloning as it threatens to eliminate that 'Factor-X', an incommunicable semi-Aristotelian essence that defines the concept of the human and one that must be defended at all costs from the mechanistic control of scientists who, intoxicated with the potential of pharmacological and genetic change, must be carefully monitored.[22] Speaking to the disquiet provoked by the term posthuman and addressing some of the ethical and philosophical concerns over the fate of the Benjaminian 'tiny, fragile human body', Judith Halberstam and Ira Livingstone offer the reassurance that the advent of the posthuman era '... does not necessitate the obsolescence of the human', neither does it, they insist, 'represent an evolution or devolution of the human. Rather it partakes in re-distribution of difference and identity.'[23]

So what interests Houellebecq, a writer best known for his tetchy accounts of the more ignominious aspects of contemporary Western life, tedious office work, sexual disappointment, masturbation and ready meals-for-one, in the idea of the posthuman? Simply stated, science, and in particular biotech-nology, might be the only cure for the social and affective misery wreaked by capitalism. In Houellebecq's work sex assumes, as we have seen, a metonymic role standing for all affective feeling and experience in a more general sense;

thus his work is necessarily 'over-sexualized' as social relations are reduced to sexual relations and 'sexuality and sex itself become the only register of anything like the political'.[24] The biopolitical subsumption of every aspect of human life to the principles of free-market exchange allows certain atavistic behaviours to re-emerge in both sexual and affective life, returning humanity to a less evolved, even primitive, way of living in which a pitiless division of winners and losers emerges. 'In this sense', Bülent Diken suggests, 'the biopolitical element is explicit in Houellebecq's work, in which the Communist Manifesto is restaged as a spectacle of bare life' and where 'the physical body appears, through sexuality, as a pure political element'.[25] No less than the death or the withering of the political is at stake here as the body and its sexuality assumes a centrality as part of what Agamben describes as the 'unpolitical primacy of sex in our unpolitical age'.[26]

In its biopolitical grip on the subject, neoliberalism portends, as Comaroff and Comaroff argue, 'the death of politics' – [a] diminution of the political to the pursuit of self or single interests disassociated 'from anything beyond themselves'.[27] In his work, Houellebecq seems then, to propose no less than an annihilation of the political and the ethical, replacing them with the determinism of science and technology, which will finally reduce us all to a monocultural, homogeneous community of one. Building on Plato's ideas of the ancient *polis* in *Politikes*, Peter Sloterdijk's 'Rules for the Human Zoo' (2009) articulates similar views to these, in particular the loss of faith in finding any humanist solution to the problem of the human condition. Arguing that we are at the end of an anthropocentric stage of history, Sloterdijk sees the advent of genomics as the dawn of a new era of biopower that will alter drastically the course of human evolution. No longer dependent on what Foucault calls the anthropotechnologies of literature, art and philosophy to understand the socio-cultural world, humanity now turns to a post-cultural world of biotechnologies for self-understanding and improvement.[28] Of course, Foucault said much the same when he described humanity as an endangered species which could disappear just as easily as 'a face drawn in sand at the edge of the sea'.[29] The posthuman vision of *Atomised* and *Possibility* is positioned, then, somewhere between this dissolving face in the sand and Nietzsche's *Übermensch* overcoming of man, a view expressed in the final words of *Atomised*: 'Having broken the filial chain that linked us to humanity, we live on [...] it is certainly true that we have succeeded in overcoming the monstrous egotism, cruelty and anger [...] vile, unhappy race of humans' (*A*, 379).

A former science student at the Institut National Agronomique Paris-Grignon, Houellebecq was very likely *au courant* with the debates on genetic cloning that were in circulation at the time of writing both *Atomised* and *Possibility*. Indeed, many of the most significant advances in biotechnology are present in these two novels. While every detail of the science used is not consistently reliable, there is, as one scientist from the CNRS has noted, a remarkable level of technical accuracy in each of the novels.[30] However, as is often the case in Houellebecq's work, the representation of the scientific solution is far from unequivocal. His 'solution' is worked out in his trademark agonistic and contrary approach, that is to say, in ways that are every bit as troublingly contradictory and difficult to pin down as are representations of religion, race and gender in his work. While both novels take on the topic of human cloning and genetic engineering, one as an end-point, the other as a more central thematic, Houellebecq's vision of a posthumanity dominated by scientific principles shows, at best, an inconsistent philosophical and ethical engagement with many contemporary theories of posthumanism. Rather, he uses the concept of posthumanism and the science underpinning it as a theoretical strategy with which to probe contemporary society, and in this way both novels enact what Fredric Jameson has described as science fiction's 'structurally unique method of apprehending the present as history'.[31]

In *Interventions*, Houellebecq has admitted with some candour that his views on science, metaphysics and social ennui may be somewhat inconsistent and conflicted but that '... the only way forward is to continue to uncompromisingly express the contradictions that tear me apart, in the knowledge that they are more than likely to be representative of my times'.[32] These contradictions abound in his presentation of the scientific solution. As we shall see, at one moment his depiction of a modern *scientia universalis* seems to half-resonate with Adorno and Horkheimer's warning in *Dialectic of Enlightenment*; whereas at others, it seems as if his thought has more in common with the libertinism of de Sade and the positivism of Comte. But if his work does show some engagement with Marxism, this is simply a surface effect as the revolution *chez* Houellebecq is not only a cold and quiet one, it is post-ideological and entirely non-dialectical; any ideological tension is reduced to fruitless contradiction or paradox rather than any fecund clash of ideas that might bring about some synthesis.[33] If there is any dialectic to be found here, it is a rotten and exhausted one, ideas reduced to ineffective contradictions and doubling-back. What if there were really no alternative or outside to the system we have created? If politics and philosophy have failed irretrievably then the only remaining position, it would seem, is complete surrender to the rational world-view of science and technology. It is far from clear, however, to what extent we, as readers, should view this technical

solution as desirable. It is highly likely, I think, that just as the representations of race, sex tourism and women in Houellebecq's work are not always
straightforwardly presented; the depiction of science, or more specifically of
the biotechnological solution as a cure for lovelessness, cannot be read entirely
at face value. A 'curious contradiction is detectable' says Angela Holzer, in
the position of science in the two novels. On the one hand, it is deployed as
a 'methodological model' and 'structural principle and theme' and, as such,
demonstrates the folly of an excessively positivist, mechanical understanding
of what Houellebecq calls 'the kingdom of intersubjective'.[34] However, and this
is where the contradictions become more noticeable, science also is presented
as a legitimate, even desirable, 'solution to social problems that are rooted in
human biology'.[35] The representation of science, as we shall see presently, in
both *Atomised* and *Possibility* is something like the Derridean *pharmakon*,
both poison and cure, vacillating between weak critique and an even weaker
resignation.

Very often in the novels, despite the 'pitiless and mechanical' reading of
the human condition, it seems as if science is the closest we might have in the
way of secular redemption in its offer of a genetic solution to the 'flaws' of this
'vile, unhappy race' (*A*, 104, 379). Thus, any kind of future ethics might only be
possible through science. Such an explicitly post-ideological or post-political
solution is consonant with a quasi-Comtean approach to social and cultural
theory which posits that humanity passes through three stages: the theological,
the metaphysical and, finally, that of the positive which represents the supremacy
of scientific knowledge and endeavour. In *Atomised* Michel Djerzinski, a
scientist with an unusually passionate interest in metaphysics, is an attentive
reader of Comte, and his genetic experiments with the concepts of human
happiness and love are profoundly influenced by the Comtean conviction that
only 'a relational, structural positivism can promise improvement'.[36] This faith
in a Comtean positivism is also, however, far from unequivocal, as the novels
also seem to advocate a reading in which science and the technocracy arising
from its sovereignty are anti-metaphysical, positivist extensions of the sexual
Darwinism that has emerged out of neoliberal logic. As Cruickshank notes,
'scientific breakthrough is linked to intellectual failure', but perhaps it would
be more accurate to say that this intellectual failure is in fact a symptom of the
wider political failure of the new world order of neoliberalism that everywhere
commodifies human life.[37]

An interview Houellebecq gave to the *Paris Review* in 2010 may go some way
to clarifying the ambiguous view of science presented in the novels. Explaining

that the scientific inspiration for *Atomised* came from reading about Alain Aspect's experiments in 1982 demonstrating the Einstein, Podolsky, Rosen (EPR) paradox in which science is used to undermine its own certainty, he says:

> ... when particles interact, their destinies become linked. When you act on one, the effect spreads instantly to the other, even if they are great distances apart. That really struck me, to think that if two things are connected once, they will be forever. It marks a fundamental philosophical shift. Ever since the disappearance of religious belief, the current reigning philosophy has been materialism, which says we are alone and reduces humanity to biology. Man as calculable as billiard balls and completely perishable. That worldview is undermined by the EPR paradox.[38]

The interdependent mixture of science and philosophy suggested here seems to revolve around an apparently paradoxical proposition. On the one hand, it seems to advocate a wholly materialistic explanation of the world, but this is countered by a residual belief in human interconnection that is not solely determined by biology and the molecular arrangement of particles. Both *Atomised* and *Possibility* seem to turn around these two apparently mutually incompatible positions. The genetic rectification of certain human 'flaws' that have been exacerbated, and in some cases actually produced, by the ubiquity of the desire-compulsion of capitalism is proffered, although, as noted, not as straightforwardly as it might first appear. Is Houellebecq really suggesting biotechnology as the sole remedy for existential disillusionment? Is science's ability to catalyse a 'metaphysical mutation' really a 'less depressing alternative to materialism', as he once suggested?[39] As a writer whose work is habitually undecidable, it so often the case in his novels that 'facetious parody' becomes one of the only conditions of 'sincerity', and so Houellebecq's scientific 'solution' must be read with some question as to whether it is endorsement or condemnation. Is this a lament for the falling away of philosophy? As one critic puts it, 'It remains unclear whether Houellebecq's narrator[s] favour the supersession of philosophy by science, or whether the indictment of philosophy serves as a nostalgic call for its renewal beyond the confines of what is knowingly – paradoxically – reduced to the homogenous mass of French Theory'.[40]

The thesis propounded in his novels is that Western modernity is a world in which the traces of Christianity, while faintly present in parts of some European countries, have, for the most part, disappeared, replaced by the demythologizing forces of secularism and consumerism which have offered the paltry consolidation of individualism as substitutes for the religious and the spiritual. Both of these novels, then, push this paradigm of disenchantment to its extreme in order to point up where we might be heading in a technological sense, but also to demonstrate that the parts that sex and shopping cannot reach – love, compassion, altruism – are simply not being nurtured in any substantial way. Compassion plays an important role in the conceptualization of love in both novels. In *Public Enemies*, Houellebecq suggests compassion, creaturely human sympathy, is a vital but imperilled quality of human nature:

> It remains a mystery that Schopenhauer alludes to only with a vague terror to the origin of compassion. For after all compassion is merely a feeling, something fragile on the face of it, although it seems to be reborn, naturally, from generation to generation [...] What if compassion disappeared? I think, in that case, humanity would disappear [...] And that the disappearance of humanity would be a good thing.[41]

Both novels suggest, then, that the only hope for a future humanity bound together by compassion, fraternity and love, lies in its technical management which, as becomes apparent in *The Possibility of an Island*, is no real hope at all.

Contemptus mundi: Lovecraft meets the *Moralistes*

Eschatological meditations on modernity in perceived terminal cultural and social decline, both *Atomised* and *Possibility* affirm that, in one way or another, 'humanity must disappear', a disappearance that will be achieved through the 'egalitarian' and 'transcendent ethics' of biogenetics, and in particular the ability to modify human DNA coding (*A*, 28, 29). Humanity gives way gradually to a new species of cloned 'neo-humans' in whom desire, jealousy, egotism and cruelty have been permanently eradicated and sexual difference is but a distant memory. Such genetic modification necessitates the ontological disappearance of extant human beings, a situation that Houellebecq, on the surface at least, finds not at all disturbing, as evidenced by his professed admiration for the 'weird fiction' writer H. P. Lovecraft in his 1991 book, *H. P. Lovecraft: Against the World, Against Life* (*Contre le monde, contre la vie*) (1991, 2005), borrowing, in fact, the title of *Atomised* (elementary particles) from Lovecraft's writing. The endlessly repeated scenarios of human and geological apocalypse integral to Lovecraft's forbidding materialist attitude suggest a cyclical entropic movement in which humanity and the notion of free will play a minuscule part in the unfolding of the cosmos:

The universe is nothing but a furtive arrangement of elementary particles. A figure in transition towards chaos. That is what will finally prevail. The human race will disappear. Other races in turn will appear and disappear. The skies will be glacial and empty traversed by the feeble light of the half-dead stars. These too will disappear. Everything will disappear. And human actions are as free and as stripped of meaning as the unfettered movements of the elementary particles. "Good, evil, morality, sentiments? Pure Victorian fictions." All that exists is egoism. Cold, intact, and radiant.[42]

While Houellebecq's reading of morality and human sentiment differs in some important ways from those in the abject universe of Cthulhu, his work shows an unmistakeable appetite for the Lovecraftian-inspired maxim that 'life is painful and disappointing' and, further, that 'we generally know where we stand in relation to reality and don't care to know any more. Humanity, such as it is, inspires only an attenuated curiosity in us'.[43] Unremittingly bleak and evacuated of any human warmth, Lovecraft's fictional universe is a 'desolate cosmos' of posthumanity in which those who survive have a stark choice either 'to be *pulverized*' or '*devoured*'.[44] Houellebecq's attraction to this world-view demonstrates a fear, palpable in both *Atomised* and *Possibility*, of an entropic return to nothing; a notably more abstractly metaphysical fear than that which underpins his anxieties around sexual competition, the decline of religion and the spread of 'unrestrained' neoliberalism and one that is expressed very clearly in a passage from *Public Enemies* in which he defends himself against charges of being a reactionary:

> ... if there is an idea, a single idea that runs through all of my novels, which goes so far as to haunt them, it is the *absolute irreversibility of all processes of decay* once they have begun. Whether this decline concerns a friendship, a family, a larger social group, or a whole society; in my novels there is no forgiveness, no way back, no second chance: everything that is lost is lost absolutely and for all time. It is more than organic, it is like a universal law that applies also to inert objects; it is literally entropic.[45]

This fear of entropy, of the changing and falling away of all things, is reminiscent of the view of the non-static world intrinsic to the processes of the dialectic as expounded by Friedrich Engels in *Socialism: Utopian and Scientific* (1878) that places 'nature at large' and 'the history of mankind or our own intellectual activity' within a larger cosmic 'picture of an endless entanglement of relations and reactions, permutations and combinations, in which nothing remains what, where, and as it was, but everything moves, changes, comes into being, and passes away …'. Engels notes that it was the Greek philosophers, in particular Heraclitus, who first alighted upon this 'primitive, naïve but intrinsically correct conception of the world' in which 'everything is and is not, for everything is fluid, is constantly changing, constantly coming into being and passing away'.[46] Interestingly, once again we find Houellebecq's ideas keeping strange and reluctant company with aspects of Marxism, but it is finally with Lovecraft's very un-Marxist misanthropic 'hatred of life' and pathological 'aversion to the modern world in particular' that he chooses to align himself.[47] Both Lovecraft and Houellebecq possess a profoundly non-ideological *contemptus mundi* presented through the medium of 'apocalyptic teleologies' emerging from a 'common Christian source'.[48]

Producing severe bouts of nausea in various protagonists in each of Houellebecq's novels, this *contemptus mundi* is not a provocation to action or to a heightened sense of moral or political responsibility in the Sartrean sense; Houellebecq's characters are emphatically not in the mould of Roquentin. The recognition that 'life is shit' produces, not a desire for social change or political insurrection, but only more of the same; a maintenance of the 'rancorous cataloguing' of the shit that assumes a post-ideological guise.[49] Each of his protagonists retreats from what they see as the execrable taint of the world into a Pascalian ascetic isolation; a move that, as more than one of Houellebecq's most perceptive critics have pointed up, owes much to the work of the seventeenth-century *Moralistes*, and in particular to the work of François de La Rochefoucauld (1631–80) and Jean de La Bruyère (1645–96).[50] 'In reading *Atomised*, Abecassis says, 'you know that you are, at heart, in the presence of a *Moraliste* of the French Augustinian variety (Arnault, Pascal, La Rochefoucauld). His is the infernal lucidity of a thinker who has thought through his subject and who cannot shake off his insights, for better or worse'.[51] Going on to describe the technique of cultural criticism in this novel as one in which 'the seventeenth-century French *Moraliste* meets the nano-cyber-molecular engineer', he concludes that this novel produces a 'very sophisticated grafting of Pauline and Pascalian anthropology' onto the moral and cultural topography of the late twentieth century.[52] The *Moraliste* methodology typically involves a close scrutiny of the flaws of contemporary society that unmasks vice underneath the patina of virtue and thus demonstrates the progressive and inevitable decline and disintegration of society in ways that are not explicitly political. Houellebecq's take on contemporary culture and society might indeed, in these terms, reveal him to be a modern *Moraliste*.

Bruno Chaouat has written of a pervasive atmosphere of 'metaphysical moroseness' in post-war France that is, he suggests, a reaction to a post-ideological, neoliberal age, a symptom of the 'fading away of an anthropological regime grounded in the shadow of the transcendent Other, the nation, the Republic, the state and the emergence of forms of communities yet to be determined' that I have been describing.[53] One might even say it is a moroseness tinged with melancholic longing for the old days of a structured *Gemeinshaft*; communities of belonging and social and kinship bonds that are so radically absent in *le monde houellebecquien* in which affective relations disappear to nothing. All of this, then, produces an unrelenting feeling of acedia; a pervasive sense of lifelessness and existential lassitude causing a movement away from any otherness or difference that is rehearsed in the idea of eternal repetition inherent in genetic cloning; a repetition, understood by Gerald Moore as the literalization of the Nietzschean concept of eternal return. Suggesting that *Possibility* presents a 'parody of the science of cloning as reconstructed eternal return', Moore sees the 'interweaving narratives' in the novel as 'meditations or variations on eternal return that are ultimately condemned to fail'.[54] Tracing the death of laughter through Nietzsche's *The Gay Science* and Henri Bergson's *Le Rire*, Moore argues that Houellebecq's novels communicate a pervasive sense of anaesthetized flatness and an ontological folding in of the self; a view that resonates with Daniel Heller-Roazen's ideas on subjectivity and sentience, in particular with a condition he calls coenesthopathy, a feeling where 'the sense of sensing has all but disappeared'.[55] Not quite the same as depression with which it shares some common features, this feeling of unresponsiveness is rather a profound sensual detachment from the materiality of the world. It is existence in a state of only partial sentience and anaesthetized affect.

The repeated scenarios of the falling away of all forms of vitality, but most particularly of that of desire and feeling or affect, into a profound state of impassive anaesthesia in Houellebecq's work comes hard on the heels of an intensive eroticism that is heavily charged with the possibility of intense suffering, always threatening to tip from the high of Eros into the not-quite-Thanatos of affective death. Without exception, pleasure turns into suffering, which in turn prompts a radical retreat from the physical world of sensuality and feeling. This is not precisely a deflation of sexual desire as some critics have suggested, but the realization that desire in its subsumed commodified form thwarts any potential for genuine human sociability and thus for love. 'If desire no longer justifies being', as Abecassis argues, 'then the last transcendental grounding of the modern individual has been pulled out from under his feet',[56] a scenario posed in slightly more anxious terms by Žižek when he suggests that the end of sexuality of the cloned posthuman entity 'far from opening up the way to pure spirituality, will simultaneously signal the end of what is traditionally designated as the uniquely human spiritual transcendence'. [57]

I turn now to examine the specific ways in which *Atomised* and *Possibility* trace this movement away from social and affective attachment into the realm of the posthuman where all difference and otherness – alterity – has been written out of human ontology. I consider the ways in which Houellebecq presents the restructuring of DNA as means of constructing a 'genetically egalitarian utopia' based on the 'freedom of indifference' and perfect ontological similitude that offers the possibility of overcoming the unruly, creaturely materiality aspects of the human body and, in so doing, quelling its metaphysical anguish.[58] Beginning with Michel Djerzinski's early experiments with human cloning that occupy the latter parts of *Atomised*, I then move on to examine *The Possibility of an Island* where the 'ontological overhaul' begun in *Atomised* is more fully developed.

A technical solution?

Atomised

Described by Žižek as 'the story of radical desublimation' and by others as a 'deeply cynical view of human possibility', *Atomised* takes its title from modern physics via H. P. Lovecraft, namely, the discovery of sub-atomic particles in quantum physics, informed by Niels Bohr's principle of complementarity.[59] Depending on its disciplinary location, the word atomization has two definitions: the first, a term used in atomic physics to describe a process during which a particle and its anti-particle collide and subsequently disappear, thus releasing energy. The second definition is drawn from modern sociology where it describes the breakdown of strong social and familial ties in society. These different, but interrelated, definitions provide a structural schema for the novel as they are reflected, to a large extent, in the divergent but corresponding responses of Bruno and Michel. As discussed, the half-brothers represent two alternative paths through the changed sexual environment of late modernity. Despite their divergent life trajectories, both Bruno and Michel arrive at more or less the same conclusions: the world in which they live is too painful to endure. More specifically, each comes to the realization that in a world where sexuality and sexual desire are traded as commodities, the possibility of love can no longer exist and that sex is the root of all human unhappiness. Having considered the libertine solution personified by the priapic Bruno Clément's attempts to join in the sexual carnival, which drives him clinically insane, let us turn now to his half-brother Michel Djerzinski, a melancholic and reclusive molecular biologist working at the Centre National de Recherche Scientifique (CNRS). Almost wholly asexual and socially reclusive, Michel wants 'nothing more than to love' and his tragic-romantic view of love spurs on his work in biogenetics, searching for a 'metaphysical mutation' that will redefine concepts of sexuality, free will and human individuality (*A*, 100). While Bruno's search for human fellowship and intimacy takes the form of a rampant, ultimately illicit, quest for increasingly elusive erotic sensation, Michel has one brief but tender relationship with his childhood sweetheart Annabelle. Like Valérie, she too kills herself, in this case after a diagnosis of ovarian cancer, bringing the total number of female suicides in this novel to three. Women have to die in Houellebecq's work so that the real task of masculine despair may begin and so it is only after Annabelle's death that Michel can begin in earnest to find a solution for 'the failure of the Event of love in contemporary Western societies'.[60]

It is somewhat ironic that it is Bruno and *not* Michel who first comes up with the idea that suggests a link between science and happiness. One night, over the course of many drinks with his half-brother, Bruno opines on Aldous Huxley: 'Everyone says *Brave New World* is supposed to be a totalitarian nightmare, a vicious indictment of society, but that's hypocritical bullshit. *Brave New World* is our idea of heaven: genetic manipulation, sexual liberation, the war against age, the leisure society. This is precisely the world we have tried— and so far failed—to create' (*A*, 187). As a libertine *manqué*, Bruno's interest in Huxley's ideas fixates upon *Brave New World*'s proposals to do away with the aggressive sexual competition that characterizes the contemporary sexual economy with its non-alpha male 'losers' pitted in an unending sexual battle with the young and the beautiful. The idea of sexual 'instant gratification' and an unabashedly pharmaceutical approach to depression and melancholia has much appeal for Bruno who habitually self-medicates with copious amounts of Xanax and Prozac.[61] Michel's interest in Huxley's dystopia differs from that of his randy half-brother. Whereas Bruno is excited by the idea of unlimited sexual experience and chemically induced happiness, Michel's interest lies in the potential of biotechnology to attend to metaphysical and philosophical questions of human consciousness. Before he refines his thinking, Michel can see no rational reason for human consciousness as it seemed to be present in certain animals 'for no apparent reason'. Sceptical of Darwinism's unshakeable determinism which reduces the subject to questions of natural selection, Michel wants to discover the 'key to understanding human action and opinion' and, more than anything, to solve the 'completely mysterious' realm of the consciousness which, frustratingly for his mechanistic scientific approach, does not seem to depend on any single factor such as 'anatomical, biochemical or cellular' causes (*A*, 268, 271). A theoretical impasse thus repeatedly arises in Michel's work as he attempts, and fails, to explain scientifically the mystery of human consciousness: 'According to Margenau's theory, human consciousness could be reduced to a field of probabilities in a Fock space, defined as a direct sum of Hilbert spaces'. What vexes Michel, however, is that he sees no evidence in this 'natural topography of Hilbert spaces that might give rise to free will' (*A*, 267). Musing on this, he realizes that the 'belief in the notions of reason and free will, which are the natural foundation of democracy, probably resulted from a confusion between the concepts of freedom and unpredictability' (*A*, 270). The question of free will soon becomes a question of predictability and this will lead him to the area of sex and sexuality as areas to be perfected by the elimination of chance and unpredictability, particulary in human sexuality. In the course of Michel's work, the search to define free will and the composition of human consciousness becomes less important to decipher, however, than the equally mysterious terrains of human sexuality.

Sexual desire is top of the list of human attributes to be demystified and rationalized by Djerzinski and his scientists' research into mitochondrial DNA: 'As soon as the genome has been completely decoded [...] humanity would have complete control of its evolution: when that happened sexuality would be seen for what it really was: a useless, dangerous and regressive function' (*A*, 320). In conversation with his colleague, Dupleschin, Michel gradually realizes that what he is seeking is nothing less than a new rational humanism, one that is post-political, post-ethical; ruled by the positivism and rationality of science it would do away with the centrality of culture: 'There is no power in the world – economic, political, religious or social – that can compete with rational certainty. Western society is primarily interested in philosophy or politics [...] it has also had a passionate love affair with literature and the arts, but nothing in its history has been as important as rational certainty' (*A*, 322). Shown to be part of the failed avant-garde utopian project that belongs to the world of 'theory', culture is rendered completely redundant in Houellebecq's brave new cloned world. In *Possibility* culture has been obliterated; nothing remains of human literary and artistic endeavours of which society had once been so proud. Before the advent of the neohumans, culture had descended into the mere pantomime of either the cruel humour of Daniel1's '100% hateful' stand-up routine of racism and viscous misogyny or the 'edgy' artist's conceptual art in which pieces of rotting meat are placed in a woman's underwear to make some predictable statement about cultural degeneration and sexuality. In the broad, and in many places, indiscriminate, sweep of Houellebecq's *pensée anti-'68*, he views culture as fundamentally part of '68's Nietzschean project emphasizing transgression which, as Moore notes, has reduced philosophy to mere laughter.[62] Culture has become emptily transgressive; ironic, knowing yet stupid, a hollow populist version of 'Nietzscheanism'. As Daniel1 observes, with so many barriers and taboos broken it is now possible to 'behave like a complete bastard with impunity' (*PI*, 10–11).

The long piece of mawkish poetry with which *Atomised* opens sets the aesthetic tone for the new species. Penned by the new race of clones who appreciate the 'suffering and joy' of their 'brave and unfortunate' predecessors but are content now to dwell in their collective genetic similitude in the crepuscular half-light of a 'perpetual afternoon' (*A*, 379), it reads:

> We live today under a new world order,
> This web which weaves together all things envelops our bodies,
> Bathes our limbs,
> In a halo of joy
> A state to which men of old acceded only through music,
> Greets us each morning as a commonplace.
> [...]
> Leaving behind a world of division,
> The way of thinking that divided us,
> Immersed in a serene, fertile delight
> Of a new Law
> Now for the first time,
> We can retrace the end of the old order. (*A*, 7–8)

The reference here to the joy attained though music is an obvious allusion to Nietzsche's *The Birth of Tragedy* (1872) in which the knowledge and fear of the abyss is assuaged by the solace of form, that is, of culture. In the posthuman ending of *Atomised*, seen even more unmistakably in *Possibility*, there is no space whatsoever for culture; in fact, creativity is expunged as an unnecessary human characteristic belonging to a past where humans needed to experience a sense of connection through a shared history of textuality and where imagination, memory and desire were still important to life. With its emphasis on diluted cultural forms, *Possibility* is, as Ben Jeffery notes, like a 'mirror-image' of the most famous scene in *Brave New World* where the Savage demands the right to be unhappy through poetry.[63] Creativity, in short, belongs to the world of potentiality and possibility, one that is little more than a nostalgic fetish for the neohumans. This desire to expunge the cultural is an act against the unpredictable otherness often invited in by creativity. Indeed, as Derek Attridge has suggested, creativity, in its purest form, is always an engagement with or movement towards a sense of otherness or alterity; a richly unpredictable gesture that contrasts with the technicalities of mere production and exchange which, he continues, introduce 'no alterity', rather they simply 'deploy existing components according to accepted norms'. Creativity, then, is 'both an act and an event' requiring the blasting of the self out of its habitual methods of understanding the world.[64] Central to this process is an engagement with otherness, a term that Attridge carefully separates from its psychoanalytic and semi-mystical uses, defining it thus: 'Otherness exists only in the registering of that which resists my usual modes of understanding, and that moment of registering alterity is a moment in which I simultaneously acknowledge my failure to comprehend … '.[65] Philosophy, literature, politics and the arts in general all adhere, in one way or another, to the sphere of creativity and as such await their disappearance in the totally managed 'rational certainty' that is facing the cloned race. The move to a conflict-free similitude is in process. Whereas in the past, history has been full of 'the most vicious, the most ridiculous conflicts' over ideas of living, be they religious, philosophical or political, the scientifically managed future of the neohumans rules out all contingency and creativity (*A*, 322).

Michel's experiments are inspired by the insights of Niels Bohr and the Copenhagen Interpretation of 1927, specifically the introduction of uncertainty around the idea of an objective scientific perspective as well as casting doubt upon 'the impossibility of any sharp separation between the behaviour of atomic objects'.[66] These extraordinary scientific breakthroughs are the catalyst for different ways of thinking about the relation of philosophy to the 'consistency and refutability' of science, specifically the theory of coherent superposition which is the state of exiting in all possible states simultaneously (*A*, 215). Michel's goal is to take the insights of quantum physics and make possible a post-sexual humanity, a process that will, he hopes, thwart the commercial aspects of sexuality that have come to define much of the misery in the West. So, 'through somewhat risky interpretations of the postulates of quantum mechanics', his aim is to render human desire obsolete and thus to 'restore the conditions which make love possible'.[67] Inspired by both the positivism of Comte and the Copenhagen interpretation, the world of the posthuman clones is divested of both joy and suffering, ruled rather by a disinterested 'reasonable intersubjectivity' in which there is no separation. 'In this space of which they are so afraid, human beings learn how to love and to die; in their mental space, separation, distance and suffering are born […] Good binds, while evil unravels. Separation is another word for evil …' (*PI*, 372).

Eschewing any modern intellectual thought outside of a strictly scientific domain, the only kind of philosophy in which Michel is interested is that of the ancient Celts and Greeks. *Three Conjectures on Topology in Hilbert Space* and *Mediations on Interweaving* and *The Clifden Notes* are shaped by the insights of Plato and Ancient Celtic art. In fact, we learn that a visit to Trinity College Library to see the Book of Kells is a 'decisive moment in the evolution of Michel Djerzinski's ideas' (*A*, 360). The medieval illuminated manuscript composed of elaborate crosses and spirals in insular majuscule tells the story of the four Gospels and stimulates Djerzinski's thinking: 'All that exists is a magnificent interweaving, vast and reciprocal' and that if this interweaving cannot be realized through 'natural' means then it must be reached through 'biophysical means' (*A*, 214, 362). This interweaving, crucially, must be devoid of the destructive forces of sexuality. Such a view of sexuality that insists upon its drives as inherently dangerous and destructive is, of course, another echo of Comte's suggestion that sexuality is 'the most disturbing of our propensities'.[68] Sex is the force that drives us, as human bodies, most insistently into and against each other, and if that fails, as it is seen to do in Houellebecq's fiction, then it must be expunged. Reproduction can be carried out by strictly technical means. In an eight-page work called 'Towards Perfect Reproduction' Michel's theory of cloning is expounded in detail: '… every cell contained within it the possibility of being perfectly copied. Every animal species, however highly evolved, could be transformed into similar species, reproduced by cloning and therefore immortal' (*A*, 370).[69] Cloning obviates any need for sex but the problem is that because sexuality has defined us as human subjects, in Houellebecq's unvarying thesis that is, then the eradication of sex will necessarily entail the eventual obliteration of every aspect of affective human behaviour; this is precisely what occurs in *Possibility* as the neohumans live an affect-free and isolated existence, completely alone with their experience of language reduced to the virtual exchange of email messages over a vast server.

In his first paradigm-altering publication, *The Topology of Meiosis*, Michel argues for the replacement of the ontology of objects with the ontology of states, thus enacting not only a scientific but also a '*metaphysical revolution*' that is able to move beyond the '*quasi-anthropological*' stage of human history (*A*, 355–6).

In such an ontology of states, a strict quantification of life without the eccentric impulses of sexuality would have the effect of 'restoring the practical possibility of human relationships' and, in due course, 'fraternity, sympathy and love' (*A*, 358–9). Central to Michel's project is the necessity for all human beings to have an identical genetic code – a prerequisite, of course, for cloning – thus posing a fundamental challenge to the notion of identity and difference so fundamental to the 'tortured, individualistic, quarrelsome' everyday lives of earlier humanity (*A*, 379). If everyone is the same, they are perfectly symmetrical and divisible creations and thus there is no longer any need for sexual difference or attraction. In this way, Michel's work allows the creation of a new strain of humanity as part of the first 'post-human civilization that breaks with the sex-death nexus and hence with the individualism and immorality that characterized the end of the twentieth century'.[70] The clones are asexual and immortal as the sexual urge to be with another body is genetically circumvented by the rolling-out of Krause corpuscles (obtained from advances in stem-cell biotechnology) and spreading them over the entire epidermis. Michel's 'biophysical' hypothesis argues that for humans to achieve happiness, then, sex must become an entirely technical and purely physiological non-event that permits the emergence of a purer form of love between human beings in which 'individuation, narcissism, malice' are banished. Sexual pleasure is thus radically demystified; if one can achieve orgasm through simply rubbing one body part against another then 'the great orgasm can be as commonly consumed and experienced as a can of Campbell's Soup'.[71] With multiple potential for auto-erotic enjoyment and *jouissance*, the self no longer requires any physical interchange with another body for either sexual pleasure or reproduction; the self pleasures the self and is thus never rejected, disappointed or disenchanted. There is no feeling of alienation or separation, no difference and no otherness.

A young scientist called Hubczejak becomes the most zealous proselytizer of Michel's work and devotes his life to its dissemination and popularization before taking it over as its 'logical successor' (*A*, 375). At first, he is called upon to defend Michel's most radical implication that humanity was a 'species that had outgrown individuality, individuation and progress' and that sexuality was simply a regressive function that had to be eradicated. 'One of the principal objections to his project' which carries Djerzinski's work into the twenty-first century, concerned, we learn, 'the suppression of sexual difference which is so central to human identity'. To this charge Hubczejak responds that his intention 'was to create a new, rational species, and that the end of sexuality as a means of reproduction in no way heralded the end of sexual pleasure …' (*A*,

374–5). By a media-savvy combination of compromise and strategic cynicism, Hubczejak renders these ideas more palatable by folding them into existing New Age thinking. Not possessing Michel's sensitivity to matters of human consciousness, Hubczejak is prone to underestimating the extent of the impact of this metaphysical change and has to come up with some hackneyed slogans in order to sell it to a sceptical public. This new sexual order is marketed as soft, peaceful and, above all, feminine. The Movement for Human Potential in 2011 bears a slogan modelled on a catalogue strap-line, 'THE FUTURE IS FEMININE' and later 'THE REVOLUTION WILL NOT BE MENTAL, BUT GENETIC' (*A*, 374, 377).

Resistance gradually melts away as most people now seemed to 'to believe in their hearts that the solution to every problem – whether psychological, sociological or more broadly human – could only be a technical solution' (*A*, 371, 376). UNESCO funds the project in 2021, and in 2029 the first of this 'new intelligent species' is created (*A*, 378). The final vision of *Atomised*, then, proposes an end to troubling individuation, sexual difference and the pursuit of any kind of otherness, sexual or ontological, in a world where science has 'cured' all metaphysical suffering. This posthuman world is shaped, as Moore points up, by the 'ethos of purely quantitative living' that no longer has any need for the sociality of politics, religion or kinship, neither for the conso-lation of culture and still less for philosophy.[72] Science alone has become the sole 'arbiter of unique irrefutable truth' and only science is able to restore a sense 'of community, of permanence, of the sacred' to a beleaguered humanity (*A*, 376–7). As suggested, it is not clear whether this presentation of science as metaphysically redemptive is a normative or critical one in *Atomised* but it is one that more fully developed in *Possibility* in which biogenetically engineered similitude is to the only way to achieve 'goodness, compassion, fidelity, and altruism' (*PI*, 53). The neohumans of *Possibility* are the direct descendants of the cloned entities at the end of *Atomised* who live affectless but peaceful lives in a barren, post-apocalyptic landscape.

The Possibility of an Island

Beginning almost precisely where *Atomised* leaves off, the narrative in *The Possibility of an Island* alternates between the hypertexted stories of Daniel24 and Daniel25, neohuman clones of the original Daniel, the transgressive, faux-Nietzschean comedian, 'a sort of Zarathustra of the middle classes', whose works include a screenplay aptly entitled *Diogenes the Cynic* (*PI*, 294). Part of the novel traces Daniel1's disillusionment with love and sex and his gradual withdrawal from the world into the Elohimite cult (a thinly disguised version of Raëlism is also described in *Lanzarote*) whose biogenetic experiments in cloning are inching ever closer to perfecting the science of the exact replication of human DNA. Devastated by sexual rejection and tired of all his worldly attachments, including sex with the nubile Esther, a variety of over-priced and useless vintage cars and his millions of Euros earned from his comedy ventures, Daniel1 visits the sect of the Elohimites.[73] Led by a distinctly un-spiritual prophet with a penchant for lewdly captioned T-Shirts (Lick my Balls) and an obsession with an anti-ageing Cretan diet, the Elohimite Church offers the possibility of eternal life through human cloning. Daniel's story is being read by the neohumans two thousand years later and is intercut with that of his two clones who recount the homogenous, wholly affectless, environment of the posthuman clones living in a post-apocalyptic world ruled over by The Supreme Sister.

Moving between the present, the near future and the distant future, the novel plots the trajectory of this new race of 'neo-humans' who, described in their infancy in *Atomised*, are now two thousand years old. While both novels offer 'scandalously unattractive dystopias', *Possibility* presents a significantly bleaker vision of posthumanity than that of *Atomised*.[74] In the earlier novel, the bioengineered entities remain recognizably human save for their augmented auto-erotic possibilities, whereas in *Possibility* human life has all but vanished, reduced to a virtual existence in which all communication and connection is carried out through the medium of machines and where all 'identity is serial' and bare life is lived out in the 'cold ecstasy of self-sufficiency'.[75] Made up of a set of cloned DNA information, the neohumans are only nominally human. Genetically unable to form any social or sexual attachments with each other and lacking in free will of any kind, theirs are lives as 'predictable as the functioning of a radiator' (*PI*, 321). Completely undifferentiated entities, the neohumans are super-rationalized units with no superfluous functions who live in a self-incorporated environment where everything and everyone is already known and communication takes place within a closed network. Science has allowed, however, some superficial differences to the composition of the cloned DNA to permit some local variations in their genomic fingerprint. For example, the neohumans are composed of their predecessors in two important genetic respects: the mechanical transmission of memory from one generation (or more properly, incarnation) to the next and the continuity of certain genetic weaknesses or psychological tendencies are passed on between all the 25 versions of the original Daniel. This bare difference has a negligible overall effect on the Daniels and functions as a ghostly trace, a distant genetic memory, of the real differences that characterized an older humanity.

In the narrative of the original storyteller, Daniel1, we learn of the formation and success of the Elohimites, a cult who use biotechnology to freeze the DNA from the original human subjects and who will refine this process to permit full genetic cloning. Millennia later, the cloned neohumans are living out their (eternal) days in individual compounds in 'total physical separation', the only communication between them taking place via computers by means of mathematical codes and limited visualization (*PI*, 302). Consuming only water and mineral salts, their physical bodies are stripped down to the barest life functions with no recognizably human digestive system and therefore producing no waste. The neohumans experience existence as a solitary, fear-free state of consciousness characterized by an unchanging homogeny and the predictability of non-event.

They are the end result of the total determinism of biogenetic science that has been able to prove that humans are little more than 'matter plus information' and the human mind is little more than a mechanical collection of 'neuronal sub-networks and dedicated synapses' that need only 'chemical refinement' to activate a full human subject with a history and individual personality (*PI*, 171). An Elohimite lecture on DNA and embryo-genesis, 'The Human Being: Matter and Information', displays a container full of plastic bags of 'unequal sizes of which the largest is water' on the stage. These bags, the audience is told, contain 'the exact chemical composition of the human being and it is only in a few quirky combinations of the genetic code, a 'few basic elements of aptitude and character that constitute our individuality and our memory' that our uniqueness as humans lies (*PI*, 170–1).

If science can intervene and correct these few elements that make us so distinctly and individually human then the more fugitive and unpredictable aspects of human subjectivity and intersubjectivity – sexuality, love, desire, memory and feeling – can be smoothed out into a state of serene one-ness by the application of the right kind of science, thus making human or neohuman life predictable, peaceful and utterly closed to the vagaries and possibilities of any possibility of otherness and difference. With no death, no difference and no affect, there is no longer any 'outside' for these self-sufficient entities. The teachings of the Supreme Sister, a nod to Auguste Comte's feminized secular Religion of Humanity and its *Nouveau Grand-Être Suprême* (New Supreme Great Being), accordingly emphasize the importance of indifference and detachment for the neohumans:

... jealousy, desire, and the appetite for procreation share the same origin, which is the suffering of being. It is the suffering of being [*la souffrance d'être*] that makes us seek out the other, as a palliative; we must go beyond this stage to reach the state where the simple fact of being constitutes in itself a permanent occasion for joy; where intermediation is nothing more than a game, freely undertaken, and not constitutive of being. We must, in a word, reach the freedom of indifference, the condition for the possibility of perfect serenity. (*PI*, 267)

Set against this frictionless existence of the neohumans is the chaotic life of Daniel1 who continues to search for some workable balance between sex and love and, like all of Houellebecq's characters, fails miserably. Simultaneously, horrified and perplexed by the 'incredible importance accorded to sexual matters among humans', the cloned Daniel25 realizes that in the twenty-first century such primitive behaviours encouraged humans to 'sacrifice its happiness, its physical well-being and even its life, in the hope of sexual inter-course alone' (*PI*, 231). When it comes to sexual matters, Daniel1 is marginally more successful than Bruno was in *Atomised*, although the two share similar proclivities in their aversion to sexual relations with middle-aged women as well as their willingness to offend by publicly transgressive behaviour. But where Bruno is finally locked away for his increasingly offensive behaviour most clearly articulated in his hateful, his right-wing pamphleteering, Daniel makes a lucrative career out of scurrilous humour as a stand-up comedian with shows such as *We Prefer the Palestinian Orgy Sluts*. Hugely successful, Daniel1 is spokesperson for his cynical young fans who fail to perceive that the 'institu-tionalised anarchy' of his shows is merely a symptom of a decayed ethical system 'centered for some decades now on competition, innovation and energy, more than on fidelity and duty'. As we know from *Atomised*, humour will save us from nothing. Transgression offers us similarly insubstantial succour and Daniel1 is fully aware that the 'putting to death of morality' had become a kind of empty ritual of transgression that operated only to reassert the dominant values of the group'; what he soon comes to realize is that '... life, fundamentally, *is not* comical' (*PI*, 32).

The opposite of this 'empty pseudo transgression' is the 'authentic' kitsch art of Vincent Greilsamer, a thoughtful and softly spoken young man who will become the second prophet of the sect, who Daniel meets on one of his first visits to the Elohimites.[76] Vincent outlines three main trends in contemporary art: gore, humour and the virtual (*PI*, 102–3). The first two of these categories are predicated on a sense of irony and distantiation from any sense of earnestness that 'leaves you doubting whether or not it has the slightest artistic value'. Then there is the concept of kitsch art which, while presenting emotion and feeling, necessitates a signalling 'by means of a meta-narration' on the part of the viewer that he or she is not fooled by this claim to seriousness: 'Everything is kitsch if you like. Music as whole is kitsch; art is kitsch, literature itself is kitsch. Any emotion is kitsch, practically by definition; but any reflection also, and even in a sense any action, the only thing that is not absolutely kitsch is nothingness' (*PI*, 103). What we end up with in the novel then, is an impoverished version of nothingness; a technically induced nothingness posing as life, what might be termed *le néant méchanique*.

Vincent's art is the realization of a very particular view of love in Houellebecq's work. As noted above, the cruelty of Daniel1's art in his vicious, apolitical stand-up routines, is welcomed by a society ever more entranced by mirthless, pointless transgression; a world in which love is becoming a distant memory. Vincent's installation art is the opposite of the transgressive gestures that have come to define modern and contemporary visual arts:

> I have chosen to create a small, easy world where you only encounter happiness. I am perfectly conscious of the regressive nature of my work; I know that it can be compared to the attitude of adolescents who, instead of confronting the problems of adolescence, dive head first into their stamp collection, their herbarium or whatever other glittering, limited, multicoloured little world they choose [...] I am a tiny little invalid child, who cannot live. I cannot come to terms with the brutality of this world: I just can't do it. (*PI*, 110)

The aesthetic setting for this installation is the 'naïve' taste in decor of the working-class of the grandparental generation, the last generation who knew how to love unselfishly and who experienced the deep bonds of familial and social attachments that, in Houellebecq's view, irrevocably disappeared after 1968 and were particularly ruinous for women like Esther, the young Spanish actress Daniel meets and who finally proves to him that love is no longer possible in a sexually liberated world. Unprotected by his cynicism, Daniel's rejection by the sexy but capricious Esther is the final push towards the dubious sect of the Elohimites. Esther's cheerful willingness to have uninhibited adventurous sex with his middle-aged body (although later this enthusiasm is shown to be faked) is the source of most of his joy in the relationship. This very quickly wanes as she is shown to epitomize the sexual amorality of her generation who manifest a complete indifference to love, pointed up in a drug-fuelled orgy at her birthday party in which Daniel is excluded from the sexual action, wandering Methuselah-like among the younger people 'like some kind of prehistoric monster with my romantic silliness, my attachments, my chains':

> As for love, it could no longer be counted on: I was undoubtedly one of the last men of my generation to love myself sufficiently little to be able to love someone else [...] There is no love in individual freedom in independence [...] love is only the desire for annihilation, fusion, the disappearance of the individual, in sort of what used to be called oceanic feeling, in something that anyway was, at least in the near future, condemned. (*PI*, 300)

For Esther and her generation there is an explicit repudiation of love and of any 'feeling of exclusivity' and 'of dependence' involved in monogamous relations. Realizing his desire to love has become hopelessly outmoded, 'like a stigmata in ancient times', Daniel concludes, not that Esther's behaviour is some kind of fruition, however imperfectly realized, of female sexual emancipation but that 'the centuries-old male project, perfectly expressed nowadays by pornographic films, that consisted in ridding sexuality of any emotional connotation in order to bring it back into the realm of pure entertainment had finally, in this generation, been accomplished' (*PI*, 241). The epitome of selfless love in its ideal state is represented in *Possibility* by Daniel's dog Fox. The state in which a dog apprehends the world and others in it is free, of course, from any existential anguish and crucially is not vulnerable to erotic obsolescence, affective ruin or boredom. The simplicity of canine rituals is something to which humanity might aspire. As Michel muses in *Atomised*: 'Life should be simple [...] something that could be lived as a collection of small, endlessly repeated rituals. Perhaps somewhat empty rituals, but they gave you something to believe in.[77] With their uninterrupted capacity for consistent daily pleasure it is the endless possibility for joy that makes a dog a 'machine for loving'; they are ideal love objects to which all three Daniels can attach themselves, 'Through dogs we pay homage to love' (*PI*, 190–1).[78]

In the 'Final Commentary, Epilogue' in *Possibility* there is a moment of resistance to the totally administered world of the neohumans in which all possibility of flux, flow and transformation has been stilled. Inspired, or perhaps corrupted, by reading Daniel1's commentary detailing the painful but still attractive texture of 'real' human life and still possessing some residual longing for another body, that of Marie23 whom he has 'met' online, Daniel25 decides to take his chances outside of the gated compounds of the 'abstract and virtual community' (*PI*, 331). Driven by the need to experience a real outside, he longs for the possibility of encountering otherness and sets out on a doomed mission to find an older version of humanity who may have survived the various catastrophic events, nuclear war, droughts and so on. Finally, Daniel25 decides to travel to the sea beyond the compound and its guarantee of eternal life. Inspired by the writing of Daniel1, he leaves behind the world of the neohumans and eternal life in the hope of understanding something of the feeling and passions of humans, 'what is best in our lives' (*PI*, 319). The smooth working of the human as machine may be pain-free and predictably serene but the possibility of something infinite and mystical continues to hold him mesmerized despite his final realization that whatever the goal might be of finite life, it will never be reached.

He begins to wander among the blasted 'ruins of a destroyed world', a post-apocalyptic landscape decimated by climatic catastrophes, with the faithful Fox by his side. Seeing the ruins of technology all around, he concludes that what was best about 'real' humanity was not art or 'philosophical or theological systems' but 'its technological ingenuity' (*PI*, 324). This outside world is inhospitable and ultimately lethal for Daniel25, and his decision to die rather than submit to this system of affectless stasis seems to suggest that the neohuman solution is no solution at all.

Notes

1 Houellebecq, *Rester Vivant*, 43.
2 *The Possibility of an Island* is henceforth abbreviated to *PI*. All page references will be given in parentheses in the main body of the text.
3 Christian Moraru, 'The Genomic Imperative: Michel Houellebecq's *The Possibility of an Island*', *Utopian Studies*,19, 2 (2008), 265–83, 268.
4 Melissa Gregg and Gregory J. Seigworth, 'An Inventory of Shimmers' in *The Affect Theory Reader* Melissa Gregg and Gregory J. Seigworth (eds) (Durham and London: Duke University Press, 2010), 2.
5 Bruno Latour, 'How to Talk About the Body? The Normative Dimension of Science Studies', *Body & Society*, 10.2 (2004), 205–29, 207.
6 Abecassis, 824.
7 Raymond Williams, *The Long Revolution* (Broadview Press, 2001 [1961]), 63–4.
8 Varsava, 146. Note that the novel's title *Les Particules élémentaires* was more literally translated as *The Elementary Particles* in the USA.
9 Richard J. Bauckham, 'Freedom in the Crisis of Modernity', in *Public Theology for the 21st Century* William F. Storrar and Andrew R. Morton (eds) (London: T&T Clark/Continuum, 2004), 80.

10	Charles Melman and Jean-Pierre Lebrun, *L'Homme sans gravité: fouir a tout prix* (Paris: Denoël, 2002), 224.

11	Ludwig Feuerbach, *Principles of the Philosophy of the Future*, trans. Manfred Vogel (Indiana: Hackett Publishing, 1966 [1843]), 1.

12	1953: James Watson and Francis Crick publish their findings on the molecular structure of the DNA-helix.

	1978: The first human to be conceived by natural cycle *in vitro fertilisation* (IVF) is born.

	1990: A consortium of researchers begins work on identification of three billion base pairs of DNA of the human genome. A first draft of the human genome is completed in February 2001.

	1997: Scientists announce that they have successfully cloned a sheep called Dolly.

	2003: The Human Genome Project is successfully completed on 12 April.

	2009: Barack Obama overturns the ban on stem cell research opening up a new era in biotechnological research.

13	For an overview of all of these viewpoints on critical posthumanism see Evelyn Fox Keller, *Refiguring Life: Metaphors of Twentieth Century Biology* (New York: Columbia University Press, 1995); Richard Doyle, *On Beyond Living: Rhetorical Transformations of the Life Sciences* (Stanford: Stanford University Press, 1997); Robert Bud, *The Uses of Life: A History of Biotechnology* (Cambridge: Cambridge University Press, 1993); Frédéric Vandenberghe, 'Posthumanism, or the Cultural Logic of Global Neo-Capitalism', translated into French as *Complexités du posthumanisme: Pour une critique de la bio-économique politique* (Paris: Harmattan, Collection Diagonale Critique, 2005). See also Bruno Latour and Michel Serres on the sociology and philosophy of science. See Steven Connor's 'Introduction', to Michel Serres, *The Five Senses: A Philosophy of Mingled Bodies* (I), trans. Margaret Sankey and Peter Cowley (London: Continuum, 2008), 1–16.

14	Steven Best and Douglas Kellner, *The Postmodern Adventure: Science, Technology and Cultural Studies at the Third Millennium* (New York and London: Guildford Press, 2001). See especially chapter 4, 'Technological Revolution and Human Evolution', in which they provide an indispensable overview of a 'number of critical mutations unfolding in the Third Millennium', distinguishing between the radical biocentrism of ecological groups, such as Earth First! who are deconstructive posthumanists, as well as a useful critical assessment of the more moderate positions. (195–6). Among the various writers and theorists considered, Best and Kellner identify a sub-group, transhumanists or extropians, who are neither anti-human nor anti-modern, but passionate believers in the spirit of the Enlightenment, especially the ideas of Condorcet. Transhumanists 'fervently embrace science and technology' regarding them not as potential enemies of an essential organic humanness but as 'positive forces' that will allow us to make 'quantum leaps in human evolution' by creating 'enhanced minds, bodies, and improved control over nature' (197).

15 Best and Kellner, 'Biotechnology, Ethics, and the Politics of Cloning', http://pages. gseis.ucla.edu/faculty/kellner/essays/biotechnologypoliticscloning.pdf [accessed 18 March 2008].

16 Donna Haraway, *Simians, Cyborgs, and Women: The Reinvention of Nature* (New York: Routledge, 1991). Haraway's work has endured in its importance and perspicacity, not only in the areas of feminist and gender studies, but also beyond, in a wider field of cultural and philosophical critique. See also her next book *Modest_Witness@Second_Millenium.FemaleMan©_Meets_OncoMouse^TM* (London: Routledge, 1997) for a detailed set of arguments about genetic modification, particularly of animals, in this case a patented mouse purposely bred to carry the breast cancer gene.

17 Katherine N. Hayles, *How We Became Posthuman: Virtual Bodies in Cybernetics, Literature, and Informatics* (Chicago: University Of Chicago Press, 1999); Eugene Hacker, 'What is Biomedia', *Configurations*, 11, 1 (2003) 47–79; *Posthuman Bodies*, (eds) Judith Halberstam and Ira Livingstone (Bloomington: Indian University Press, 1995); Rosi Braidotti, *Nomad Subjects: The Uses of Life: A History of Biotechnology* (Cambridge: Cambridge University Press, 1993); Bruno Latour, *Pandora's Hope: Essays on the Reality of Science Studies* (Cambridge: Harvard University Press, 1999); and Keith Ansell-Pearson, *Viroid Life: Perspectives on Nietzsche and The Transhuman Condition* (New York: Routledge, 1997). See also Ray Kurzweil's *The Age of Spiritual Machines: When Computers Exceed Human Intelligence* (Cambridge: MIT Press, 1999) for its influential arguments on the interface between human and artificial intelligence. On extropianism see Kurzweil, *The Singularity is Near: When Humans Transcend Biology* (New York: Viking Penguin, 2005) and also his *The Age of Spiritual Machines: When Computers Exceed Human Intelligence* (New York: Penguin, 2000) that has been influential in this field.

18 Jeremy Rifkin, *The Biotech Century: Harnessing The Gene and Remaking the World* (New York: Tarcher/Putnam, 1998), 236–7.

19 Paul Rabinov and Nikolas Rose, 'Biopower Today', *BioSocieties*, 1 (2006), 195–217.

20 Felipe Fernández-Armesto, *So You Think You're Human?* (Oxford and New York: Oxford University Press, 2004), 1. For a sceptical view of biotechnology and in particular of human cloning see Rifkin; for a bio-conservative view see Leon Kass's 'The Wisdom of Repugnance', in *Flesh of My Flesh: The Ethics of Human Cloning*, ed. Gregory Pence (Lanham, Maryland: Rowman and Littlefield, 1998), 13–37; and Nikolas Rose, *The Politics of Life Itself: Biomedicine, Power, and Subjectivity in the Twenty-First Century* (Princeton: Princeton University Press, 2007).

21 Francis Fukuyama, *Our Posthuman Future: The Consequences of the Biotechnical Revolution* (London: Profile Books, 2002), 7; *The End of History and the Last Man* (New York: The Free Press, 1992).

22 See also Fredric Jameson, 'Progress versus utopia: Or, can we imagine the future', *Science-Fiction Studies*, 27 (1982), 147–58.

23 Halberstam and Livingstone, 10.

24 Diken, 63.

25 Ibid., 62.

26 Giorgio Agamben, *Homo Sacer: Sovereign Power and Bare Life* (Stanford University Press, 1998), 135

27 Jean and John Comaroff, 'Millennial Capitalism: First Thoughts on a Second Coming', *Public Culture*, 12, 2 (2000), 291–343, 322.

28 See Hub Zwart, 'From Utopia to Science: Challenges of Personalised Genomics Information for Health Management and Health Enhancement', *Medicine Studies*, 1, 2 (2009), 155–66; Peter Sloterdijk, 'Rules for the Human Zoo: A Response to the Letter on Humanism', *Environment and Planning D: Society and Space*, 27.1 (2009), 12–28, http://www.xs4all.nl/~rekveld/tech/Sloterdijk_RulesForTheHumanZoo.pdf

29 Foucault, *The Order of Things* (New York: Random House, 1994), 387.

30 Commenting on Houellebecq's account of how science, and in particular, molecular biology will overtake ethics and philosophy as formative discourses, Roger K. Malina notes: 'The sometimes purple prose is laced with scientifically accurate descriptions of human biology, psychology and anatomy [...] The discussion of the impact of Einsteinian relativity, quantum mechanics, chaos theory, and molecular biology are well thought out and interesting.' *Leonardo*, 32, 2 (1999), 147–8, 147.

31 Fredric Jameson, *Archaeologies of the Future: The Desire Called Utopia and Other Science Fictions* (London: Verso, 2005), 31.

32 *Interventions*, 118.

33 Bowd, 31.

34 *Public Enemies*, 144.

35 Angela Holzer, 'Science, Sexuality, and the Novels of Huxley and Houellebecq', *Comparative Literature and Culture*, 5, 2 (2003), 1–11, 6.

36 Alexander Riley, 'In the Trenches of the War between Literature and Sociology: Exploring the Scandalous Sociology of Modernity in the Novels of Michel Houellebecq', *International Journal of Contemporary Sociology*, 431, 1 (2006), 104–24, 112.

37 Cruickshank, 139.

38 Susannah Hunnewell, 'The Art of Fiction', http://www.theparisreview.org/interviews/6040/the-art-of-fiction-no-206-michel-houellebecq [accessed January 2011]. Aspect's 1982 experiment tested the idea of quantum interconnectedness originally proposed by Albert Einstein, Boris Podolsky, and Nathan Rosen in 1935.

39 Hunnewell, 'The Art of Fiction'.

40 Gerald Moore, 'Gay Science and (No) Laughing Matter: The Eternal Returns of Michel Houellebecq', *French Studies*, 1 (2011), 45–60, 50, 53.

41 *Public Enemies*, 169.

42 *H.P. Lovecraft: Contre le monde, contre la vie* (Paris: Editions du Rocher, 1991);

H.P. Lovecraft: Against the World, Against Life, trans. Dorna Khazeni (San Francisco: Believer Books, 2005), 32.

43 *Lovecraft*, 29.

44 Ibid., 33.

45 *Public Enemies*, 111.

46 Frederick Engels, *Socialism: Utopian and Scientific* (Chicago: Charles H. Kerr & Co., 1908), http://www.gutenberg.org/files/39257/39257-h/39257-h.htm [accessed 18 April 2012].

47 *Lovecraft*, 57.

48 Abecassis, 823

49 Nicholas Sabloff, 'Of Filth and Frozen Dinners', *The Common Review*, 5, 3 (2006), 51.

50 On the French *moralistes* see A. J. Krailsheimer, *Studies in Self-Interest from Descartes to La Bruyère* (Oxford: Clarendon Press, 1962) and also Odette de Mourgues, *Two French Moralists: La Rochefoucauld, La Bruyère* (Cambridge: Cambridge University Press, 1978).

51 Abecassis, 822.

52 Ibid., 804.

53 Bruno Chaouat, 'Moroseness in Post-cold War France', *Yale French Studies*, 116/117 (2009), 125–38, 127, 137.

54 Moore, 53.

55 Daniel Heller-Roazen, *The Inner Touch: Archaeology of a Sensation* (New York: Zone Books, 2007), 286.

56 Abecassis, 821, 822.

57 Žižek, 'Masturbation, or Sexuality in the Atonal World', (2008), http://www.lacan. com/symptom/?page_id=247 [accessed 18 May 2011].

58 Moraru, 268.

59 See Žižek; and Varsava, 160.

60 Žižek.

61 Studies have shown that France 'holds the dubious distinction of being the world leader in the per capita consumption of psychotropic medications'. Jennifer Willging, 'Another Prozac Nation: The Problem of Psychotropic Medication Consumption in Contemporary France', *Contemporary French Civilization*, 33, 1 (2009), 1–22, 1.

62 Moore, 45.

63 Jefferey, 60.

64 Attridge, 25–6.

65 Ibid., 27.

66 Jørgen Kalckar, Niels Bohr, Léon Rosenfeld, Erik Rüdinger, Finn Aaserud, *Foundations of Quantum Physics II (1933–1958)* (Amsterdam: Elsevier Press, 1996), 210.

67 Angela Holzer, 'Science, Sexuality, and The Novels of Huxley and Houellebecq',

CLC Web: Comparative Literature and Culture, 5, 2 (2003),1–11, 6, http://docs.lib. purdue.edu/clcweb/vol5/iss2 [accessed 23 April 2011].

68　Auguste de Comte, *An Appeal to Conservatives*, 75.

69　Of course, the idea that such a simple causality exists between genes and the variegated terrains of human sexuality is a rather untrustworthy interpretation of genome science as it erroneously conflates sexuality and sexual desire, reducing both to a matter of tinkering with DNA.

70　Bowd, 35.

71　Abecassis, 807.

72　Moore, 58.

73　The Elohimites are actually a disguised version of the actual sect of the 'UFO religion' the Raëlians. Set up by ex-racing driver Claude Vorilhon in 1974, Raëlism is difficult to define as a movement as it comprises a motley mixture of New Age thinking, a belief in the existence of extraterrestrials, eschatology and a strong advocation of scientific cloning through nanotechnology. Houellebecq undertook extensive research on the sect in preparation for *The Possibility of an Island*.

74　Brinkmann, 1387.

75　Moraru, 276.

76　Moore, 45.

77　*Atomised*, 100.

78　Houellebecq himself has a dog, his beloved Pembroke Corgi, Clément, with whom he has been frequently photographed. He has made several comments to interviewers conveying his deep affection for Clément: 'It is always hard to abandon him', he told Andrew Hussey, a reporter from *The Observer*, Sunday 6 November 2005. See Delphine Grass, 'Domesticating Hierarchies, Eugenic Hygiene and Exclusion Zones: The Dogs and Clones of Houellebecq': *La Possibilité d'une île*', *L'Esprit créateur*, 52, 2 (2012), 127–40.

Conclusion

You could quibble forever whether men were more or less happy in previous centuries. You could comment on the disappearance of religions, of the feeling of love [...] the loss of our sense of the sacred, the crumbling of social ties [...] But it remains the case that, on the level of consumption, the pre-eminence of the twentieth century was indisputable.[1]

'It has now become easier', writes Jameson, 'to imagine the end of the world than the end of capitalism'.[2] The end of the world, or more accurately the end of humanity, is precisely what is finally imagined in Houellebecq's novels that have been considered here. This, then, is the literature of despair. Unable to conceive of anything that might be outside of capitalism or any point of meaningful or effective resistance to it, Houellebecq's writing demonstrates what Susan Buck-Morss argues is neoliberalism's capacity to eliminate 'the very possibility of critical thinking', central to which is a continuing human openness to the idea and possibility of otherness and alterity.[3] The end of the human world imagined in these novels is reached through a brief period of libertine participation that produces an irreversible cauterization of affect leading to social and sexual atomization and then to a total sloughing off of all human attachments and affiliations. This process of detachment reaches its apotheosis in *The Possibility of an Island* where there is an absolute separation from any recognizably human world. With every sense of the political discounted, the only solution offered to the affective misery wreaked by capitalism is a biogenetic one enabling the anaesthetizing of all feeling and the stilling of all thought and, most crucially, removing the need for any kind of otherness or alterity.

The difficulty of encountering alterity, anything outside of the citadel of the self, is central to all of Houellebecq's writing. Both *Atomised* and *Possibility* trace humanity's retreat from the contingency and potentiality of everyday affective life into the perfectly functioning technical existence of clones who are no longer buffeted by the whims of affect, as every trace of organic, creaturely feeling has been bioengineered out of their biological schema. With affect gone, there is no interrelatedness or connection, as there is no longer a social body to which these new entities belong. There is no more culture, no society to speak of, no more sex and above all, no more sense of otherness. Eating, secreting and existing in complete isolation, the neohumans have only the faintest trace of the memory of human laughter and happiness in the shape of Daniel1's writing, read by his Daniel25 incarnation as a ghostly archive of the ruins of 'real' humanity. This life-story of the original Daniel speaks of the frictionless, affectless, undifferentiated world-without-desire to come two millennia later: 'I no longer feel any hate in me, nothing to cling to any more, no more landmarks or clues [...] There is no longer any real world, no world, no human world, I am outside time, I no longer have a past or future, I have no more sadness, plans, nostalgia, loss or hope ...' (PI, 304). Unable, and eventually unwilling, to connect to any other body, Houellebecq's protagonists retreat from affective potentiality into almost total somatic isolation where all human life is identical; 'corrected' human entities exist painlessly in vanishingly small physical and phenomenological spaces with no flux, flow and transformation – existence is reduced to what might be called 'bare life'.

The asexual, posthuman space that culminates in The Possibility of an Island has been in the making across all four novels considered here and is the conclusion of the working through of the hypothesis set out in Whatever; namely, that the extension of the domain of neoliberal capitalism produces irreversibly ruinous effects on human affective life. This ruination is seen most particularly in the sexual domain as it is in sexuality and its attendant potential for intimacy and feeling that it is most keenly registered. With its sphere of emotional attachment and affective belonging, sexuality is, as we have seen, the site at which capital most acutely meets biopolitical life and, as such, is one of the most vulnerable spaces to the affective reach of neoliberal capitalism, where emotional sensibilities are transformed into resources to form an integral part of human capital. This incursion of capital into the innermost worlds of our subjectivity – our desires, dreams and fears – leaves nothing untouched in its subsuming wake and increasingly, Houellebecq suggests in his oeuvre, there is no outside to this subsumption. The transformation of the myriad nuances and singular fragilities of the affective human world into a material one defined by exchange and profit is on its way to full totality and part of this is the gradual writing out of any possibility of resistance to this system. For the subject who is sensitive to this lack of outside, living produces almost unbearable suffering as it becomes acutely aware of itself as an increasingly deprived consciousness. Incrementally then, the novels shut off any possibility of any alterity to this vision, choosing instead complete disaffiliation from the social and withdrawal into an ontological similitude that requires no outside or difference; a post-philosophical world where the rational determinism of science and technology contours human life. The posthuman world presented in *The Possibility of an Island* has given up on 'real' human communion and collectivity. Living in carefully managed isolation in a state of supreme reason and indifference, the neohuman entities are the products of Houellebecq's 'cold revolution', one in which 'sociability had had its day'. 'Perhaps that crude imbecile Hegel', Daniel1 says, 'had, at the end of the day, seen things correctly' and that all humans were merely the 'servant[s] *of the cunning of reason*' (*PI*, 299, 300). *Possibility* is, then, the end point of Houellebecq's recurring thesis of an escalating anomie in which the number of possibilities in human life are inexorably on the wane in a process of shrivelling up and contraction, and which are finally brought to a standstill in the monadic entities of the neohumans.

Whether Houellebecq's vision of 'bare life' is to be understood as warning or as resignation gives rise to several questions, of course. Does this posthuman vision suggest that acquiescence to the neoliberal state of affairs is inevitable and unavoidable? Or is Houellebecq rather warning us, using the debased register of the world we inhabit, of the dangers we surely face? Is the suggestion that there really is no alternative to this metaphysical and affective desubjectification finally a deeply conservative one? Or, is the peaceful existence of the neohumans desirable, even utopian? On the face of it at least, their existence might appear something of a utopian space; free from individuation and narcissism and thus from any sense of economic, sexual, or metaphysical struggle, there is a strict equivalence and egalitarianism between the posthuman entities. In this way, the vagaries of humanity will disappear and in its place an improved, technically corrected, post-ideological posthumanism will be created in which all human affect and striving is replaced by serene indifference and ontological similitude. This is, however, a vision that teeters on the line between utopia and dystopia and might be regarded as a rather cagey, but in many ways typically Houellebecquian, manoeuvre.

Seen positively, Houellebecq's work demonstrates what might happen to humanity if we continue down the current ideological road and, for many readers, this warning is an important part of the allure of *le monde houellebecquien*. Attracted to his novels by their urgent engagement with their subject, that of the total subsumption of the human life world into the desymbolizing circuits of exchange and competition, we are continually waiting, even if we are not fully conscious of this, for something resembling a 'solution' to become visible. Undeterred perhaps even by his 'modest proposal' of sex tourism, misogyny and anti-Islamic comments, we are persuaded by the conviction of his vision to go along with many of the controversies and outrages in the work in the persistent hope that we might be offered some kind of workable critique of the world described. In other words, we hope that Houellebecq's work is all a timely caution that, if left unchecked, capitalism will continue to swallow up our lives, loves and feelings and feed them into the machine of exchange.

However, the solution we are offered is no solution at all as what we end up with is a post-ideological, posthumanism that points up the lack of conceivable ethical or political alternatives to the rationalization of the lifeworld. There is only more of the same to come, Houellebecq suggests, and the only way out of this is the creation of a post-historical, non-human world that is, in the end, no world at all and offers us only a vision of an endlessly regressive humanity. In its failure to imagine another possibility for the world other than an affectless posthumanity, Houellebecq's work may be said to exemplify that which is most at risk under the reign of neoliberalism: progressive and creative critical thinking itself. 'To be truly radical', as Raymond Williams said, 'is to make hope possible rather than despair inevitable'. Despair is not only inevitable in Houellebecq's work, it is without anticipation of either hope or redemption.

Notes

1 *Possibility*, 17.
2 Fredric, Jameson, *The Seed of Time* (New York: Columbia University Press, 1994), xii.
3 Susan Buck-Morss, *Thinking Past Terror: Islamism and Critical Theory on the Left* (London: Verso, 2003), 65–6.

Bibliography

Abdel-Illah, Salhi, 'Un racisme chic et tendance', *Libération*, 4 September 2001, 6

Abecassis, Jack I., 'The Eclipse of Desire: L'Affaire Houellebecq', *MLN*, 115, 4, French Issue (2000), 801–26

Adorno, Theodor W., *Minima Moralia: Reflections on a Damaged Life* (London: Verso, 1999)

Adorno, Theodor W. and Max Horkheimer, *Dialectic of Enlightenment* (London: Verso, 1997)

Agamben, Giorgio, *The Time That Remains: A Commentary on the Letter to the Romans*, trans. Patricia Dailey (Stanford: Stanford University Press, 2005)

—*Homo Sacer: Sovereign Power and Bare Life* (Stanford University Press, 1998)

Ahmed, Sara, 'Affective Economies', *Social Text*, 22, 2 (2004), 117–39

Allwood, Gill, *French Feminisms: Gender and Violence in Contemporary Theory* (London: Routledge, 1998)

Amans, Thomas, 'Love, Hate, and Dissolution: A Contextualization of the Representation of Women in the Novels of Michel Houellebecq', in Melanie Hackney and Aaron Emmitte (eds), *Sexuality, Eroticism, and Gender in French and Francophone Literature* (Newcastle upon Tyne: Cambridge Scholars Publishing, 2011)

Amin, Ash, *Post-Fordism: A Reader* (London: Blackwell, 1994)

Anderson, Perry, 'Dégringolade', *London Review of Books*, 26, 17, 2 September 2004, 3–9

Ansell-Pearson, Keith, *Viroid Life: Perspectives on Nietzsche and the Transhuman Condition* (New York: Routledge, 1997)

Appignanesi, Lisa, 'Liberté, égalité and fraternité: PC and the French', in Sarah Dunant, ed., *The War of the Words: The Political Correctness Debate* (London: Virago, 1994), 145–63

Apter, Emily, 'Mobile Citizens, Media States: A Panel at the 2000 MLA Convention', *PMLA*, 117, 1 (2002), 79–83

Arènes, Claire and Jacques Arènes, 'Michel Houellebecq: prophète des temps finissants', *Études*, 404, 6 (2006), 796–803

Armus, Seth, 'The American Menace in the Houellebecq Affair', *French Politics and Society*, 17, 2 (1999), 34–42

Aron, Raymond, *The Elusive Revolution,* trans. Gordon Clough (New York: Praeger, 1969)

Arrabal, Fernando, *Houellebecq* (Paris: Cherche Midi, 2005)

Arrighi, Giovanni, *The Long Twentieth Century: Money, Power and the Origins of our Times* (London: Verso, 1994)

Artières, Philippe and Michel Zancarini-Fournel (eds), *68, Une Histoire collective* (Paris: La Découverte, 2008)

Attridge, Derek, *The Singularity of Literature* (London: Routledge, 2004)

Audier, Serge, *La pensée anti-'68: Essai sur une restauration intellectuelle* (Paris: La Découverte, 2008)

Augé, Marc, *Non-Places: Introduction to an Anthology of Supermodernity* (London: Verso: 1995)

Authier, Christian, 'Houellebecq: la mort à crédit de l'Occident', *L'Opinion Indépendante*, 19 November 2002

Badinter, Elisabeth, *XY: De l'identité masculine* (Paris: Odile Jacob, 1992)

Badré, Frédéric, 'Une Nouvelle Tendance en littérature', *Le Monde*, 3 October 1998, 14

Banville, John, 'Futile Attraction: Michel Houellebecq's Lovecraft', *Artforum International*, 1 April 2005

Bardolle, Olivier, *La literature à vif: Le cas d'Houllebecq* (Paris: Esprit des péninsules, 2004)

Barnes, Julian, 'Hate and Hedonism: The Insolent Art of Michel Houellebecq', *The New Yorker*, 7 July 2003, http://www.newyorker.com/archive/2003/07/07/030707crbo_books; originally published in French as 'Haine et hédonisme; L'art insolent de Michel Houellebecq', *Les Inrockuptibles*, special issue Houellebecq (2005), 30–5

Barry, Kathleen, *The Prostitution of Sexuality* (New York and London: New York University Press, 1995)

Barthes, Roland, 'The Death of the Author', *Image-Music-Text*, trans. Stephen Heath (New York: Hill and Wang, 1977)

Bauckham, Richard J., 'Freedom in the Crisis of Modernity', in William F. Storrar and Andrew R. Morton (eds), *Public Theology for the 21ˢᵗ Century* (London: T&T Clark/Continuum, 2004)

Baudrillard, Jean, *For a Critique of the Political Economy of the Sign* (London: Telos Press, 1981, [1972])

—*Symbolic Exchange and Death* (London: Sage, 1993)

—*The Consumer Society: Myths and Structures*, trans. Chris Turner (London: Sage, 1998, [1970])

—'The Ecliptic of Sex', in *Seduction*, trans. Brian Singer (London: Macmillan, 1988)

—*The System of Objects* (London: Verso, 1996, [1968])

—*The Vital Illusion*, ed. Julia Witwer (New York: Columbia University Press, 2000)

Bauman, Zygmunt, *Globalization: The Human Consequences* (New York: Columbia University Press, 1998)

—*Postmodernity and Its Discontents* (New York: New York University Press, 1997)

Baumgardner, J. and A. Richards, 'Feminism and femininity: Or How We Learned to Stop Worrying and Love the Thong', in A. Harris and M. Fine (eds), *All About the Girl* (London: Routledge, 2004), 59–69

Baverez, Nicolas, *La France qui tombe* (Paris: Perrin, 2004)

Bell, Shannon, *Reading, Writing, and Rewriting the Prostitute Body* (Bloomington: Indiana University Press, 1994)

Benjamin, Walter, 'Capitalism as Religion', in *Selected Writings: 1938–1940* (Cambridge, MA: Harvard University Press, 1996)

Bennett, David, 'Libidinal Economy, Prostitution and Consumer Culture', *Textual Practice*, 24, 1 (2010), 93–121

Berger, Peter and Stanley Pullberg, 'Reification and the Sociological Critique of Consciousness', *New Left Review*, 35 (1996), 56–77

Berman, Paul, 'Depressive Lucidity', *New Republic*, 223, 21 (20 November 2000), 25–9.

Best, Beverly, '"Fredric Jameson Notwithstanding": The Dialectic of Affect', *Rethinking Marxism*, 23, 1 (2011), 60–82

Best, Steven and Douglas Kellner, 'Biotechnology, Ethics, and the Politics of Cloning', http://pages.gseis.ucla.edu/faculty/kellner/essays/biotechnologypoliticscloning.pdf [accessed 18 March 2008]

Best, Victoria, 'Eros and Extimité: Viewing the Pornographic Self in Bataille, Cixous and Houellebecq', in Silke Horskotte and Esther Peeren (eds), *The Shock of the Other: Situating Alterities* (Amsterdam: Rodopi Press, 2007), 93–104

Bewes, Timothy, *Cynicism and Postmodernity* (London: Verso, 1997)

—*Reification, or the Anxiety of Late Capitalism* (London: Verso, 2002)

Biemann, Ursula, 'Remotely Sensed: A Topography of the Global Sex Trade', *Feminist Review*, 70, 1 (2002), 75–88

Bienczyk, Marek, 'Sur quelques éléments (particuliers) de l'art Romanesque', *L'Atelier du roman*, 18 (June 1999), 33–9

Biron, Michel, 'L'Effacement du personnage contemporain: l'exemple de Michel Houellebecq', *Études françaises*, 41, 1 (2005), 27–41

Bisnel, François, 'Le fabuleux destin de Michel H.', *L'Express*, 30 August 2001

Boal, Iain and Michael Watts, 'The Liberal International', *Radical Philosophy*, 140 (2006), 40–44

Bohr, Niels, Jørgen Kalckar, Léon Rosenfeld, Erik Rüdinger, and Finn Aaserud, *Foundations of Quantum Physics II (1933–1958)* (London: Elsevier Press, 1996)

Boltanski, Luc and Ève Chiapello, *The New Spirit of Capitalism* (London: Verso, 2005)

Bonefeld, W., R. Gunn and K. Psychopedis (eds), *Theory and Practice* (London: Pluto, 1992)

de Bord, Guy, *The Society of the Spectacle*, trans. Donald Nicholson-Smith (New York: Zone Books, 1967)

Bottomore, Tom, Laurence Harris, V. G. Kiernan and Ralph Miliband (eds), *A Dictionary of Marxist Thought* (Cambridge: MA: Harvard University Press, 1983)

Bourdieu, Pierre, 'Neo-liberalism, the Utopia (Becoming a Reality) of Unlimited Exploitation' in *Acts of Resistance: Against the New Myths of Our Time* (Cambridge: Polity Press, 1998), 94–106

—*Distinction: A Social Critique of the Judgment of Taste,* trans. Richard Nice (Cambridge: Harvard University Press, 1984)

—'La Domination Masculine', *Actes de la recherche en sciences socials*, 84 (1990), 2–31

—*Interventions 1961–2001: Science sociale et action politique* (Marseilles: Agone, 2002)

—'A Reasoned Utopia and Economic Fatalism', *New Left Review*, 227 (1998), 125–30

—'A Utopia of Endless Exploitation', *Le Monde Diplomatique*, December 1998, http://mondediplo.com/1998/12/08bourdieu

Bourdieu, Pierre and Loïc Wacquant, 'New-Liberal Speak: Notes on the New Planetary Vulgate', *Radical Philosophy*, 105 (2001), 2–5

Bourg, Julian, *From Revolution to Ethics: May '68 and Contemporary French Thought* (Montreal & Kingston: McGill-Queen's University Press, 2007)

Bourriaud, Nicolas, Christophe Duchatelet, et al., 'Houellebecq et l'ère du flou', *Le Monde*, 10 October 1998

Bourriaud, Nicolas, Jean-Yves Jouannais and Jacques-François Marchandis, 'An Interview with Michel Houellebecq: "I have little faith in Freedom"', trans. Dawn M. Cornelio, *Sites: Journal of Twentieth-Century/Contemporary French Studies*, 3, 2 (1999), 242–52

Bowd, Gavin, 'Michel Houellebecq and the Pursuit of Happiness', *Nottingham French Studies*, 4, 2 (2002), 28–39

—ed., *Le Monde de Houellebecq* (Glasgow: Glasgow University Press, 2006)

Braedley, Susan and Meg Luxton (eds), *Neoliberalism and Everyday Life* (McGill: Queen's University Press, 2010)

Braidotti, Rosi, *Nomad Subjects: The Uses of Life: A History of Biotechnology* (Cambridge: Cambridge University Press, 1993)

Brenner, Neil, Jamie Peck and Nik Theodore, 'Variegated Neoliberalization: Geographies, Modalities, Pathways', *Global Networks*, 10, 2 (2010), 182–222

Bridet, Guillaume, 'Michel Houellebecq and les montres molles', *Littérature*, 151 (2008), 6–20

Brinkmann, Svend, 'Literature as Qualitative Inquiry: The Novelist as Researcher', *Qualitative Inquiry*, 15, 8 (2009), 1376–94

Brown, Wendy, 'Neoliberalism and the End of Liberal Democracy', *Theory & Event*, 7, 1 (2003), 1—21

Bud, Robert, *The Uses of Life: A History of Biotechnology* (Cambridge: Cambridge University Press, 1993)

Budgen, Sebastian, 'A New Spirit of Capitalism', *New Left Review* (January–February 2000), http://newleftreview.org/II/1/sebastian-budgen-a-new-spirit-of-capitalism

Butler, Judith, 'Merely Cultural?', *New Left Review*, 227 (January–February 1998), 33–44

—*The Psychic Life of Power: Theories in Subjection* (Stanford: Stanford University Press, 1997)

Butt, Ronald, 'Mrs Thatcher: The First Two Years', *The Sunday Times*, 3 May 1981

Buvik, Per, 'Faut-il brûler Michel Houellebecq?', *Hesperis: Revue de littérature contemporaine*, 4 (1999), 81–6

Caldwell, Christopher, 'Enraged by Licentiousness ... and Indulging in it', *Wall Street Journal*, 15 November 2001

Cannon, Steve and Hugh Dauncey (eds), *Popular Music in France from Chanson to Techno: Culture, Identity, and Society* (Aldershot: Ashcroft Publishing, 2003)

Canto-Sperber, Monique, 'Le Sexe et la vie d'une femme', *Esprit*, March–April 2001, 270–89

Capuid, M., *Voluptuous Yearnings: A Feminist Theory of the Obscene* (London: Rowman and Littlefield, 1994)

Ceccaldi, Lucie, *L'Innocente* (Paris: Scali), 2008

Céline, Louis-Ferdinand Destouches, *Journey to the End of the Night* (London: Calder, 2004)

Chabet, Georges, 'Michel Houellebecq: Lecteur d'Auguste Comte', *Revue Romane*, 27, 2 (2002), 187–204

Chaouat, Bruno, 'Moroseness in Post-Cold War France', *Yale French Studies*, 116/117 (2009), 125–38

Chaplin, Tamara, *Turning on the Mind: French Philosophers on Television* (Chicago: University of Chicago Press, 1997)

Chaput, Catherine, 'Rhetorical Circulation in Late Capitalism: Neoliberalism and the Overdetermination of Affective Energy', *Philosophy and Rhetoric*, 43, 1 (2010), 1–25

Clark, Alex, 'Atom bomb', *The Guardian*, 13 May 2000

Clément, Murielle Lucie, *Houellebecq: sperme et sang* (Paris: L'Harmattan, 2003)

—'Masculin versus féminin chez Michel Houellebecq', *L'esprit créateur*, 44 (2004), 28–39

Cloonan, William, 'Literary Scandal, Fin du Siècle, and the Novel in 1999', *The French Review*, 74, 1 (October 2000), 14–30

Comaroff, Jean and John Comaroff, 'Millennial Capitalism: First Thoughts on a Second Coming', *Public Culture*, 12, 2 (2000), 291–34

de Comte, Auguste, *An Appeal to Conservatives*, (Kessinger Legacy Reprints, 2003, orig. pub. 1889), 75.

Connor, Steven, *Michel Serres' The Five Senses: A Philosophy of Mingled Bodies* (I), trans. Margaret Sankey and Peter Cowley (London: Continuum, 2008), 1–16

Coward, David, 'The newest barbarism', *Times Literary Supplement*, 16 September 2005, 21–2

Cowley, Jason, '*Atomised*', *The Times*, 7 July 2001

—'French kisses … and the rest: *Platform* by Michel Houellebecq', *Observer Review*, 11 August 2002, 16

Crangle, Sara and Peter Nicholls (eds), *On Bathos* (London: Continuum, 2010)

Critchley, Simon, *Very Little, Almost Nothing* (London and New York: Routledge, 1997)

Crowley, Martin, 'Houellebecq: The Wreckage of Liberation', *Romance Studies* 20, 1 (2002), 17–28

—'Low Resistance', in Sara Crangle and Peter Nicholls (eds), *On Bathos* (London: Continuum, 2010)

—'Michel Houellebecq: Misery, pornography, utopia', in Victoria Best and Martin Crowley (eds), *The New Pornographies: Explicit Sex in Recent French Fiction and Film* (Manchester: Manchester University Press, 2012)

—'Postface à la transgression, or: Trash, Nullity and Dubious Literary Resistance',
    Dalhousie French Studies, 87 (2009), 1–11

Cruickshank, Ruth, 'L'Affaire Houellebecq: Ideological Crime and fin de millénaire
    Literary Scandal', French Cultural Studies, 1, 1 (2003), 101–16

—Fin de millénaire French Fiction: The Aesthetics of Crisis (Oxford: Oxford University
    Press, 2009)

Dammam, Dominique, et al. (eds), Mai–Juin 68 (Paris: Editions de l'Atelier, 2008)

De Haan, Martin, 'Entretien avec Michel Houellebecq', C.R.I.N., 43, 1 (2004), 22

De Lillo, Don, Underworld (London: Picador, 1998)

Debray, Régis, 'A Modest Contribution to the Rites and Ceremonies of the Tenth
    Anniversary' trans. John Howe, New Left Review, 115 (1979), 46

Deleuze, Gilles, Spectres of Marx: The State of Debt, The Work of Mourning, and The
    New International, trans. Peggy Kamuf (London: Routledge, 2006)

Deleuze, Gilles and Felix Guattari, A Thousand Plateaus: Capitalism and Schizophrenia:
    Volume II (Minneapolis: University of Minnesota Press, 1984)

—Anti-Oedipus: Capitalism and Schizophrenia: Volume I (London: Athlone, 1983)

—'Capitalism: A very special delirium', Chaosophy, ed. Sylvère Lotringer, Autonomedia/
    Semiotexte (1995), 119–50

Delphy, Christine, 'Nouvelles du MLF: Libération des femmes an dix', Questions
    féministes, 2 (1981), 59–74

Demonpion, Denis, 'Houellebecq malgré lui', L'Express, 22 August 2003

Derrida, Jacques, Specters of Marx (New York and London: Routledge, 1994)

Despentes, Virginie, Baise-Moi (Paris: Editions Grasset & Faquelle, 1999)

Dewey, Joseph, Steven G. Kelman and Irving Malin (eds), UnderWorlds: Perspectives on
    Don DeLillo's Underworld (Newark: University of Delaware Press, 2002)

Diken, Bülent, 'Houellebecq, or, the Carnival of Spite', Journal for Cultural Research, 11,
    1 (2007), 57–73

Dion, Robert and Élisabeth Haghebaert, 'Le cas de Michel Houellebecq et la
    dynamique des genres littéraires', French Studies, 55 (2001), 509–24

Doezema, Jo, '"Ouch!" Western Feminist "Wounded Attachment" to the "Third World
    Prostitute"', Feminist Review, 67, 1 (2001), 16–38

Dooley, Mark and Richard Kearney (eds), Questioning Ethics: Contemporary Debates in
    Continental Philosophy (London: Routledge, 1999)

Downing, Lisa, 'French Cinema's New "Sexual Revolution": Postmodern Porn and
    Troubled Genre', French Cultural Studies, 15 (2004), 265–80

Doyle, Richard, On Beyond Living: Rhetorical Transformations of the Life Sciences
    (Stanford: Stanford University Press, 1997)

Duchen, Claire, Feminism in France: From May '68 to Mitterrand (London and New
    York: Routledge, 1986)

Dufour, Dany-Robert, The Art of Shrinking Heads: On the New Servitude of the
    Liberated in the Age of Total Capitalism, trans. David Macey (London: Polity Press,
    2008)

Eakin, Emily, 'Le Provocateur', *The New York Times Magazine*, 10 September 2000

d'Estaing, Valéry Giscard, *Démocratie française* (Paris: Arthème Fayard, [1976] 1979)

Edwards, Richard, *Contested Terrain: The Transformation of the Workplace in the Twentieth Century* (New York: Basic Books, 1979)

Elst, Koenraad, 'Afterword, The Rushdie Affair's Legacy', http://koenraadelst.bharatvani.org/articles/misc/rushdie.html

Engels, Frederich, *Socialism: Utopian and Scientific* (Chicago: Charles H. Kerr & Co, 1908)

Faludi, Susan, *Backlash: The Undeclared War Against American Women* (New York: Doubleday, 1991)

Feehily, Gerry, 'A World on the Brink of Collapse', *New Statesman*, 130, 4542, 18 June 2001, 56

—'The Man who Fell to Earth', *New Statesman*, 131, 4599, 5 August 2002, 36–7

Feigenbaum, Harvey and Jeffrey Henig, 'The Political Underpinnings of Privatization: A Typology', *World Politics*, 46, 2 (1994), 185–208

Fernández-Armesto, Felipe, *So You Think You're Human?* (Oxford and New York: Oxford University Press, 2004)

Ferry, Luc and Alain Renaut, *French Philosophy of the Sixties: An Essay on Antihumanism*, trans. Mary Schakenber Cattap (Amherst: University of Massachusetts Press, 1990)

Feuerbach, Ludwig, *Principles of the Philosophy of the Future*, trans. Manfred Vogel (Indiana: Hackett Publishing, 1966 [1843])

Fisher, Mark, *Capitalist Realism* (London: Zero Books, 2009)

Forster, E. M., *Aspects of the Novel* (London: Penguin, 1927)

Foucault, Michel, *The Birth of Biopolitics: Lectures at the College de France, 1978–79*, trans. Graham Burchell (Chicago: Chicago University Press, 2008)

—*The History of Sexuality, Volume 1: An Introduction*, trans. Robert Hurley (New York: Vintage Books, 1980)

Fourcade-Gourinchas, Marion and Bob Hancke, 'Revisiting the French Model: Coordination and Restructuring in French Industry', in Peter A. Hall and David Soskice (eds), *Varieties of Capitalism* (New York: Oxford University Press, 2001)

Fourcade-Gourinchas, Marion and Sarah Babb, 'The Rebirth of the Liberal Creed: Paths to Neoliberalism in Four Countries', *American Journal of Sociology*, 108, 3, (2002), 533–79

Frank, Thomas, *One Market Under God: Extreme Capitalism, Market Populism, and the End of Economic Democracy* (New York: Random House, 2000)

—*The Conquest of Cool: Business Culture, Counterculture, and the Rise of Hip Consumerism* (Chicago: University of Chicago Press, 1997)

Fraser, Nancy, 'Feminism and the Cunning of History', *New Left Review*, 56 (2009), 97–117

—'Heterosexism, Misrecognition and Capitalism: A Response to Judith Butler', *New Left Review*, 1, 228 (1998), 140–49

Frey, Hugo and Benjamin Noys, 'Reactionary Times', *Journal of European Studies*, 37, 3 (2007), 243–253

Fukuyama, Francis, *Our Posthuman Future: Consequence of the Biotechnology Revolution* (London: Profile Books, 2002)

—*The End of History and the Last Man* (New York: The Free Press, 1992)

Gambino, Ferruccio, 'A Critique of the Fordism of the Regulation School', *thecommoner*, 12 (2007), 39–62

Gantz, Katherine. 'Strolling with Houellebecq: The Textual Terrain of Postmodern Flânerie', *Journal of Modern Literature*, 28, 3 (2005), 149–61

Garcin, Jérôme, 'Un entretien avec Michel Houellebecq: "Je suis un prophète amateur"', *Le Nouvel Observateur*, 2129, August 2005, www.houellebecq.info/presse/205-garcin.doc

Gardels, Nathan, 'Cloning: Central Planning of the 21st Century?', *New Perspectives Quarterly*, 18, 1 (Winter 2001), 56

Genette, Gérard, *Paratexts: Thresholds of Interpretation* (Cambridge: Cambridge University Press, 1997)

—*Seuils* (Paris: Seuil, 1987)

Gent, Paul, 'Human nature: a particle guide', *The Sunday Telegraph*, Sunday 29 April 2000

Gentleman, Amelia, 'Summertime, and living is not easy for French racked with self-doubt', *The Guardian*, 10 August 2004, http://www.guardian.co.uk/world/2004/aug/10/france.ameliagentleman

George, Susan, 'Emerging Opportunities for Structural Change' (1999), http://www.globalexchange.org/resources/econ101/neoliberalismhist

Giddens, Anthony, *The Consequences of Modernity* (Cambridge: Polity, 1991)

Gildea, Robert, 'Forty years on: French writing on 1968 in 2008', *French History*, 23, 1 (2009), 109–18

Gill, Rosalind and Andy Pratt, 'In the Social Factory: Immaterial Labour, Precariousness, and Cultural Work', *Theory, Culture & Society*, 25 (2000), 1–30

Giroux, Henry, *Against the Terror of Neoliberalism: Politics Beyond the Age of Greed* (Boulder, CO: Paradigm Press, 2008)

Gloguen, Philippe, 'Le Routard s'en prend à Michel Houellebecq', *Le Monde*, 22 August 2001, 24

Gobille, Boris, et al., 'Mai '68 en quarantaine' (2008), http://colloque-mai68.ens-lsh.fr

Goffmann, Erving, *Interaction Ritual: Essays on Face-to-Face Behaviour* (New York: Anchor Books, 1967)

Golsan, Richard and Ralph Schoolcraft, 'Paradoxes of the Postmodern Reactionary: Michel Rio and Michel Houellebecq', *Journal of European Studies*, 37 (2007), 349–71

Gopnik Adam, 'Noel Contendere', *The New Yorker*, 28 December, 1998, 64

Gordon, Daniel A., 'Liquidating May '68? Generational Trajectories of the 2007 Presidential Candidates', *Modern and Contemporary France*, 16, 2 (2008), 143–59

Grass, Delphine, 'Domesticating Hierarchies, Eugenic Hygiene and Exclusion Zones: The Dogs and Clones of Houellebecq's *La Possibilité d'une île*', *L'Esprit Créateur*, 52, 2 (2012), 127–40

—'Houellebecq and the Novel as a Site of Epistemic Rebellion', in 'French Literature, Knowledge, and the Problem of Housing', http://www.ucl.ac.uk/opticon1826/archive/issue1/VfPHoullebecq.pdf

Grauby, Françoise, 'La Vie en noir: le discours célibataire dans *Plateforme* de Michel Houellebecq', *New Zealand Journal of French Studies*, 24, 2, (2003) 29–42

Gray, John, *False Dawn: The Delusions of Global Capitalism* (London: Granta Books, 1999)

Green, Patricia, 'Thailand: Tourism and the Sex Industry', *Women*, 54 (2001), 20

Gregg, Melissa and Gregory J. Seigworth (eds), 'An Inventory of Shimmers' in *The Affect Theory Reader* (Durham and London: Duke University Press, 2010)

Guenaire, Michel, 'Beauté cou coupé', *Le Monde*, 4 February 1999

Guillebaud, Jean-Claude, *La tyrannie du plaisir* (Paris: Seuil, 1998)

Habermas, Jürgen, *Toward a Rational Society: Student Protest, Science and Politics*, trans. Jeremy J. Shapiro, (Boston: Beacon Press, 1970)

Hacker, Eugene, 'What is Biomedia', *Configurations*, 11, 1 (2003), 47–79

Halberstam, Judith and Ira Livingstone (eds), *Posthuman Bodies* (Bloomington: Indian University Press, 1995)

Halimi, Serge, 'France: Sarkozy's Old Familiar Song', *Le Monde diplomatique*, http://mondediplo.com/2007/06/02france

Hall, Stuart, 'Brave New World', *Socialist Review*, 91, 1 (1991), 57–84

—'The Meaning of New Times', in Stuart Hall and Martin Jacques (eds), *New Times: The Changing Face of Politics in the 1990s* (London: Lawrence and Wishart, 1989)

Hancke, Bob, 'Revisiting the French Model: Coordination and Restructuring in French Industry', in Peter A. Hall and David Soskice, (eds) *Varieties of Capitalism* (New York: Oxford University Press, 2001) 307–34

Haraway, Donna, *Modest_Witness@Second_Millenium.FemaleMan©_Meets_OncoMouse™* (London: Routledge, 1997)

—*Simians, Cyborgs, and Women: The Reinvention of Nature* (New York: Routledge, 1991)

Hardt, Michael, 'Affective Labor', *Boundary 2*, 26, 2 (1999), 89–100

—'The Violence of Capital', *New Left Review*, 48 (2007), 153–160

Hardt, Michael and Antonio Negri, *Empire* (Cambridge: Harvard University Press, 2000)

Harkin, James, 'Review of *Atomised*, by Michel Houellebecq', *New Statesman*, 129, 4487 (22 May 2000), 57

Harvey, David, *A Brief History of Neoliberalism* (Oxford: Oxford University Press, 2007)

—*The Condition of Postmodernity: An Enquiry into the Origins of Social Change* (Cambridge, MA: Blackwell, 1990)

Hayles, Katherine, N., *How We Became Posthuman: Virtual Bodies in Cybernetics, Literature, and Informatics* (Chicago: University of Chicago Press, 1999)

Hect, Emmanuel, 'Ben Jalloun flingue Houellebecq', *L'Express*, 20 August 2010

Heller-Roazen, Daniel, *The Inner Touch: Archaeology of a Sensation* (New York: Zone Books, 2007)

Hennessy, Rosemary, *Profit and Pleasure: Sexual Identities in Late Capitalism*, (New York: Routledge, 2000)

Hobsbawm, Eric, *On the Edge of the New Century* (New York: The New Press, 2000)

Holzer, Angela, 'Science, Sexuality, and the Novels of Huxley and Houellebecq', *Comparative Literature and Culture*, 5, 2 (2003), 1–11

Hooper, Charlotte, *Manly States: Masculinities, International Relations, and Gender Politics* (New York: Columbia University Press, 2001)

Houellebecq, Michel, *Atomised*, trans. by Frank Wynne (London: Vintage, 2000)

—'En finir avec le désir', *Les Inrockuptibles*, 161 (19–25 August), 16–20

—*Extension du domaine de la lutte* (Paris: Maurice Nadeau, 1994)

—*H. P. Lovecraft: Contre le monde, contre la vie* (Paris: Editons du Rocher, 1999)

—*Interventions* (Paris: Flammarion, 1998)

—Interview with Christian Autheir, *Houelle* (May 2002), 6–11

—*La Carte et le territoire* (Paris: Flammarion, 2010)

—*La Possibilité d'un île* (Paris: Fayard, 2005)

—*Lanzarote*, trans. Frank Wynne (London: Vintage, 2004)

—*Les Particules éleméntaires* (Paris: Flammarion, 1998)

—*Plateforme* (Paris: Flammarion, 2001)

—*Platform*, trans. Frank Wynne (London: Vintage, 2003)

—*Public Enemies: Dueling Writers Take on Each Other and the World* (New York: Random House, 2011)

—*Rester vivant méthode* (Paris: La Différence, 1991) (*How to Stay Alive: A Method*); and later published as *Rester vivant et autres textes* (Paris: Librio, 1998)

—*The Art of Struggle*, trans. Delphine Grass and Timothy Mathews (London: Herla, 2010)

—*The Map and the Territory*, trans. Gavin Bowd (London: Heinemann, 2011)

—*The Possibility of an Island*, trans. Gavin Bowd (London: Weidenfeld & Nicholson, 2005)

—*Whatever*, trans. by Paul Hammond (London: Serpent's Tail, 1998)

Houellebecq, Michel and Bernard-Henri Lévy, *Ennemis publics* (Paris: Flammarion & Grasset, 2008)

Howell, Chris, *Regulating Labor: The State and Industrial Labor Relations Reform in Postwar France* (Princeton, NJ: Princeton University Press, 1992)

Hunnewell, Susannah, 'Michel Houellebecq, The Art of Fiction', *The Paris Review*, 206 (Fall 2010)

Hussey, Andrew, 'Animal Omega: The Dubious Moral Universe of Michel Houellebecq', *Planet Magazine*, 142, 9 December 2001

—'Agent Provocateur', *The Observer*, Sunday 6 November 2005

Huston, Nancy, 'Writers and Writing: Michel Houellebecq: The Ecstasy of Disgust', *Salmagundi* (2006), 20–39

—*Professeurs de désespoir* (Paris: Actes Sud, 2004)

Huxley, Aldous, *Brave New World* (London: Penguin, 1992)

Illouz, Eva, *Cold Intimacies: The Making of Emotional Capitalism* (London: Wiley 2007)

Irigaray, Luce, *Speculum of the Other Woman*, trans. Gillian C. Gill. (New York: Cornell University Press, 1985)

James, Simon, and Nicholas Saul (eds), *The Evolution of Literature: Legacies of Darwin in European Cultures* (Amsterdam: Rodopi, 2011)

Jameson, Fredric, *Archaeologies of the Future: The Desire Called Utopia and Other Since Fictions* (London: Verso, 2005)

—*Marxism and Form* (Princeton, NJ: Princeton University Press, 1974)

—*Postmodernism, or, the Cultural Logic of Late Capitalism* (Durham, NC: Duke University Press, 1991)

—'Progress versus Utopia: Or, can we imagine the future', *Science-Fiction Studies*, 27 (1982), 147–58

—'Reification and Utopia in Mass Culture', *Social Text*, 1 (1979), 130–48

Jeffery, Ben, *Anti-Matter: Michel Houellebecq and Depressive Realism* (Winchester: Zero Book, 2011)

Jenson, Jane, 'Representations of Difference: The Varieties of French Feminism', *New Left Review*, 180 (1990), 127–60

Kurzweil, Ray, *The Age of Spiritual Machines: When Computers Exceed Human Intelligence* (Cambridge: MIT Press, 1999)

—*The Singularity is Near: When Humans Transcend Biology* (New York: Viking Penguin, 2005)

Jessop, Bob, 'From Micro-powers to Governmentality', *Political Geography*, 26 (2007) 34–40

—'Post-Fordism and the State' in Bent Gaeve, *Comparative Welfare Systems* (London: MacMillan, 1996), 165–85

Jones, Jonathan, 'Artistic License to Thrill: Houellebecq's *The Map and the Territory*', http://www.guardian.co.uk/artanddesign/jonathanjonesblog/2011/oct/03/ michel-houellebecq-map-and-territory

Judt, Tony, *Marxism and the French Left: Studies in Labour and Politics in France, 1830–1981* (Oxford: Clarendon, 1986)

Juvin, Hervé, *The Coming of the Body* (London: Verso, 2010)

Kakutani, Michiko, 'Unsparing case of Humanity's Vileness', *The New York Times*, 10 November 2000

Kalckar, Jørgen, Niels Bohr, Léon Rosenfeld, Erik Rüdinger, Finn Aaserud, *Foundations of Quantum Physics II (1933–1958)* (Amsterdam: Elsevier Press, 1996)

Kandall, Jonathan 'Jacques Derrida, Abstruse Theorist, Dies at 74', *The New York Times*, 10 October 2004

Karwowski, Michael, 'Michel Houellebecq: French Novelist for Our Times', *Contemporary Review*, 283 (2003), 4–46

Kass, Leon 'The Wisdom of Repugnance', in Gregory Pence, ed., *Flesh of My Flesh: The Ethics of Human Cloning*, Rowman & Littlefield, 1998)

Keller, Evelyn Fox, *Refiguring Life: Metaphors of Twentieth Century Biology* (New York: Columbia University Press, 1995)

Kellner, Douglas and Steven Best, *The Postmodern Adventure: Science, Technology and Cultural Studies at the Third Millennium* (New York and London: Guildford Press, 2001)

Kiersey, Nicholas J., 'Everyday Neoliberalism and the Subjectivity of Crisis: Post-Political Control in an Era of Financial Turmoil', *Journal of Critical Globalization Studies*, 4 (2011), 23–44

Kołakowski, Lesek, *Main Currents of Marxism, Vol. 1* (Oxford: Oxford University Press, 1978)

—*Modernity on Endless Trial* (Chicago: University of Chicago Press, 1990)

Krailsheimer, A. J., *Studies in Self-Interest from Descartes to La Bruyère* (Oxford: Clarendon Press, 1962)

Kristeva, Julia, *Powers of Horror* (New York: Columbia University Press, 1982)

Kuisel, Richard, *Capitalism and the State in Modern France: Renovation and Economic Management in the Twentieth Century* (Cambridge: Cambridge University Press, 1981)

Kumar, Krishan, *From Post-Industrial to Post-Modern Society: New Theories of the Contemporary World* (London: Blackwell, 1995)

Lapaque, Sébastien, 'Houellebecq: les critiques divisés', *Le Figaro littéraire*, 6, 9 (2001)

Latour, Bruno, *Pandora's Hope: Essays on the Reality of Science Studies* (Cambridge: Harvard University Press, 1999)

—'How to Talk About the Body? The Normative Dimension of Science Studies', *Body & Society*, 10, 2–3 (2004), 205–29

Lazzarato, Maurizio, 'From Capital-Labour to Capital-Life', *Ephemera*, 4, 3 (2004), 187–207

—'Immaterial Labour' in Virno and Hardt (eds), *Radical Thought in Italy A Potential Politics* (Minneapolis: University of Minnesota Press, 1996) 133–47

Lefebvre, Henri, *Critique of Everyday Life* (London: Verso, 1991)

—*Everyday Life in the Modern World* (New Brunswick, NJ: Transaction, 1984)

—*The Production of Space*, trans. D. Nicholson-Smith (Oxford: Blackwell, 1974)

Lefol, Sébastien and Anthony Palou, 'Faut-il condamner Michel Houellebecq?', *Le Figaro*, 31 August 2001

Le Goff, Jean-Pierre, *Mai '68, l'héritage impossible* (Paris: La Découverte, 2006)

Lemke, Thomas, 'The Birth of Bio-Politics': Michel Foucault's Lecture at the Collège de France on Neo Liberal Governmentality', http://www.thomaslemkeweb.de/engl.%20 texte/The%20Birth%20of%20Biopolitics%203.pdf

—*Foucault, Governmentality, and Critique* (London: Paradigm Books, 2012)

Lepape, Pierre, 'Dernière station avant le désert', *Le Monde des livres*, 28 August 1998

Le Quesne, Nicholas, 'War of Words', *Time*, 22 September 2002

Lezard, Nicholas, 'Pick of the Week: Atom Bomb: You're not Meant to Like This', *The Guardian*, 24 February 2001

Lilla, Mark, 'Houellebecq's Elementary Particles', *New Perspectives Quarterly*, 18, 1 (2001), 53–60

—ed., *A New French Thought Political Philosophy* (New Jersey: Princeton University Press, 1994)

Lilley, Sasha, 'On Neoliberalism: An Interview with David Harvey', *Monthly Review* (June 2006), http://mrzine.monthlyreview.org/2006/lilley190606.html

Lindenberg, Daniel, *Le Rappel à l'ordre: Enquête sur les nouveaux réactionnaires* (Paris: Éditions du Seuil, 2002)

Lipovetsky, Gilles, '"Changer la vie" ou l'irruption de l'individualisme transpolitique', *Pouvoirs*, 39 (1986) 91–100

—*Hypermodern Times* (Cambridge: Polity Press, 2005)

—*Le Crépuscule du devoir: L'Ethique indolore des nouveaux temps démocratique* (Paris: Gallimard, 1992)

—*L'Ère du vide: Essais sur l'individualisme contemporain* (Paris: Folio, 1989)

—'May '68, or The Rise of Transpolitical Individualism', in Mark Lilla, ed., *A New French Thought Political Philosophy* (New Jersey: Princeton University Press, 1994)

Lloyd, John, 'Is man too wicked to be free?', *New Statesman*, 16 December 2002

Lloyd, Vincent, 'Michel Houellebecq and the Theological Virtues', *Literature and Theology*, 23, 1 (2009), 84–98

Loingsigh, Aedín Ní, 'Tourist Traps Confounding Expectations in Michel Houellebecq's *Plateforme*', *French Cultural Studies*, 16, 1 (2005)

Lukács, Georg, *History and Class Consciousness: Studies in Marxist Dialectics*, trans. Rodney Livingstone (Boston: MIT Press, 1971)

—'Reification and the Consciousnesses of the Proletariat', in Imre Szeman and Timothy Kaposy (eds), *Cultural Theory: An Anthropology* (London: Wiley-Blackwell, 2011)

Lyotard, Jean-François, *The Postmodern Condition: A Report on Knowledge* (Manchester: Manchester University Press, 1984)

Madar, Chase, Review of *Interventions*, *Times Literary Supplement*, 22 October 1999, 36

Malina, Roger F., Review of *Les Particules élémentaires*, *Leonardo*, 32, 2 (1999), 147–8

Mann, Stefan, 'From friendly turns toward trade – on the interplay between cooperation and markets', *International Journal of Social Ethics*, 35 (2008), 326–37

Mapp, Nigel and David Cunningham (eds), *Adorno and Literature* (London: Continuum, 2006)

Marcuse, Herbert, 'Aggressiveness in Advanced Industrial Society', in *Negations: Essays in Critical Theory* (Boston: Beacon Press, 1968), http://www.wbenjamin.org/marcuse.html [accessed 30 June 2011]

—*Negations: Essays in Critical Theory* (Boston: Beacon Press, 1968)

—*One Dimensional Man: Studies in the Ideology of Advanced Industrial Society* (Boston: Beacon Press, 1964)

Marian, Michel, 'France 1997–2002: Right-Wing President, Left-Wing Government', *Political Quarterly*, 73, 3 (2002), 258–65

Marks, John, 'L'Affaire Sokal' in John Marks and Enda McCaffrey (eds), *French Cultural Debates* (Melbourne: Monash Romance Studies, 2001), 80–93

Marr, Andrew, 'We're all doomed … except for middle aged French philosophers', *The Observer*, 2 May 2000

Martel, Frédérick, 'Michel Houellebecq: C'est ainsi que je fabrique mes livres', *La Nouvelle Revue Française* 548 (1999), 197–209

Martin, Tim, 'The Michel Houellebecq Phenomenon', *The Daily Telegraph*, 29 September 2011

Marx, Karl and Friedrich Engels, *The Communist Manifesto* (London: Polity Press, 2008, [1948])

Marx, Karl, *The Eighteenth Brumaire of Louis Bonaparte* (New York: International, 1963)

—'From The Economic and Philosophical Manuscripts of 1844', *Karl Marx A Reader*, ed. Jon Elster (New York: Cambridge University Press, 1988), 35–46

—*Poverty of Philosophy* (Chicago: Charles H. Kerr and Company, 1920, [1847])

Masson, Sophie, 'The Strange Case of Michel Houellebecq', *The Social Contract* (Winter 2003–4), 110–13

McGrath, Melanie, *The Evening Standard*, 8 May 2000

McNamara, Liam, 'Michel Houellebecq and the Male Novel of Ressentiment', *Journal of Mundane Behaviour*, 3, 1, (2002), 127–45

McRobbie, Angela, *The Aftermath of Feminism* (London: Sage, 2009)

Meeks, James, 'Every Boy's Young Dream', *London Review of Books*, 24, 2, (14 November 2002), 26–7

Meizoz, Jérôme, *L'œil sociologue et la littérature* (Genève: Slaktine Érudition, 2004)

—*Postures littéraires: Mises en scène modernes de l'auteur* (Genève: Slatkine, 2007)

Melman, Charles and Jean-Pierre Lebrun, *L'Homme sans gravité: fouir a tout prix* (Paris: Denoel, 2002)

Michallat, Wendy, 'Modern life is still rubbish: Houellebecq and the Refiguring of "reactionary" Retro', *Journal of European Studies*, 37 (2007), 313–31

Minc, Alain, *L'Avenir en face* (Paris: Seuil, 1984)

Modleski, Tania, *Feminism without Women: Culture and Criticism in a Postfeminist Age* (New York: Routledge, 1991)

Monnin, Christian, 'Extinction du domaine de la lutte: l'œuvre romanesque de Michel Houellebecq', *Atelier du roman*, 32, (2002), 128–37.

Moor, Louise, 'Posture polémique ou polémisation de la posture?: Le cas de Michel Houellebecq' *COnTEXTES*, 10 (2012), http://contextes.revues.org/4921

Moore, Gerald, 'Gay Science and (no) Laughing Matter: The Eternal Returns of Michel Houellebecq', *French Review*, 65, 1 (2011), 45–60

Moore, Steven, 'Getting Physical', *Washington Post Book World*, 31, 3 (January 2001), 7

Moraru, Christian, 'The Genomic Imperative: Michel Houellebecq's *The Possibility of an Island*', *Utopian Studies*, 19, 2 (2008), 65–283

Morin, Edgar, 'Mai 68: Complexité et ambiguïté', *Pouvoirs*, 39 (1986), 71–80

Morrey, Douglas, 'Michel Houellebecq and the international sexual economy', *Portal*, 1, 2, http://ep'ess.lib.edu.au/journals/portal/index.php

—'Sex and the Single Male: Houellebecq, Feminism and Hegemonic Masculinity', *Yale French Studies*, 116/117 (2010), 141–52

—'Houellebecq, Genetics and Evolutionary Psychology', in Nicholas Saul and Simon J. James (eds), *The Evolution of Literature: Legacies of Darwin in European Cultures*, 227–38

Morrison, Donald, *Que reste-t-il de la culture française?* suivi de Antoine Compagnon, *Le Souci de la grandeur* (Paris, Denoël, 2008)

Morrison, Donald and Antoine Compagnon, *The Death of French Culture* (London: Polity, 2010)

Mortimer, Armine K., 'The Third Closet: Sollers's War', *Yale French Studies*, 'Turns to the Right?', 116/117 (2009), 169–82

de Mourgues, Odette, *Two French Moralists: La Rochefoucauld, La Bruyère* (Cambridge: Cambridge University Press, 1978)

Musil, Robert, *The Man Without Qualities*, vol. 2, trans. Sophie Wilkins (New York: Vintage, 1996)

Nalleau, Eric, *Au secours, Houellebecq revient!* (Paris: Chiflet & Cie, 2005)

Naqui, Fatima, *The Literary and Cultural Rhetoric of Victimhood, Western Europe 1970-2005* (London: Palgrave Macmillan, 2005)

Negra, Diane and Yvonne Tasker, *Interrogating Postfeminism: Gender and the Politics of Popular Culture* (Durham, NC: Duke University Press, 2007)

Negri, Antonio, 'Interpretation of the Class Situation Today: Methodological Aspects' in *Open Marxism*, Vol. 2, W. Bonefeld, R. Gunn and K. Psychopedis (eds) (London: Pluto, 1992)

—'Value and Affect', *boundary*, 26 (1999), 77–88

Noguez, Dominique, 'Ce qui compte', *Nouvelle revue française*, 557 (2001), 61–7

—*Houellebecq en fait* (Paris: Fayard, 2003)

—'La Rage de ne pas lire', *Le Monde*, 29 October 1998

—'Le Style de Michel Houellebecq', *L'Atelier du roman*, 18 (1999)

—'Le Style de Michel Houellebecq: Fin', *L'Atelier du roman*, 20 (1999), 129–37

Noudelmann, François and Andre Piggott, 'A Turn to the Right: "Genealogy" in France Since the 1980s', *Yale French Studies*, 116/117, (2009), 7–19

Nussbaum, Martha, *Sex and Social Justice* (Oxford: Oxford University Press, 1999)

Orthofer, Michael, 'On Michel Houellebecq', *The Complete Review*, 11, 2 (August 2010), http://www.complete-review.com/quarterly/vol11/issue2/houellebecq.htm

Pence, Gregory, ed., *Flesh of My Flesh: The Ethics of Human Cloning* (Lanham, Maryland: Rowman and Littlefield, 1998)

Petit, Marc, 'Nouvelle tendance, vieux démons', *Le Monde*, 10 October 1998

Pettman, Jan Jindy, 'Body Politics: International Sex Tourism', *Third World Quarterly*, 18, 1 (1997), 93–108

Picq, Françoise, 'Sauve qui peut, le MLF', *La Revue d'en face*, 11, 4 (1981), 11–24

Polyani, Karl, *The Great Transformation* (Boston: Beacon Press, 1954)

Power, Nina and Alberto Toscano, 'The Philosophy of Restoration: Alain Badiou and the Enemies of May', *Boundary 2*, 36, 1 (2009), 27–46

Prada, Juan Martin, 'Affective Link: Policies of Affectivity, Aesthetics of Biopower', http://www.vinculo-a.net/english_site/text_prada.html

Prasad, Monica, 'Why Is France So French? Culture, Institution, and Neoliberalism, 1974–1981', *The American Journal of Sociology*, 111 (2005), 357–407

Proguidis, Lakis, 'Preuves irréfutables de la non-existence de la société', *De l'autre côté du brouillard* (Québec: Éditions Nota Bene, 2001)

Quinn, Anthony, 'One Thinks the Other Doesn't', *The New York Times*, 10 November 2000

Rabinov, Paul and Nikolas Rose, 'Biopower Today', *BioSocieties*, 1 (2006), 195–217

Ramonet, Ignacio, *Le Monde diplomatique*, January 1995, http://www.monde diplomatique.fr/1995/01/RAMONET/1144

Read, Jason, 'A Genealogy of Homo-Economicus: Neoliberalism and the Production of Subjectivity', *Foucault Studies*, 6 (2009), 25–36

—*The Micro-Politics of Capital: Marx and the Prehistory of the Present* (New York: SUNY Press, 2003)

Reader, Keith (with Khursheed Wadia), *The May 1968 Events in France: Reproductions and Interpretations* (New York: St Martin's Press, 1993)

—*The Abject Object: Avatars of the Phallus in Contemporary French Theory, Literature and Film* (Amsterdam and New York: Rodopi, 2006)

Redonnet, Marie, 'La Barbarie postmoderne', *Art Press*, 244 (1999), 60–4

Remy, J., M. Dagouat, and D. de Saint Pern, 'Qu'est-ce qu' un homme aujourd'hui?' *L'Express*, 12 August 1993, 26–39

Renaut, Alain and Luc Ferry, *La pensée 68: Essai sur l'anti-humanisme contemporain* (Paris: Gallimard, 1985).

—*French Philosophy of the Sixties: An Essay on Anti-Humanism*, trans. Mary Schnackenberg Cattani (Boston: University of Massachusetts Press, 1990)

Riding, Alan, 'Arts Abroad: Roman à Gripe Stirs Flames Among the French', *The New York Times*, 2 March 1999

—'Author Charged for Islam Remarks Acquitted', *The New York Times*, 23 October 2002

Rifkin, Jeremy, *The Biotech Century: Harnessing The Gene and Remaking the World* (New York: Tarcher/Putnam, 1998)

Riley, Alexander, 'In the Trenches of the War between Literature and Sociology: Exploring the Scandalous Sociology of Modernity in the Novels of Michel Houellebecq', *International Journal of Contemporary Sociology*, 431, 1 (2006), 104–24

Robitaille, Martin, 'Houellebecq, ou l'extension d'un monde étrange', *Tangence*, 76 (2004), 87–103

da Rocha Soares, Corina, 'Michel Houellebecq, Amélie Nothomb et Jacques Chessex: Performances sous contexts médiatisés', *Carnets, Cultures littéraires: Nouvelles performances et développement* (2009), 207–20, http//:carnets.web.ua.pt

Rosanvallon, Pierre, *La démocratie inachevée: Histoire de la souveraineté du peuple en France* (Paris: Gallimard, 2000, 2003)

Rose, Nikolas, *The Politics of Life Itself: Biomedicine, Power, and Subjectivity in the Twenty-First Century* (Princeton: Princeton University Press, 2007)

—*Powers of Freedom* (Cambridge: Cambridge University Press, 1999)

Ross, Kristin, 'Establishing Consensus: May '68 in France as Seen from the 1980s', *Critical Inquiry*, 28, 3 (2002), 650–76

—*Fast Cars, Clean Bodies: Decolonization and the Reordering of French Culture* (London and Cambridge, MA: MIT Press, 1996)

—*May '68 and its Afterlives* (Chicago: University of Chicago Press, 2002)

Rowbotham, Sheila, *Promise of a Dream: A Memoir of the 1960s* (London: Allen Lane, 2000)

Rubin, Gayle, 'The Traffic in Women: Notes on the Political Economy of Sex', in Rayna R. Reiter ed., *Toward an Anthropology of Women* (New York: Monthly Review Press, 1975)

Rubin, Merle, 'A Perfect Genetic Future', *Christian Science Monitor*, 92, 240 (2 November 2000)

Rushdie, Salman, 'A Platform For Closed Minds', *The Guardian*, 28 September 2002, 7

Sabloff, Nicholas, 'Of Filth and Frozen Dinners', *The Common Review*, 5, 3, (2007), 50

Salles, Alain, 'Des associations musulmanes veulent poursuivre en justice Michel Houellebecq', *Le Monde*, 8 September 2001

Sallis, James, 'Michel Houellebecq, The Elementary Particles', *Review of Contemporary Fiction*, 21, 1 (2001), 19–197

Sartre, Jean Paul, *Nausea* (New York: New Directions, 1964)

—*What is Literature? And Other Essays*, trans. by Bernard Frechtman (Cambridge: Harvard University Press, 1988)

Savary, Nicolas, 'Houellebecq, le désir, le destin', *L'Atelier du roman*, 18, June 1999, 67–72

Savigneau, Josiane, 'Houellebecq et l'Occident', *Le Monde* (Le Monde des livres), 31 August 2001, 1

—'Michel Houellebecq, écrivain, évoque l'influence de Schopenhauer et sa vision d'un avenir determine par la technique', *Le Monde*, 21 August 2005

Schmidt, Vivien, *From State to Market? The Transformation of French Business and Government* (Cambridge: Cambridge University Press, 1996)

Schober, Rita, 'Weltsicht und Realismus in Houellebecq's *Les Particules éleméntaires*', *Romantische Zeitschrift für Literaturgeschichte*, 25, 1 (2001), 177–211

Schoolcraft, Ralph and Richard Golsan, 'Paradoxes of the Postmodern Reactionary Michel Rio and Michel Houellebecq', *Journal of European Studies*, 37 (2007), 349–71

Schuerewegen, Franc, 'Scènes de cul' in Sabine van Wesemael, ed., *Michel Houellebecq* 91–8.

Seabrook, Jeremy, *Travels in the Skin Trade: – Tourism and the Sex Industry* (London: Pluto Press, 1996)

Segal, Victoria, '*Atomised* by Michel Houellebecq', *The Times*, 10 March 2001

Seidman, Michael, *The Imaginary Revolution: Parisian Students and Workers in 1968* (New York and Oxford: Berghahn Books, 2004)

Sénécal, Didier, 'Entretien avec Michel Houellebecq' (2001), http://www.lire.fr/ entretien.asp/

—'Houellebecq fidèle à lui-même', *L'Express*, July/August 1999

Sennett, Richard, *The Culture of the New Capitalism* (New Haven and London: Yale University Press, 2006)

Sloterdijk, Peter, 'Rules for the Human Zoo: A Response to the Letter on Humanism', *Environment and Planning D: Society and Space*, 27, 1 NO: 1 (2009), 12–28, http:// www.xs4all.nl/~rekveld/tech/Sloterdijk_RulesForTheHumanZoo.pdf

Smart, Barry, *Economy, Culture and Society: A Sociological Critique of Neo-liberalism* (Buckingham/Philadelphia, PA: Open University Press, 2003)

Smith, Timothy, *France in Crisis: Welfare, Inequality and Globalization since 1980* (Cambridge: Cambridge University Press, 2004)

Sollers, Philipe, *Éloge de l'infini* (Paris: Gallimard, 2001)

Stein, Lorin, 'What to Read in October', *Salon*, 23 October 2000

Steiner, Liza, *Sade-Houellebecq, du boudoir au sex-shop* (Paris: Editions L'Harmattan, 2009)

Steintrager, James A., 'Liberating Sade', *The Yale Journal of Criticism*, 18, 2 (2005), 351–79

Strange, Susan, *The Retreat of the State: The Diffusion of Power in the World Economy* (Cambridge: Cambridge University Press, 1996)

Sturrock, John, 'Agitated Neurons', *London Review of Books*, 21, 2, 21 January 1999

Tahourdin, Adrian, 'Generation '68', *Times Literary Supplement*, 23, 15 January 1999,

Tait, Theo, 'Gorilla with Mobile Phone', *London Review of Books*, 28, 3, 9 February 2006

Tasker, Yvonne and Diane Negra, *Interrogating Postfeminism: Gender and the Politics of Popular Culture* (Durham, NC: Duke University Press, 2007)

Tebbs, Paul, '*Atomised* by Michel Houellebecq', *The Daily Telegraph*, 24 February 2001, 2

Théret, Bruno, 'Néo-libéralisme, inégalités sociales et politiques fiscales de droite et de gauche dans la France des anneés 1980', *Revue française de science politique* 41, 3 (1991), 342–81

Touraine, Alain, *Beyond Neoliberalism*, trans. David Macy (Cambridge: Polity Press, 2001)

Treanor, Paul, 'Neoliberalism: Origins, Theory, Definition', http:/web.inter.nl.net.users/ Paul.Treanor/neoliberalism

Tremblay, Isabelle, 'L'emploi du stéréotype dans le roman *Extension du domaine de la lutte* ou l'extinction de l'altérité', *Symposium*, 59, 4 (2006), 225–36

Turner, Jenny, 'Club Bed', *The New York Times*, 20 July 2003

Vandenberghe, Frédéric, 'Posthumanism, or the Cultural Logic of Global Neo-Capitalism', (*Complexitiés du posthumanisme: Pour une critique de la bio-économique politique* (Paris: Harmattan, 2005)

Vaneigem, Raoul, *The Revolution of Everyday Life* (London: Rebel Press, 2010)

Van Renterghem, Marion, 'Esprit divisè par les nouveaux réactionnaires', *Le Monde*, 28 January 2003

—'Le Procès Houellebecq', *Le Monde*, 8 November 1998

—'"Well-beck" vu par le "New York Times"', *Le Monde*, 11 March 1999

Van Wesemael, Sabine, 'L'ère du vide' *RiLUnE*, 1 (2005), 85–97

—*Michel Houellebecq: Le plaisir du texte* (Paris: L'Harmattan, 2005)

—ed., *Michel Houellebecq: Études réunies par Sabine Van Wesemael* (Amsterdam: Rodopi, 2004)

Varsava, Jerry, 'The Dialectics of Self and Community in Toni Morrison and Thomas Pynchon', *Contemporary Literature*, 4 (2002), 794–803

—'Utopian Yearnings, Dystopian Thoughts: Houellebecq's *The Elementary Particles* and the Problem of Scientific Comunitarianism', *College Literature*, 32, 4 (2005), 145–67

Viard, Bruno, 'Houellebecq du côté de Rousseau et de René Girard', *Houelle*, 2 (1999), 10–11

—'Houellebecq du côté de Rousseau', *C.R.I.N.: Cahiers de recherches des instituts néerlandais de langue et de littérature française*, 43, 1 (2004)

—*Houellebecq au laser: La faute à Mai '68* (Nice: Editions Ovadia, 2008)

Virno, Paolo and Michael Hardt (eds), *Radical Thought in Italy* (Minneapolis: University of Minnesota Press, 1996)

von Hayek, Friedrich, *The Road to Serfdom* (London: Routledge, 2005, orig. pub. 1944)

Wagner, Walter, 'Le bonheur du néant: une lecture schopenhauerienne de Houellebecq', in Murielle Lucie Clément and Sabine van Wesemael (eds), *Houellebecq sous la loupe* (Amsterdam: Rodopi, 2007), 109–22

Waldberg, Michel, *La Parole putanisée* (Paris: La Différence, 2002)

Wassenaar, Ingrid, '*Whatever*: Michel Houellebecq and the Future of French Literature', paper presented at the British Academy Postdoctoral Fellowship Symposium London, 3 April 2001

Weber, Max, *The Protestant Ethic and the Spirit of Capitalism* (London: Routledge, 2005, [1930])

Weiss, Margot, 'Gay Shame and BDSM Pride: Neoliberalism, Privacy, and Sexual Politics', *Radical History Review*, 100 (2008), 86–101

Weitzmann, Marc, 'Houellebecq, aspects de la France', *Le Monde*, 7 September 2001

—'L'entretien des Inrocks', *Les Inrockuptibles*, 16 (April 1996), 56–9

Westerbrook, John, 'Cultivating Kitsch: Cultural bovéism', *Sites: The Journal of Contemporary French Studies* (2002), 424–35

Wichterch, Christa, *The Globalized Woman: Reports from a Future of Inequality*, trans. Patrick Camiller (London: Zed Books, 2000)

Wieviorka, Michel, *Le printemps du politique: Pour en finir avec le déclinisme* (Paris: Robert Laffont, 2007)

Willging, Jennifer, 'Another Prozac Nation: The Problem of Psychotropic Medication Consumption in Contemporary France', *Contemporary French Civilization*, 33, 1 (2009), 1–22

Williams, Raymond, *Marxism and Literature*, (Oxford: Oxford University Press, 1977)

—*The Long Revolution* (Broadview Press, 2001 [1961])

Winnubust, Shannon, 'The Queer Thing about Neoliberal Pleasure: A Foucauldian Warning', *Foucault Studies*, 14 (2012), 79–97

Winter, Joshua, 'France: into the void', *New Statesman*, 131, 4586, 6 May 2002, 25–7

Wood, James, 'Love Actually', *The New Republic Online*, 14 September 2006, http://www.powells.com/review/2006_09_14

Worton, Michael, 'A dog's life (poodles excepted)', *The Guardian*, 29 October 2005

Wynne, Frank, 'Terribleman', http://www.frankwynne.com

Žižek, Slavoj, *First as Tragedy, Then as Farce* (London: Verso, 2009)

—'Masturbation, or Sexuality in the Atonal World', *Lacan.com*, 2008, http://www.egs.edu/faculty/slavoj-zizek/articles/masturbation-or-sexuality-in-the-atonal-world

Zwart, Hub, 'From Utopia to Science: Challenges of Personalised Genomics Information for Health Management and Health Enhancement', *Medicine Studies*, 1, 2 (2009), 155–66

Index

Lightning Source UK Ltd.
Milton Keynes UK
UKOW05f0713151016

285289UK00001B/67/P